JOURNAL FOR THE STUDY OF THE NEW TESTAMENT
SUPPLEMENT SERIES
88

Executive Editor
Stanley E. Porter

JSOT Press
Sheffield

The Birth of the Lukan Narrative

Narrative as Christology in Luke 1–2

Mark Coleridge

Journal for the Study of the New Testament
Supplement Series 88

Almae Matri Patrisque
Memoriae Piae

Copyright © 1993 Sheffield Academic Press

Published by JSOT Press
JSOT Press is an imprint of
Sheffield Academic Press Ltd
343 Fulwood Road
Sheffield S10 3BP
England

Typeset by Sheffield Academic Press
and
Printed on acid-free paper in Great Britain
by Biddles Ltd
Guildford

British Library Cataloguing in Publication Data

A catalogue record for this book is available
from the British Library

ISBN 1-85075-447-0

CONTENTS

PREFACE

What is published here by the good graces of Sheffield Academic Press is a slightly modified version of a doctoral thesis presented to the Pontifical Biblical Institute in Rome. The thesis was submitted in May 1991 and defended finally in April 1992. A good deal of literature in the field of narrative criticism has appeared since early 1991, but I have decided to include little of it in a work that already contains abundant notes and bibliography.

The writing of a thesis is in some ways a very solitary task; yet in other ways it could hardly be more communal. My name may appear on the work, but many others were part of its composition. I mention first Jean-Noël Aletti SJ, the supervisor, who guided the work from its inception. His professional skill and rigour were matched only by his personal generosity and patience. The same was no less true of John Kilgallen SJ, the second reader. To them and to all at the Biblicum I am deeply grateful.

Various communities offered me their hospitality in the writing of the thesis. I thank especially the Jesuit communities in Cambridge, MA, where Jerome Neyrey SJ was a great help, and in Chantilly. To the Dominican community of the Ecole Biblique in Jerusalem I am also indebted. While in Jerusalem I had the good fortune to be with Francis Moloney SDB. He knows, I hope, how much I have valued his support and stimulation through our time together both at Catholic Theological College, Melbourne, and elsewhere. Through my years in Rome as a doctoral student, I lived and worked as chaplain with the Marist Brothers, and that was a singular blessing. In particular, I thank Brian Wanden FMS and John McDonnell FMS for their unfailing sensitivity and truly fraternal support.

The roots of the work lie in Australia: it was Archbishop Little of Melbourne who first suggested that I turn to the study of Scripture. In thanking him, I would thank the whole Church of Melbourne without whose magnificent support not a word of this could have been written.

Finally I turn to my family, to whom I owe a unique debt of affection and gratitude. I was never more conscious of this than when my father died in the early days of my doctoral studies. To his memory and to my beloved mother I dedicate this work.

Mark Coleridge
Melbourne
Christmas 1992

Abbreviations

AB	Anchor Bible
AJBI	*Annual of the Japanese Biblical Institute*
AsSeign	*Assemblées du Seigneur*
AusBR	*Australian Biblical Review*
BAGD	W. Bauer, W.F. Arndt, F.W. Gingrich and F.W. Danker, *Greek-English Lexicon of the New Testament*
BDF	F. Blass, A. Debrunner and R.W. Funk, *A Greek Grammar of the New Testament*
Bib	*Biblica*
BJRL	*Bulletin of the John Rylands University Library of Manchester*
BK	*Bibel und Kirche*
BR	*Biblical Research*
BT	*The Bible Translator*
BZ	*Biblische Zeitschrift*
CBQ	*Catholic Biblical Quarterly*
EstBíb	*Estudios bíblicos*
ExpTim	*Expository Times*
Forum	*Forum and Facets*
GL	*Geist und Leben*
HTS	Harvard Theological Studies
IDB	G.A. Buttrick (ed.), *Interpreter's Dictionary of the Bible*
IndTS	*Indian Theological Studies*
Int	*Interpretation*
ITQ	*Irish Theological Quarterly*
JAAR	*Journal of the American Academy of Religion*
JBL	*Journal of Biblical Literature*
JETS	*Journal of the Evangelical Theological Society*
JR	*Journal of Religion*
JSNTSup	*Journal for the Study of the New Testament*, Supplement Series
JSOTSup	*Journal for the Study of the Old Testament*, Supplement Series
JTS	*Journal of Theological Studies*
LB	*Linguistica Biblica*
NovT	*Novum Testamentum*
NRT	*Nouvelle revue théologique*
NTS	*New Testament Studies*
OTG	Old Testament Guides

PG	J. Migne (ed.), *Patrologia Graeca*
PL	J. Migne (ed.), *Patrologia Latina*
RB	*Revue Biblique*
RevExp	*Review and Expositor*
RHPR	*Revue d'histoire et de philosophie religieuses*
RivB	*Rivista biblica*
RSR	*Recherches de science religieuse*
RSV	Revised Standard Version
SBL	Society of Biblical Literature
ScEccl	*Sciences ecclésiastiques*
Str–B	[H. Strack and] P. Billerbeck, *Kommentar zum Neuen Testament aus Talmud und Midrasch*
TDNT	G. Kittel and G. Friedrich (eds.), *Theological Dictionary of the New Testament*
ThWAT	G.J. Botterweck and H. Ringgren (eds.), *Theologisches Wörterbuch zum Alten Testament*
TS	*Theological Studies*
TTod	*Theology Today*
TWNT	G. Kittel and G. Friedrich (eds.), *Theologisches Wörterbuch zum Neuen Testament*
ZNW	*Zeitschrift für die neutestamentliche Wissenschaft*

Chapter 1

THE NARRATIVE TURN

A Shift in Lukan Studies

From History to Art

In his commentary on the Acts of the Apostles, Ernst Haenchen suggests that if Lukan scholarship has in recent times been concerned to study Luke first as historian and second as theologian, then perhaps the time is ripe for the study of Luke as artist.[1] Until the appearance of Hans Conzelmann's *Die Mitte der Zeit*,[2] Lukan studies were largely absorbed with the question of Luke as historian and the closely allied question of sources. But with the rise of redaction criticism and the ascendancy of Conzelmann, the focus shifted more to questions of the theological thrust and temper of Luke.[3]

1. E. Haenchen, *The Acts of the Apostles: A Commentary* (trans. B. Noble, G. Shinn, H. Anderson, R. Wilson; Oxford: Basil Blackwell, 1971), pp. 91-92.

2. H. Conzelmann, *Die Mitte der Zeit: Studien zur Theologie des Lukas* (Tübingen: Mohr, 1954; ET *The Theology of St. Luke* [trans. G. Buswell; Philadelphia: Fortress Press, 1982]).

3. The following is a sample of the plethora of studies which might be cited: C.K. Barrett, *Luke the Historian in Recent Study* (London: Epworth Press, 1961); H. Flender, *St. Luke: Theologian of Redemptive History* (Philadelphia: Fortress Press, 1967); S. Brown, *Apostasy and Perseverance in the Theology of Luke* (Rome: Biblical Institute Press, 1969); T. Schramm, *Der Markus-stoff bei Lukas: Eine literarkritische und redaktionsgeschichtliche Untersuchung* (Cambridge: Cambridge University Press, 1971); I.H. Marshall, *Luke: Historian and Theologian* (Exeter: Paternoster Press, 1970); J. Jervell, *Luke and the People of God: A New Look at Luke–Acts* (Minneapolis: Augsburg, 1972); S.G. Wilson, *The Gentiles and the Gentile Mission in Luke–Acts* (Cambridge: Cambridge University Press, 1973); E. Franklin, *Christ the Lord: A Study in the Purpose and Theology of Luke–Acts* (Philadelphia: Westminster Press, 1975); E. Rasco, *La teologia de Lucas: Origen, desarollo, orientaciones* (Rome: Gregorian University Press, 1976); J. Drury, *Tradition and Design in Luke's Gospel* (London: Darton, Longman & Todd, 1976);

More recently, however, there have been signs of a further shift of attention of the kind signalled by Haenchen, with the focus moving this time to the work of Luke as artist.[1] This had never been entirely absent from the interest of scholars such as Henry Cadbury and Martin Dibelius, whose work on Lukan language and style retains its relevance;[2] but more recent studies of Luke as artist have moved in somewhat different directions. Monographs have appeared, each in its own way breaking new ground;[3] and other contributions more modest

A. George, *Etudes sur l'oeuvre de St. Luc* (Paris: Gabalda, 1978); H. Dömer, *Das Heil Gottes: Studien zur Theologie des lukanischen Doppelwerks* (Bonn: Peter Hanstein, 1978); R.J. Dillon, *From Eye-Witnesses to Ministers of the Word* (Rome: Biblical Institute Press, 1978); R. Maddox, *The Purpose of Luke–Acts* (Edinburgh: T. & T. Clark, 1982).

1. In his review of the second volume of Joseph Fitzmyer's commentary on the Third Gospel, Charles Talbert specifies 1974 as the turning point in Lukan studies, with Paul Minear's lectures of that year (to appear later as *To Heal and Reveal: The Prophetic Vocation according to Luke* [New York: Seabury, 1976]) the emblematic statement signalling a new methodological departure (C.H. Talbert, Review of *The Gospel of Luke Vol. II [X–XXIV]*, by J.A. Fitzmyer, *CBQ* 48 [1986], pp. 336-38). Talbert suggests four main points of difference between Lukan studies in the period 1954–74 (i.e. from Conzelmann to Fitzmyer) and Lukan studies after 1974: (1) a focus upon larger textual units rather than the traditional pericopae, (2) more attention to the Third Gospel within itself than in comparison with Mark and Matthew, (3) less interest in reconstructing the tradition, even to the point of tracing it to the historical Jesus, and more interest in addressing the canonical form of the text, and (4) less of a concern to dialogue with Conzelmann and his followers and more interest in a dialogue with classical rhetoric and modern literary criticism.

2. Cadbury's most influential works are *The Style and Literary Method of Luke* (Cambridge, MA: Harvard University Press, 1920) and *The Making of Luke–Acts* (London: Macmillan, 1927). For a soundly argued caution against a false modernizing of Cadbury's work, see B. Roberts Gaventa, 'The Peril of Modernizing Henry Joel Cadbury', in K.H. Richards (ed.), *Society of Biblical Literature Seminar Papers 1987* (Atlanta: Scholars Press, 1987), which also has a full bibliography of Cadbury's work on Luke–Acts. Dibelius's most interesting and, in this context, most significant work is *Aufsätze zur Apostelgeschichte* (ed. H. Greeven; Göttingen: Vandenhoeck & Ruprecht, 1951).

3. Among these are the following: C.H. Talbert, *Literary Patterns, Theological Themes and the Genre of Luke–Acts* (Missoula, MT: Scholars Press, 1974); L.T. Johnson, *The Literary Function of Possessions in Luke–Acts* (Missoula, MT: Scholars Press, 1977); R. Meynet, *Quelle est donc cette parole? Lecture 'rhétorique' de l'évangile de Luc (1-9; 22-24)* (Paris: Cerf, 1979); D.L. Tiede, *Prophecy and History in Luke–Acts* (Philadelphia: Fortress Press, 1980);

in length and scope have also made their mark.[1] Lukan studies have also been influenced by work done on other Gospels, such as the work on Mark's Gospel by Frank Kermode, David Rhoads and Donald Michie, Jack Dean Kingsbury on Matthew,[2] and R. Alan Culpepper's

A. Gueuret, *L'engendrement d'un récit: L'Evangile de l'enfance selon saint Luc* (Paris: Cerf, 1983); R.J. Karris, *Luke: Artist and Theologian—Luke's Passion Account as Literature* (New York: Paulist Press, 1985); R.C. Tannehill, *The Narrative Unity of Luke–Acts: A Literary Interpretation*. I. *Luke* (2 vols.; Philadelphia: Fortress Press, 1986); J.M. Dawsey, *The Lukan Voice: Confusion and Irony in the Gospel of Luke* (Macon: Mercer University Press, 1986); J.B. Tyson, *The Death of Jesus in Luke–Acts* (Columbia: University of South Carolina Press, 1986); M.C. Parsons, *The Departure of Jesus in Luke–Acts: The Ascension Narratives in Context* (JSNTSup, 21; Sheffield: JSOT Press, 1987); J.-N. Aletti, *L'art de raconter Jésus Christ: L'écriture narrative de l'évangile de Luc* (Paris: Seuil, 1989).

1.   Again a sample must suffice to indicate the growing swell: G. Nuttall, *The Moment of Recognition: Luke as Story-Teller* (London: Athlone Press, 1978); J.L. Resseguie, 'Point of View in the Central Section of Luke (9:51–19:44)', *JETS* 25 (1982), pp. 41-47; J.-N. Aletti, 'Jésus à Nazareth (Lc 4,16-30): Prophétie, Ecriture et Typologie', in F. Refoulé (ed.), *A Cause de l'Evangile* (Paris: Cerf, 1985), pp. 431-51; K.R.R. Gros Louis, 'Different Ways of Looking at the Birth of Jesus', *Bible Review* 1.1 (1985), pp. 33-40; D. Hamm, 'Sight to the Blind: Vision as Metaphor in Luke', *Bib* 67 (1986), pp. 457-77; J.M. Dawsey, 'What's in a Name? Characterization in Luke', *BTB* 16 (1986), pp. 143-47; M.C. Parsons, 'Narrative Closure and Openness in the Plot of the Third Gospel: The Sense of an Ending', in K.H. Richards (ed.), *Society of Biblical Literature Seminar Papers 1986* (Atlanta: Scholars Press, 1986), pp. 201-23; J.-N. Aletti, 'Luc 24,13-33: Signes, accomplissement et temps', *RSR* 75 (1987), pp. 305-20; J. Drury, 'Luke', in R. Alter and F. Kermode (eds.), *The Literary Guide to the Bible* (Cambridge, MA: Belknap/Harvard University Press, 1987), pp. 418-39; S.M. Sheeley, 'Narrative Asides and Narrative Authority in Luke–Acts', *BTB* 18.3 (1988), pp. 102-107; J.P. Heil, 'Reader-Response and the Irony of Jesus before the Sanhedrin in Luke 22:66-71', *CBQ* 51.2 (1989), pp. 271-84; G.W. Ramsey, 'Plots, Gaps, Repetitions and Ambiguity in Luke 15', *Perspectives in Religious Studies* 17 (1989), pp. 33-42; M.A. Powell, 'The Religious Leaders in Luke: A Literary-Critical Study', *JBL* 109 (1990), pp. 93-110.

2.   F. Kermode, *The Genesis of Secrecy: On the Interpretation of Narrative* (Cambridge, MA: Harvard University Press, 1979). Worth noting too is H. Gardner's reply to Kermode in 'Narratives and Fictions', in her *In Defence of the Imagination* (Oxford: Oxford University Press, 1982), pp. 111-37, in which she rejects what she calls Kermode's 'gnostic solipsism'. D. Rhoads and D. Michie, *Mark as Story: An Introduction to the Narrative of a Gospel* (Philadelphia: Fortress Press, 1982). See also D. Rhoads, 'Narrative Criticism and the Gospel of Mark', *JAAR* 50 (1982), pp. 411-34; J.D. Kingsbury, *Matthew as Story* (Philadelphia:

study of the Fourth Gospel.[1] Harder to measure but present nonetheless has been the influence of the study of the Hebrew Bible by
literary critics such as Erich Auerbach,[2] Robert Alter,[3] Meir
Sternberg[4] and Kenneth Gros Louis.[5]

The Rise of Narrative Criticism

To understand more clearly the nature of the shift now apparent in
Lukan studies, a still wider context needs to be set. This is because the
influences converging in the current shift come not only from within
the field of biblical study, but also, and in some ways more particularly, from the field of literary criticism. It is an intriguing phenomenon of the present time that literary critics are turning their
attention to the writings of the Bible,[6] and that biblical critics are
turning theirs to the methods and insights of literary criticism. In
particular, it is the study of the novel which has generated the study
now known as narratology;[7] and it is this study that offers a range of
new perspectives and questions to the study of biblical narrative.[8] The

Fortress Press, 1986).
    1. R.A. Culpepper, *Anatomy of the Fourth Gospel: A Study in Literary Design*
(Philadelphia: Fortress Press, 1983).
    2. E. Auerbach, *Mimesis: The Representation of Reality in Western Literature*
(trans. W. Trask; Garden City, NY: Anchor Books, 1957).
    3. R. Alter, *The Art of Biblical Narrative* (New York: Basic Books, 1981).
    4. M. Sternberg, *The Poetics of Biblical Narrative: Ideological Literature and the
Drama of Reading* (Bloomington: Indiana University Press, 1985).
    5. See his various contributions, on both OT and NT, in K.R.R. Gros Louis,
J.S. Ackermann and T.S. Warshaw (eds.), *Literary Interpretations of Biblical
Narratives* (Nashville: Abingdon Press, 1974) and K.R.R. Gros Louis and J.S.
Ackermann (eds.), *Literary Interpretations of Biblical Narratives Volume II*
(Nashville: Abingdon Press, 1982).
    6. As well as Sternberg, Alter, Kermode and Gros Louis noted above, other
literary critics to enter the biblical arena in recent times are Northrop Frye, Gabriel
Josipovici, Meike Bal, Harold Bloom, Geoffrey Hartman, J. Hillis Miller, Stephen
Prickett, Roland Barthes, Réné Girard, Julia Kristeva and George Steiner.
    7. The term is a neologism of French provenance coined to describe the attempt
to discern the poetics or system of narrative in general. Narrative therefore is understood as a system in a way which is often, though not always, under the influence of
structuralism. This study owes a debt to narratology but is not a narratological exercise. Rather than work from text to theory as narratology does, the attempt here is to
move from theory to text.
    8. Some of the works more influential in the field of biblical studies would be

last twenty years have been an unusually hectic and fruitful period in the study of narrative, a time in which the pressure of insights from disciplines such as text linguistics, speech-act theory and communication theory has prompted an array of new questions which the study of biblical narrative can scarcely avoid.[1]

The convergence of influences such as these has produced, at least in the field of NT study, what has come to be known as narrative criticism.[2] In the way it seeks to trace the creative work of the evangelist

the following: W. Booth, *The Rhetoric of Fiction* (Harmondsworth: Peregrine Books, 1987); R. Scholes and R. Kellogg, *The Nature of Narrative* (New York: Oxford University Press, 1966); B. Uspensky, *A Poetics of Composition: The Structure of the Artistic Text and Typology of a Compositional Form* (trans. V. Zavarin and S. Wittig; Berkeley and Los Angeles: University of California Press, 1973); W. Iser, *The Implied Reader: Patterns of Communication in Prose Fiction from Bunyan to Beckett* (Baltimore and London: Johns Hopkins University Press, 1978); *idem, The Act of Reading: A Theory of Aesthetic Response* (Baltimore and London: Johns Hopkins University Press, 1980); G. Genette, *Narrative Discourse: An Essay in Method* (trans. J. Lewin; Ithaca, NY: Cornell University Press, 1978); *idem, Nouveau discours du récit* (Paris: Seuil, 1983); S. Chatman, *Story and Discourse: Narrative Structure in Fiction and Film* (Ithaca, NY: Cornell University Press, 1980); S. Rimmon-Kenan, *Narrative Fiction: Contemporary Poetics* (London: Methuen Books, 1983); P. Ricoeur, *Temps et récit* (3 vols.; Paris: Seuil, 1983, 1985, 1988).

1. Roman Jakobson is the presiding spirit in communication theory and has had his influence too on speech-act theory, on which see J.L. Austin, *How to Do Things with Words* (London and New York: Oxford University Press, 1962); J.R. Searle, *Speech Acts: An Essay in the Philosophy of Language* (Cambridge: Cambridge University Press, 1969); M.L. Pratt, *Toward a Speech Act Theory of Literary Discourse* (Bloomington: Indiana University Press, 1977). For an account of the impact of linguistics on biblical studies, see P. Cotterell and M. Turner, *Linguistics and Biblical Interpretation* (London: SPCK, 1989).

2. The pedigree of the term is a little hard to trace. It seems to appear for the first time in N.R. Petersen, *Literary Criticism for New Testament Critics* (Philadelphia: Fortress Press, 1978), p. 40, but with its more specific and now widely accepted sense in Rhoads, 'Narrative Criticism'. It tends not to be common currency in OT study and has no exact parallel in literary-critical parlance. The most concise and recent introduction to the field is M.A. Powell, *What is Narrative Criticism?* (Minneapolis: Fortress Press, 1990), in which he makes it clear that the single rubric 'narrative criticism' embraces a wide variety of perspectives and approaches, of which the example offered in this study is not the most purist or doctrinaire. For various assessments of the production and prospects of narrative criticism, see: R.M. Frye, 'Literary Criticism and Gospel Criticism', *TTod* 36 (1979), pp. 207-19;

understood as more than the arranger of received materials, narrative criticism aligns itself with redaction criticism. But where redaction criticism seeks to trace the work of the evangelist primarily as theologian, narrative criticism is more concerned with the work of the evangelist as artist, which is not to say that it ignores the theological question. It simply approaches it differently.

With its concern to identify the distinctive theology of the evangelists, redaction criticism is inevitably more interested in content than in form. In some of its manifestations, particularly those more heavily influenced by the New Criticism,[1] the opposite might be said of narrative criticism—that it is more concerned with form than content. But at least in the example of narrative criticism offered here the assumption is that content and form, theology and technique, the 'what' and the 'how' of the biblical text, are inseparable, the one determining the other in a ceaseless oscillation.

While not adopting a Romantic sense of the evangelist as totally free—'creative', that is, in the sense that he is not bound in any way by the constrictions of tradition or culture—narrative criticism extends redaction criticism's sense of the evangelist's creativity. It focuses more upon the choices that any writer, including the evangelist, is forced to make in order to shape a narrative.[2] At the simplest

---

N.R. Petersen, 'Literary Criticism in Biblical Studies', in R.A. Spencer (ed.), *Orientation by Disorientation: Studies in Literary Criticism and Biblical Literary Criticism* (Pittsburgh: Pickwick Press, 1980), pp. 25-50; P. Perkins, 'Crisis in Jerusalem? Narrative Criticism in New Testament Studies', *TS* 50.2 (1989), pp. 296-313; W.H. Kelber, 'Gospel Narrative and Critical Theory', *BTB* 18 (1988), pp. 130-37; R. Fowler, 'Using Literary Criticism on the Gospels', *Christian Century* 99.19, pp. 626-29; M. Gerhart, 'The Restoration of Biblical Narrative', *Semeia* 46 (1989), pp. 13-29; T. Longman, *Literary Approaches to Biblical Interpretation* (Grand Rapids: Zondervan, 1987); S.D. Moore, *Literary Criticism and the Gospels: The Theoretical Challenge* (New Haven and London: Yale University Press, 1989).

1.   For discussion of the origin, character and fate of the New Criticism, see G. Graff, *Literature against Itself: Literary Ideas in Modern Society* (Chicago: Chicago University Press, 1979); and for discussion of the New Criticism's influence on biblical studies in particular, see L. Poland, *Literary Criticism and Biblical Hermeneutics: A Critique of Formalist Approaches* (Chico, CA: Scholars Press, 1985).

2.   This does not imply that there is no difference of genre between the Gospels and, say, the modern novel. What it does imply is that there are certain basic points at which, for all the difference of genre, the evangelist and the novelist converge in the production of their texts.

level, the writer must decide what to include and what to exclude; and once those decisions have been made, he or she must decide how to frame and arrange the chosen elements. With specific reference to the infancy narratives of the NT, Kenneth Gros Louis suggests a set of questions as a basis for narrative criticism:

> How do Matthew and Luke decide what elements to select? What questions go through a writer's mind as he considers his sources and subjects? For Matthew and Luke, perhaps questions like these: How will the birth be described? What is the audience like? How much does it know?. . . Into what narrative context should the birth be set? Which events, of the many known, should be emphasised? Which characters should be included and which ones emphasised? Who should speak? What should they say? Should the sources be made known? In what ways should the birth set the pattern and tone of the rest of the narrative. . . ?[1]

To identify the Lukan answers to questions such as these and to attempt an explanation of what prompts them is one of the chief goals of the example of narrative criticism found in this study.[2]

One of the underlying assumptions of such an approach is that the evangelist is in control of his material, that however much he may use received sources and traditions he is more master than slave of the elements of his text. This would mean, for instance, that were fissures, gaps or elisions to appear in the text, the initial assumption would be that the author wants them to be there, and the critical question therefore is 'why?' There will of course be times when the critic can no longer maintain an assumption of this kind.[3] At that point, there is no choice but to abandon the initial assumption and to assume instead either a failure of the author to master his sources or corruption in the textual tradition. But it is a question of what initial assumption the critic brings to the task; and narrative criticism begins with the assumption that the evangelist has over his material a control which if not absolute is nonetheless real.

---

1. Gros Louis, 'Different Ways', p. 34.
2. Or, as Gros Louis puts it ('Different Ways', p. 34): 'Our problem is to see how. . . Luke answered their questions—those of any writer—by looking at the narratives and then asking why certain choices, why certain decisions, were made'.
3. The paradigm example is the notice in 1 Sam. 13.1 that Saul was one year old when he began to reign. Even the most resourceful or devious critic would be hard put to explain that one in terms of narrative strategy: textual corruption has to be the answer.

This implies that the text as it stands is understood as a coherent unity. An assumption of this kind is strikingly at odds with the basic assumption of much historical-critical exegesis that a text is a deeply fissured collection of a diversity of elements, which may with enough care and erudition be identified in such a way that the archaeology of the text may be traced. Narrative criticism's assumption of textual unity does not deny that a text includes a variety of elements, nor that a long process of redaction may underlie the final form of the text. But this final form, which is narrative criticism's chief concern, is assumed at least initially to have unity and coherence even though there may indeed be fissures and gaps. The task of the narrative critic is to offer an account of the text's unity and coherence which includes and attempts to explain the fissures and gaps, rather than ignoring or denying them, or simply noting them and leaving them unresolved, or seeking to explain them solely in terms of the archaeology of the text.

At the same time, as Stephen Moore has cautioned from a deconstructionist viewpoint,[1] there is a need to guard against a too glib assumption of textual unity, which may in fact conceal the exegete's search for a false comfort:

> The view of the biblical text (specifically the gospel text) which narrative critics are urging is ultimately a comforting one. It reassures us that in the wake of a long history of fragmentation, exposure of internal contradictions and the like, it is now possible, using the methods of literary criticism, to see that the gospel narratives do after all possess wholeness and internal consistency.[2]

Moore queries the lengths to which narrative criticism is forced to go in order to insist upon the unity of a text in which there are 'cracks and crevices that result... from the conflation of sources'. 'The more one is prepared to home in on the cracks and crevices', he writes, '...the more unusual the account of the authorial intention one will have to resort to to fill in these widened cracks'.[3] There is no doubt that Moore has a point, and that the deconstructionist critique of narrative criticism—of which he is the most articulate voice[4]—cannot

---

1. S.D. Moore, 'Are the Gospels Unified Narratives?', in K.H. Richards (ed.), *Society of Biblical Literature Seminar Papers 1987* (Atlanta: Scholars Press, 1987), pp. 443-58.

2. Moore, 'Unified Narratives?', p. 454.

3. Moore, 'Unified Narratives?', p. 452.

4. In a series of articles (as well as the one just cited, see 'Negative

simply be dismissed out of hand. But what is odd is that although Moore peers through the lens of poststructuralism he speaks in defence of a more orthodox account of authorial intention than post-structuralism will allow and also a readier acceptance that source material at times gets the better of the evangelist. At that point, Moore seems to run with the hare and hunt with the hounds: he seeks to defend a hermeneutic which the poststructuralist criticism underlying his critique has long since abandoned.

If narrative criticism does not set the search for either authorial intention or the archaeology of the text at the heart of its hermeneutic, neither does it reject them out of hand. They are however moved from the centre and are no longer the linchpin of interpretation.[1] What stands at the heart of the hermeneutic implied by narrative criticism is an attention to the way in which the narrative works as a process of communication (from author via text to reader).[2] However

Hermeneutics, Insubstantial Texts: Stanley Fish and the Biblical Interpreter', *JAAR* 54 [1986], pp. 401-13; 'Narrative Commentaries on the Bible: Context, Roots, and Prospects', *Forum* 3.3 [1987], pp. 29-62; 'Doing Gospel Criticism as/with a "Reader"', *BTB* 19.3 [1989], pp. 85-93) and now in his monographs, *Literary Criticism,* and *Mark and Luke in Poststructuralist Perspectives: Jesus Begins to Write* (New Haven and London: Yale University Press, 1992), Moore has shown himself adept at posing the pertinent question to narrative criticism and playing a significant part therefore in setting its agenda.

1.   From a hermeneutic point of view, the question of authorial intention is more delicate than the question of the archaeology of the text. The problem with authorial intention is that it takes no account of what Paul Ricoeur has called 'the surplus of meaning', i.e. that part of meaning in any text which exceeds authorial intention and rises from the play of language itself—on which see his comments on authorial intention in *Interpretation Theory: Discourse and the Surplus of Meaning* (Forth Worth: Texas Christian University Press, 1976), pp. 29-30, 75-76, 99-100 n.5. In saying that I do not put authorial intention at the heart of my hermeneutic in this study, I am claiming to address the surplus of meaning in the infancy narrative. This does not mean that I exclude authorial intention as an important goal of interpretation; it means rather that the search for authorial intention cannot exhaust the act of interpretation. An implication of this is that the actual author of the Third Gospel (whoever he may have been) and the narrator that he creates are not identical. The narrator (of whom I speak habitually in this study) is more akin to what narratology calls the implied author, though that is a term I have chosen not to use.

2.   For a more detailed account of the reading process implied here, see Chatman, *Story and Discourse*, p. 267, where he draws heavily upon the model of communication proposed by Roman Jakobson.

'disunified' the formation of the text may have been, it still has a unity as a process of communication. Moreover, the reading process will demand of readers that they make unified sense of what they read, whatever the mess of the text's origins might be. The drive to coherence is an invariable of the reading process.[1]

The Shape of the Study

The Choice of Text

Some may judge it unwise or unnecessary to turn once more to a text which at times seems exhausted by the attention it has drawn. But the choice of text for this study is governed by four chief factors.

First, a piece of NT narrative has been chosen because the study of NT narrative—at least from a narrative-critical point of view—cannot match the range and sophistication of the study of OT narrative which, drawing often on the best Jewish scholarship in both the biblical and literary arenas, has produced interpretations of such quality (for example the work of Alter and Sternberg) that the value of the approach is there for all to see. But this cannot be said of the study of NT narrative, which is less mautre and has yet to produce interpretations of such range and quality.

This is not to belittle or patronise those who have been first in the field of NT narrative criticism. But the problem with the early ventures was precisely that they were first in the field. NT narrative

---

1.   On which see for example Iser, *Act of Reding*, pp. 122-30, where he discusses what he calls 'consistency-building' by the reader. A systematic attention to the reading process is a characteristic of reader-response criticism of which Iser has been a leading exponent. Reader-response criticism appeared first on the literary-critical horizon in the 1960s, by and large as a reaction to the relentless textual formalism of the New Criticism which had commanded the field from the 1930s until the 1950s. Through the 1970s, reader-response criticism became more dominant, until by the early 1980s it had displaced New Critical formalism as the commanding force. Its fortunes may have waned in the meantime, though not without leaving behind 'a new sense of what it means to be a reader—and a critic' (Moore, 'Doing Gospel Criticism', p. 85). This study is by no means a full-blown example of reader-response criticism, though it will attend to the role of the reader in the rhetorical transaction. Iser proposes as the two poles of the act of communication 'textual structures' and 'structured acts of comprehension' (Iser, *Act of Reading*, p. 107): in these terms, this study will focus more on the 'textual structures' than on the 'structured acts of comprehension'.

criticism is a much younger discipline than the study of OT narrative, and the impression at times is that NT critics, trained in other ways, are busy learning new skills, but skills that are not learnt quickly or easily. One result of this is that literary theory, not quite mastered or digested as it is in the best of OT narrative analysis, can dominate interpretation, so that the work illuminates the text less than it does the labyrinth of literary theory.[1]

An underlying assumption of this study is that NT narrative criticism has come to a point where maturity will mean that it will submerge narratological theory and attend more directly to texts. The weakness of a pioneering work like Culpepper's *Anatomy of the Fourth Gospel* is that it seems at times the servant of theory,[2] and the strength of a more recent work like Aletti's *L'art de raconter* is that its solid theoretical base is unobtrusive, with theory clearly at the service of interpretation of the text. This study seeks in its own way to follow suit, and so contribute to the maturing process of the narrative approach in NT studies.

A second factor governing the choice of text is that although the Lukan infancy narrative is by universal reckoning a classic example of NT narrative, and despite the massive historical critical attention it has drawn, it remains all but virgin territory for narrative criticism. Though often acclaimed for its artistry, it remains to be seen how at the level of narrative technique the artistry of Luke 1–2 operates and how at the same level it sets the Lukan narrative in motion.

Thirdly, Luke 1–2 is a continuous text of considerable length. Almost all NT narrative critical studies have addressed an entire Gospel, or selected pericopae of a Gospel, or a single pericope. But it

1.   There is also a figure like Stephen Moore, competent in his command of both literary theory and of NT narrative criticism, but whose dual competence has yet to produce interpretation which matches his theoretical expositions or his accounts of the status quo in NT narrative criticism. See, for example, his brief and very tentative move to interpretation in *Literary Criticism*, pp. 159-67, and his more swashbuckling performance in *Mark and Luke in Poststructuralist Perspectives*, which tells the reader more of deconstructionist modes of reading than it does of the Gospel texts. At times, Mark and Luke are swamped by the wild, dionysian voices echoing down the corridors of Moore's own text, so much does the smart and glittering prose draw attention to itself.

2.   Culpepper traces the design of the Fourth Gospel under the following headings: Narrator and Point of View, Narrative Time, Plot, Characters, Implicit Commentary, and the Implied Reader.

is hard to find a study of monographic length that addresses a continuous NT narrative text larger than the single pericope and smaller than an entire Gospel. Hence the choice of a continuous text of 132 verses.

Finally, to choose so well-worked a text is a solid test of any method. If a narrative critical approach can generate some measure of new insight into the Lukan infancy narrative, then it will have shown itself a useful addition to the instruments of NT study.

The Profile of the Argument

In 19.44, the Lukan Jesus is shown weeping over Jerusalem 'because you did not know the time of your visitation' (ἀνθ' ὧν οὐκ ἔγνως τὸν καιρὸν τῆς ἐπισκοπῆς σου); and in 7.16 the Lukan narrator has the people of Nain glorify God 'because [he] has visited his people' (ὅ τι ἐπεσκέψατο ὁ θεὸς τὸν λαὸν αὐτοῦ). Earlier still in the Gospel, Zechariah blesses God 'because he has visited and worked redemption for his people' (ὅτι ἐπεσκέψατο καὶ ἐποίησεν λύτρωσιν τῷ λαῷ αὐτοῦ, 1.68), and later in the Benedictus Zecheriah extols the divine mercy 'by which he has visited us' (ἐν οἷς ἐπισκέψεται ἡμᾶς, 1.78). Strategically placed texts such as these suggest that questions concerning the shape of the divine visitation and the recognition of it are central to the narrative of Luke–Acts.[1]

The general claim in this study is that the first two chapters of the Third Gospel set the Lukan narrative[2] in motion and lay the ground for all that follows by articulating in narrative form a vision of both

---

1. ἐπισκέπτομαι occurs 11 times in the NT, 7 times in Luke; and only Luke associates it with the divine visitation. ἐπισκοπῆς occurs 4 times in the NT, twice in Luke. In the LXX, ἐπισκέπτομαι translates the frequently found פקד on which see the articles by G. André, 'פקד', *ThWAT*, VI, pp. 708-23, and H. Beyer, 'ἐπισκέπτομαι', *TDNT*, II, pp. 599-622. In the biblical context, the word has the nuance not just of a visit, but also of care (Ps. 8.4). With specific reference to the divine visitation, it may refer to either individuals or Israel, and may indicate judgment or grace or both. Yet it alway implies God's demonstration of lordship, which in the Lukan context is tied to the coming of the messiah. It might be asked whether the notion of divine visitation is any more central than other typically Lukan notions such as salvation or peace. My point is that the notion of divine visitation is the general rubric of which other notions such as salvation or peace are specifications. In narrative terms, this means that the divine visitation is the 'what' of the story and other equally Lukan notions the 'how'.

2. The phrase 'the Lukan narrative' will be used throughout this study to refer to Luke–Acts understood as a single narrative arc.

the divine visitation and human recognition of it, and this as a way of preparing for the birth of a distinctively Lukan christology. The two seminal questions generating the Lukan infancy narrative are these: how does God visit his people, and how is one to recognize his visitation? The first of these questions is theological, the second epistemological.[1] In addressing these two questions, this study will read the infancy narrative first as theology and epistemology—but this in order to read it eventually and climactically as christology, albeit a christology that comes only slowly through a process of narration.[2]

The study will show how the infancy narrative offers an account of the divine visitation which has at its heart a dynamic of promise-fulfilment: God appears as one who before he acts announces what he will do. Once the promise is made, a process of fulfilment begins, a process of which the infancy narrative itself recounts only the first steps, and a process which will not be complete even by the end of Acts. To this process of promise-fulfilment there corresponds a process of human recognition which has a dynamic of faith-interpretation—faith in the promises and interpretation of the signs of fulfilment.[3]

1. Given how frequently the word 'epistemological' (rather than 'gnoseological' or 'hermeneutical') will recur in the study, it would be as well to avert confusion immediately. The *Concise Oxford Dictionary* defines epistemology as 'the theory of the method or grounds of knowledge'. In this study it is used to indicate the way in which the Lukan narrator constructs in the telling of his tale a profile of the kind of knowledge (its method and grounds) required in order to recognize the moment of the divine visitation. On the need to address the Lukan epistemology more attentively and for his own attempt to do so (again through the lens of deconstruction), see S.D. Moore, 'Luke's Economy of Knowledge', in D.J. Lull (ed.), *Society of Biblical Literature Seminar Papers 1989* (Atlanta: Scholars Press, 1989), pp. 38-56.

2. This is in contrast to earlier studies which have tended to read the infancy narrative primarily as history and christology. Chronologically, the interest in the infancy narrative as history is prior to interest in it as christology; but in a work such as Brown's *Birth of the Messiah*, attention to history and christology merge to produce a work which is the high-water mark of historical-critical study of the text. This study will come to the infancy narrative as christology but in a quite different key, attending less to the OT background (*behind the text*) and the retrojection of later NT christology (*in front of the text*) and more to how the narrator shapes a christology in the act of narration (*within the text*).

3. It would be as well to clarify immediately what is meant by 'signs' in this study. In the infancy narrative, there are none of the great signs which appear once the narration of the public ministry of Jesus begins, and Jesus himself never

The study will then show how the infancy narrative builds to the point where in the last episode Jesus becomes interpreter of the embryonic sign of fulfilment which he himself is; that is, he reveals the coherence between who he is and what he does. The study will argue that far from being a later addition of secondary interest and importance, the last episode of the infancy narrative (Lk. 2.41-52) is the climactic point of the infancy narrative in which theology and epistemology converge to produce a distinctively Lukan christology which will prove decisive for the Third Gospel. Trajectories that begin in the first episode and course through the infancy narrative converge in the figure of Jesus in the last episode, and do so in a way that creates a fusion of narrative and christology. In the Lukan context, this is the more precise way of describing the inseparability of form and content.

The Organization of the Work

Whatever the complexities of the infancy narrative, the study itself is simply composed. In the belief that narrative art in contrast to pictorial art is more a temporal than a spatial phenomenon,[1] I have sought to follow the temporal sequence rather than the spatial organization of the text.[2] Therefore after this introductory chapter the chapters of the study will follow in broad outline the seven episodes of the infancy narrative, without entering into intricate consideration of segmentation and structure.[3] The study has two parts corresponding to the two

---

appears in the infancy narrative as the σημεῖον he will later prove to be. But there are in the infancy narrative the first signs of fulfilment of the divine promise—signs which look to the great signs of the public ministry and beyond, but which are not the same.

1.   On narrative as a time-art, see the remarks of M. Sternberg, *Expositional Modes and Temporal Ordering in Fiction* (Baltimore and London: Johns Hopkins University Press, 1978), p. 34. It is perhaps worth adding that the distinction between the temporal and spatial dimensions of a narrative text should not be overdrawn.

2.   Moore claims with good reason that 'biblical scholars tend to conceive the text in spatial terms' ('Narrative Commentaries', p. 49). Hence, for example, Culpepper chooses to describe his work as an 'anatomy', the metaphor suggesting a static text lying corpse-like on a marble slab, the interpreter advancing scalpel in hand.

3.   Commentators vary in their reckoning of the number of episodes in the infancy narrative, sometimes preferring to join 1.26-38 with 1.39-56, thus com-

chapters of the infancy narrative, which will be referred to through-out, as they have been already, as the two phases of the narrative.

This chapter has made it clear that in different ways a study such as this does not take shape in a vacuum. There is throughout—for the most part in the notes—an attempt to enter into conversation with earlier studies of the infancy narrative. This presents three problems, however, the first of which is that the literature on the infancy narra-tive is so vast that any attempt to engage the entire corpus is doomed before it starts. The various works engaged here represent only a fraction of the entire corpus. At the same time it should be said that a reading of the vast bulk of the entire corpus shows that though the works are many the opinions are few.

A second problem is that many earlier studies—especially those in the historical-critical mode—move from such different premises and therefore ask such different questions that a direct engagement is difficult. There is more the sense of studies moving along parallel lines rather than converging from different angles in a way which would make fruitful dialogue a possibility.

A third problem already noted is that to this point there has been such meagre narrative-critical study of the infancy narrative that the chances for dialogue are very limited on that front. Aletti has a chap-ter in *L'art de raconter*; Tannehill has a still briefer treatment in *Narrative Unity*; and Gueuret's *L'engendrement,* though monographic in length, is a semiotic rather than a narrative-critical study of the text. This study, as a full length narrative-critical study of the infancy narrative, seeks to offer a more fully articulated voice with which future works may converse. In the search for that voice and in the

puting six rather than seven. Some (e.g. Dibelius, Galbiati, Burrows) see the infancy narrative as containing three large movements, while others (e.g. Gächter, Lyonnet, Laurentin) prefer two movements. For a full discussion of the various possibilities, see R. Laurentin, *Structure et théologie de Luc 1–2* (Paris: Gabalda, 1957), pp. 23-33, in the course of which he notes that 'la souplesse du procédé de composi-tion. . . laisse place à quelques hésitations pour un décompte des scènes' (p. 25). At different points of the infancy narrative there are also bridge-verses (notably 2.21 and 2.40) which may be assigned to one pericope or another with equally good reasons for either choice. See the comments of R. Funk, *The Poetics of Biblical Narrative* (Sonoma, CA: Polebridge Press, 1988), pp. 85, 164, on the necessity of segmenta-tion for interpretation, which in the light of vv. 21 and 40 seem overstated. If inter-pretation depends upon segmentation, then the interpreter's task in the infancy narrative (especially its last three episodes) is very daunting indeed.

attempt to see how the narrative is born, we turn to the path traced by the art of the Lukan narrator.

Part I

THE INCEPTION OF THE NARRATIVE

Chapter 2

INTRODUCING FAITH AND INTERPRETATION IN LUKE 1.5-25

Beginning a Narrative

If Plato is right that the beginning is the chief thing in any process,[1] then it is surprising that this first episode of the Lukan narrative has drawn such meagre critical attention.[2] Admittedly Lk. 1.5-25 is the beginning of the beginning; but it is as if the critics, in their rush to the following episodes which at least in a doctrinal sense are more decisive, have been content to skim these early verses. Yet it is not only Plato who hints that the episode may be worth more than a passing glance. In more recent times and with specific reference to narrative, Menakhem Perry has described in detail what he calls 'the primacy effect' in literary texts, stressing in his description the exceptional and enduring importance of the narrative's opening in establishing the ground rules of the rhetorical transaction.[3]

This suggests that the question of which elements a narrator chooses to introduce in the opening scene of a narrative is neither trivial nor preliminary. There is never anything inevitable about the way a narrative begins: a narrator may start anywhere, and where to begin is therefore a matter of choice. In later episodes, the narrator is to some extent determined in his or her choice by what has gone before. There is already a momentum in the narrative and the reader has already

1. Plato, *Republic* 2.377b.

2. In his 'Gospel Infancy Narrative Research from 1976–1986: Part II', *CBQ* 48 (1986), pp. 660-80, Raymond Brown needs only a paragraph to deal with this first episode, where succeeding episodes command pages.

3. M. Perry, 'Literary Dynamics: How the Order of a Text Creates its Meanings', *Poetics Today* 1 (1979), pp. 35-64 and 311-61. Perry discusses the interplay between the primacy effect and the recency effect, with later information either reinforcing or (as is more usual) modifying initial impressions. On this, see Rimmon-Kenan, *Narrative Fiction*, p. 120.

been engaged. But in the first episode nothing has gone before: there is no momentum and the reader has yet to be engaged. This untrammelled freedom of choice makes the opening episode more difficult for the narrator in the telling, and more interesting and important for the critic in the reading.[1]

The first episode sets the Lukan narrative in motion by articulating in narrative form the rudiments of both the divine visitation and the human recognition of it. God's visitation is understood as both promise and fulfilment—a fulfilment of past promises and a revelation of new promises, the fulfilment of some of which begins in the episode itself. Correspondingly, human recognition of God's visitation is understood as faith in the promise and interpretation of the signs of fulfilment. In placing before the reader this double understanding of the divine visitation and human recognition of it the first episode lays the ground for the infancy narrative, which in its first phase will focus upon faith in the promise and in its second upon interpretation of the signs of fulfilment.

Setting the Scene: Luke 1.5-10

The Handling of Time
The narrator begins by going back in time, back to the days of King Herod; but the retrospect is more contrived than this, since both the style of introduction[2] and the language suggest not the reign of

---

1.   It is a commonplace of narratology that narrator and author need to be distinguished. This is certainly true of a great deal of modern literature, but it is less true of biblical literature, in the analysis of which such distinctions, too rigidly enforced, can be more of a hindrance than a help, introducing complexity but not clarity. For the purposes of this study, author and narrator are not distinguished. A further distinction made at times is the distinction between critic and reader (on which see G. Steiner, ' "Critic"/"Reader" ', *New Literary History* 10 [1979], pp. 423-52), with the critic assumed to have a freedom and knowledge not granted to the (implied) reader. Again, while not denying the validity, even the necessity of such a distinction in many contexts, this study does not make capital of it.

2.   Compare the similar introductory formulae in (LXX) Ezra 1.1 (καὶ ἐν τῷ πρώτῳ ἔτει Κυρίου τοῦ βασιλέως Περσῶν...); Esth. 1.1 (...ἐν ταῖς ἡμέραις Ἀρταξέρξου... ἐν αὐταῖς ταῖς ἡμέραις ὅτε ἐθρονίσθη ὁ βασιλεὺς Ἀρταξέρξης ἐν Σούσοις τῇ πόλει); Isa. 1.1 (...ἐν βασιλείᾳ Ὀζίου καὶ Ιωαθαμ καὶ Αχαζ καὶ Εζεκιου, οἵ ἐβασίλευσαν τῆς Ιουδαίας); Jer. 1.2 (...ἐν ταῖς ἡμέραις Ιωσια υἱοῦ Αμως βασιλέως Ιουδα ἔτους τρισκαιδεκάτου

Herod, but the more distant past of the OT.[1] The first two chapters of the Lukan narrative will understand the events they recount as fulfilments of past promises. Therefore, in order to begin the narration of the fulfilment, the narrator turns back to the time of the promise; and that entails a move back beyond the line of Christian tradition evoked in the prologue[2] into the world of the OT. The implication is that the events of the narrative will not be rightly understood unless seen as the fulfilment of past promises; and the assumption is that the reader knows the OT well enough to recognize the echoes that the narrator now builds into the narrative. This is clearly no narrative for beginners.[3]

Introducing the Characters
The evocation of the world of the OT grows stronger with the introduction of two of the key characters, Zechariah and Elizabeth. The narration is purely external, with only the circumstances of their life

ἐν τῇ βασιλείᾳ αὐτοῦ); Dan. 1.1 (ἐν ἔτει τρίτῳ τῆς βασιλείας Ιωακιμ βασιλέως Ιουδα...); Hos. 1.1 (...ἐν ἡμέραις Οζιου καὶ Ιωαθαμ καὶ Αχαζ καὶ Εζεκιου βασιλέων Ιουδα καὶ ἐν ἡμέραις Ιεροβοαμ υἱοῦ Ιωας βασιλέως Ισραηλ); Amos 1.1 (...ἐν ἡμέραις Οζιου βασιλέως Ιουδα καὶ ἐν ἡμέραις Ιεροβοαμ τοῦ Ιωας βασιλέως Ισραηλ); Mic. 1.1 (...ἐν ἡμέραις Ιωαθαμ καὶ Αχαζ καὶ Εζεκιου βασιλέων Ιουδα); Zeph. 1.1 (...ἐν ἡμέραις Ιωσιου υἱοῦ Αμων βασιλέως Ιουδα); Hag. 1.1 (ἐν τῷ δευτέρῳ ἔτει ἐπὶ Δαρείου τοῦ βασιλέως...); Zech. 1.1 (ἐν τῷ ὀγδόῳ μηνὶ ἔτους δευτέρου ἐπὶ Δαρείου...).

1. See F. O'Fearghail, 'The Imitation of the Septuagint in Luke's Infancy Narrative', *Proceedings of the Irish Biblical Association* 12 (1989), pp. 61-62, where he points out how the presentation of Zechariah and Elizabeth is reminiscent of 1 Kgs 1.1-2: ἄνθρωπος ἦν ἐξ... καὶ ὄνομα αὐτῷ Ελκανα... καὶ τούτῳ δύο γυναῖκες, ὄνομα τῇ μιᾷ Αννα... καὶ τῇ Αννα οὐκ ἦν παιδίον. He goes on to note that the report of their Torah-piety, while not the same as formulaic expressions found in Deuteronomy (e.g. Deut. 30.10), has a strongly Septuagintal ring to it, as does the report of their advancing years—judging both phrases Lukan creations in imitation of the LXX rather than direct borrowings from it.

2. In the prologue, the narrator pledges himself to tell the tale καθὼς παρέδοσαν ἡμῖν οἱ ἀπ᾽ ἀρχῆς αὐτόπται καὶ ὑπηρέται γενόμενοι τοῦ λόγου.

3. The narrator has already made this clear in the prologue with the reference to περὶ ὧν κατηχήθης λόγων τὴν ἀσφάλειαν. Whoever Theophilus may have been, he already knows a good deal. On information presupposed in narrative, see G. Prince, *Narratology: The Form and Functioning of Narrative* (Berlin, New York and Amsterdam: Mouton Publishers, 1982), pp. 41-47.

revealed:[1] they are husband and wife, they are both of priestly lineage,[2] both are notable for their Torah-piety, and they are childless. Nothing is disclosed of their inner life,[3] nor does the narrator offer any evaluation or interpretation of their situation. Yet the echoes of the OT and the mention of their childlessness stir in the reader the memory of divine interventions on behalf of childless couples in the OT, stretching back to Abraham and Sarah at the beginning of the biblical story.[4]

As the narrative begins, a knowledge gap is set between the readers and the characters. For the first but not the last time in the infancy narrative, readers are set in a position where they may know more than the characters, which means that readers and characters will follow different paths to the point of recognition of the divine visitation.[5] The narrator invites the readers to remember the biblical story

---

1. It is true that characterization in ancient literature is not what we find in modern fiction, even though the claim that the Bible's characterization is always external is hard to sustain. The Bible can provide astonishingly nuanced and convincing characters (for example David), but still does not have the sense of the individual that we find in modern fiction. The mention of external narration raises the question of focalization in narrative. In his chapters on Mood and Voice (*Narrative Discourse*, pp. 161-262), Genette distinguishes 'focalization' (i.e. the consciousness that takes in the narrative) and 'voice' (the discourse that tells the narrative). In those terms, external narration refers to voice rather than focalization. See too Meike Bal's treatment of focalization in, *Narratology: Introduction to the Theory of Narrative* (Toronto: University of Toronto Press, 1985), pp. 100-14. For the most part in the Lukan infancy narrative the voice of the omniscient narrator chooses to remain external to the characters; and from a narrative-critical viewpoint, the question is why.

2. Both the *Protoevangelium of James* and the *Armenian Infancy Gospel* have Zechariah not just a priest, but the High Priest, presumably because they thought that anything less was unworthy of the father of the precursor.

3. Compare again the *Armenian Infancy Gospel* 3.5 which gives a detailed description of Zechariah's emotional state.

4. The line includes Jacob and Rachel (Gen. 30.22-24), Manoah and his wife (Judg. 13.3-25) and Elkanah and Hannah (1 Sam. 1.1-20).

5. See Aletti, *L'art de raconter*, pp. 79-80, where drawing on the terminology of T. Todorov (*La notion de la littérature et autres essais* [Paris: Seuil, 1987], p. 54) he describes the Lukan narrative in these terms: 'Récit doublement gnoséologique: 1) pour les personnages du récit, qui doivent reconnaître les voies de Dieu, 2) pour le lecteur qui, sachant presque tout, du moins beaucoup plus que les personnages, sur l'identité de Jésus et le type de messianisme en jeu, va voir qui le reconnaît et comment, qui le rejette et pourquoi'.

to the point where a sense of what is to come in the narrative will stir in the readers in a way denied to the characters. Good reading will demand good remembering. But the narrator is discreet in his invitation to the readers. It is implied in the mode of narration rather than stated explicitly: the readers are left free.

The third character introduced in these early verses is the corporate character of the People (ὁ λαός), who will play a more than casual role in the drama.[1] They are introduced in v. 10 as 'the whole multitude of the People' (πᾶν τὸ πλῆθος τοῦ λαοῦ), an exaggeration which is both rhetorical and theological. It is not only the entire biblical past, stretching back to Abraham, which provides the context for the introduction of Zechariah and Elizabeth and the narrative's beginning, but also the present hope of the entire People, grounded upon the biblical past and implied in their prayer.[2] Whatever the story of Zechariah and Elizabeth may be, it will unfold within the twin context of Israel's biblical past and the religious life of the People now. Whatever the private future of Zechariah and Elizabeth may be, it will touch the very public future of 'the whole multitude of the People'.

The choice of the Temple as the scene of the action allows the nar-

---

1.   Among others, A. Casalegno (*Gesù e il Tempio: Studio redazionale di Luca-Atti* [Brescia: Morcelliana, 1984], p. 32) points to the chiastic structuring of vv. 5-25, which highlights the role of ὁ λαός:

> A   vv. 5-7 Introduction of the childless couple.
> B   vv. 8-10 Priestly service; Zechariah enters; ὁ λαός at prayer.
> C   vv. 11-20 Apparition and dialogue between Gabriel and Zechariah.
> B'   vv. 21-23 ὁ λαός waiting; Zechariah emerges; finishes his service.
> A'   vv. 24-25 Elizabeth conceives; her reaction.

It can help to see that the passage is arranged in this way (for example, that references to ὁ λαός flank the central section), though what it fails to reckon with is the temporal flow of the narrative, which is not read according to the rhythm of the spatial organization that a structure such as the above reveals.

2.   Gueuret (*L'engendrement*, pp. 44-46) suggests that the prayer of ὁ λαός is an expression of their desire which moves in two directions: 'entrer en communication avec Dieu et combler un manque non explicité' (p. 45). Yet the narrator does not stress this aspect of their prayer, nor does he give any hint of what the content of the prayer might have been—even though, according to *Targum Canticum* 4.16 the prayer of the People during the incense-offering was: 'May the merciful God enter the holy place and accept with favour the offering of his people'. But in introducing ὁ λαός the narrator's interest does not lie in the content of their prayer.

rator to underscore the paradoxical nature of the divine visitation in two ways. It allows him first to situate the visitation at the heart of Judaism, and yet in a way that looks beyond the Temple cult. Secondly, it allows him to situate the visitation in the midst of the People—to bring to light its public dimension—and yet at the same time to have it hidden in the sanctuary with only Zechariah and the angel—to bring to light the private dimension.[1]

Narrating the Promise: Luke 1.11-17

The Angelic Apparition: Luke 1.11-12

According to prescription, Zechariah goes to the Temple to take his place in the ongoing rhythms of the cult; and 'according to custom' (κατὰ τὸ ἔθος), he wins the lot to burn incense. All this is in line with convention.[2] But as soon as he enters the sanctuary the unconventional erupts. The Temple and its cult are immediately transcended as the angel appears in v. 11. The cultic action is never narrated, since, as the narrator has it, it is not through the Temple cult that God visits his people. The narrator locates the divine visitation in the Temple, but does not link it to the cultic action.[3]

---

1. According to *m. Tam.* 5-7, Zechariah would not have been alone in burning the incense; and yet the narrator gives no hint of anyone accompanying him into the sanctuary. Brown (*Birth of the Messiah*, p. 263) suggests rightly if somewhat tentatively that 'the isolation of Zechariah is part of his storytelling technique'.

2. Although winning the lot was quite an event in the life of a priest. Once he had won the right, he became ineligible until all the priests of his division had taken their turn. This meant normally that a priest would win the right only once in his life.

3. Not only is the burning of incense never narrated, but neither is the priestly blessing which normally brought the rite to a conclusion. This has led some (for example E. Schweizer, *The Good News according to Luke* [trans. D.E. Green; London: SPCK, 1984], p. 378; J. Fitzmyer, *The Gospel according to Luke* [AB, 28a; Garden City, NY: Doubleday, 1985], p. 1590; Parsons, *Departure of Jesus*, p. 74; Brown, *Birth of the Messiah*, p. 280) to suggest that the blessing which Zechariah cannot give when he emerges from the sanctuary is given finally by Jesus in 24.50. But there are difficulties with this. First, Jesus is not presented as a priest in the Third Gospel (see Dillon, *From Eye-Witnesses*, p. 176, and I.H. Marshall, *The Gospel of Luke: A Commentary on the Greek Text* [Exeter: Paternoster Press, 1978], p. 909); and secondly, if Zechariah could not give the blessing because dumb, one would expect the ascending Jesus to say something, when in fact the narrator has him gesticulating but wordless. If the blessing were only a matter of gesture (as 24.50 implies), then there was no problem for Zechariah. The non-narra-

As in similar OT scenes, an anonymous heavenly messenger appears.[1] Also standard in OT annunciation scenes is the fear which is reported as Zechariah's reaction. This is the first inside view of a character that the narrator has offered,[2] though it is so standard an OT reaction to the irruption of the numinous that it offers no very penetrating insight into Zechariah. But at least the narrator, having moved the narrative inside the sanctuary, also moves inside his character in one of the few moments in which he infringes his rule of external narration.

Zechariah's fear implies a recognition of what is happening (an irruption of the numinous), but he cannot yet know why. He stands before a sign which demands interpretation. At this point, the narration is set in a strongly visual key: the angel remains silent, but his location is visualized with surprising detail (ἑστὼς ἐκ δεξιῶν τοῦ θυσιαστηρίου τοῦ θυμιάματος),[3] and the narrator has Zechariah

tion of the blessing in 1.5-25 does not look to a gigantic inclusion spanning the entire Gospel, but to the transcendence of the Temple cult within the episode itself.

1. In the OT, 'the angel of YHWH' appears frequently (though never to a priest or in the sanctuary as here), but almost always anonymously. The only angels named in the OT are Michael and Gabriel (in the book of Daniel which is late and apocalyptic). Others are named in the apocryphal literature. See the comment of Fitzmyer, *Luke*, p. 324. For a detailed presentation of what he calls 'Biblical Annunciations of Birth', see Brown, *Birth of the Messiah*, pp. 156-57, where he nominates five steps: (1) the *appearance* of an angel of the Lord (or appearance of the Lord), (2) *fear* or prostration of the visionary confronted by this supernatural presence, (3) the divine *message* (with its eight elements), (4) an *objection* by the visionary as to how this can be or a request for a sign, and (5) the *giving of a sign* to reassure the visionary. But see also the rejoinder of E.W. Conrad, 'The Annunciation of Birth and the Birth of the Messiah', *CBQ* 47 (1985), pp. 656-63, where he concludes that '[t]he rather complex form that Brown analyzes as 'Biblical Annunciation of Birth' is open to question. NT tradition appears to have created a model from OT texts where the relevant material was more complex and scattered than is suggested by Brown' (p. 662).

2. In offering an inside view, the narrator reveals either the thoughts or feelings of a character, and so retires from a position of external narration. On the effect of inside views in narrative, see Booth, *Rhetoric of Fiction*, pp. 163-164, 245-249.

3. The detail introduces into the narrative what Bovon, following Roland Barthes, has called 'l'effet du réel' ('Effet du réel et flou prophétique dans l'oeuvre de Luc', in *A cause de l'Evangile* [Paris: Cerf, 1985], pp. 349-60). Bovon asks: 'De quoi s'agit-il? D'une manière d'écrire réaliste; plus précisément de l'art de noter un détail, de signaler un événement singulier, de donner ainsi l'histoire racontée la couleur et les contours du vrai' (p. 353). This is more necessary given that nothing is said of who the angel is or what he looks like.

upset by what he *sees*. In order to know why the angel has appeared, Zechariah needs to hear: the narration needs to move into an aural mode. The sign must be interpreted.

Announcement and Interpretation: Luke 1.13-17

The silent angel speaks in v. 13, as the narrator for the first time has one of his characters move into direct speech. He has a vested interest in retiring behind the veil of direct speech as heaven speaks for the first time. It is better that the heavenly messenger be allowed to speak in his own right, lest there be any suggestion that he speak not so much as God's messenger but as the narrator's puppet.[1] Therefore, as heaven speaks for the first time, the narrator effaces himself still more.

Important from a narrative point of view is that the angel announces what God intends to do. This immediately gives to the divine visitation a dynamic of promise-fulfilment: God first announces what he intends doing and then does it. Here we have one of the ground rules of the Lukan narrative which the narrator is keen to establish without delay.

Also important from a narrative point of view is how the announcement is made. The angel not only announces an imminent event, but also interprets it and does so by returning to the past: Zechariah will have a son, but the son will be the promised precursor of God's eschatological salvation. In interpreting the birth, the angel adopts the language of Scripture in a way which suggests that right understanding of the promise and its fulfilment will depend upon a right reading of the signs of the biblical past. The episode as a whole began by evoking the biblical past and suggesting therefore that in order to understand the events filling the Lukan narrative readers must begin by looking backwards. What is true of the episode and the Lukan narrative as a whole is seen to be true of vv. 13-17: to understand the present and the future it portends one must look backwards.

But there is also a question of how readers look backwards. The narrator composes the angel's speech as a tapestry of either citations or echoes from the entire OT, with Torah, Prophets and Writings all finding their place.[2] The decision to compose the speech in this way

---

1. On this in OT narrative—but with implications for NT narrative—see Alter, *Art of Biblical Narrative*, pp. 63-87.

2. From the Torah, we have Gen. 16.11-12; 17.19; Num. 6.3; Lev. 10.9; from the Prophets (Former and Latter) Judg. 13.4; 2 Kgs 2.9-10; 1 Sam. 1.11; Dan. 10.12; Mal. 2.6; 3.1, 24; and from the Writings Sir. 48.10. Other echoes and motifs

means that in order to cover the entire OT the narrator is led to include elements which seem to add little to the speech except length.[1] The angel's announcement looks beyond the particular moment of vv. 13-17 to the entire sweep of biblical history, all of which is understood as a promise now coming to fulfilment in this particular moment. The divine visitation has a dynamic of promise-fulfilment not only in the Lukan narrative or by narratorial fiat; it has always had the same dynamic, as the whole of Scripture testifies. God is working now as he has always worked.

This implies an understanding of Scripture in its entirety as a promise in search of fulfilment.[2] In the angel's speech, therefore, we have the rudiments of a biblical hermeneutic which will come to full flower later in the Lukan narrative.[3] Placing the speech in the mouth of an angel gives the hermeneutic an authority transcending the narrator's authority. It bears the authority of heaven itself. It is also true that placing the angel in the sanctuary suggests that this understanding of the Bible, far from being alien or exotic, comes from the heart of Judaism itself.

As far as Zechariah is concerned the angel might well stop after v. 14, but in fact he has barely begun. What follows is the interpretation of the birth, which comprises the bulk of the speech. Zechariah may think he knows the meaning of the promise: an answer to his prayer and a son for him and his wife. What the angel offers, however, is an interpretation much broader in scope: the son will be the

are less specific and therefore harder to tie to any particular text. For a consideration of the various possibilities, see O'Fearghail, 'The Imitation of the Septuagint', pp. 63-64.

1. It is not clear, for instance, what v. 17cd (ἐπιστρέψαι καρδίας πατέρων ἐπὶ τέκνα καὶ ἀπειθεῖς ἐν φρονήσει δικαίων) adds to the speech, until we see that it is the one point at which the narrator inserts a clear echo of the sapiential literature of the OT. Apart from the general reminiscence, there is the specific echoing of Sir. 48.10.

2. On the Lukan understanding of the prophetic function of the Torah, see Conzelmann, *Theology*, p. 159 n. 1, which is part of his discussion of the Lukan biblical hermeneutic (*Theology*, pp. 157-62).

3. It will take a decisive turn in 4.16-30, where not only is the hermeneutic of Scripture as promise reinforced, but Jesus is established as the unique hermeneut (on which see Aletti, *L'art de raconter*, pp. 39-61); and it will come to full maturity in 24.13-35 (on which see again Aletti, *L'art de raconter*, pp. 177-98).

one to prepare a people for 'the Lord' (ὁ κύριος).[1]

As the interpretation of the birth unfolds, Zechariah is slowly elided. The focus is clearly on him in v. 13ab (μὴ φοβοῦ Ζαχαρία, διότι εἰσηκούσθη ἡ δέησίς σου), but then it broadens to include Elizabeth and 'the many' (πολλοί) who will share the joy of John's birth. From v. 15 onwards, it is John who is the focus of the speech, though in the climactic 'to make ready for the Lord a people prepared' (ἑτοιμάσαι κυρίῳ λαὸν κατεσκευασμένον) of v. 17, it is God whose shadow moves fleetingly to centre stage. By the end of the oracle, Zechariah has been backgrounded. Heaven itself has interpreted the angelic apparition and announcement; and it has done so by gathering up the past and turning to the future in a way which looks far beyond Zechariah.

Narrating the Reactions: Luke 1.18-25

The Demand for a Sign: Luke 1.18

In vv. 11-17, the narrator has begun to shape his vision of the divine visitation. Now at v. 18 he turns to the question of what is required for recognition of the moment of God's visitation? It is no accident that the key word in Zechariah's question is the verb 'to know' (γνώσομαι). A kind of knowledge is required, but what kind? It is that question to which the narrator turns in v. 18.

The first thing worth noting about Zechariah's response is that the narrator chooses to put into his mouth the question of Abraham in Gen. 15.8.[2] He who is like Abraham in his childlessness is made to sound like him in his question. But why? Does the narrator wish to present Zechariah as like Abraham, even identical to him? Are the two questions as alike as the wording suggests? Or are they different?

---

1. This fits a pattern for Zechariah. Coming to the Temple for routine service, he wins the right to enter the sanctuary; entering the sanctuary, he meets an angel; and receiving the promise of a son, he learns that the son is to be the precursor of ὁ κύριος. Locked for most of his life in a world where reality fell short of expectation, Zechariah's expectation is surpassed at every turn once the narration of the divine visitation begins.

2. There Abraham asks: δέσποτα κύριε, κατὰ τί γνώσομαι ὅτι κληρονομήσω αὐτήν; The second part of Zechariah's response—the statement which follows his question—also echoes statements by Abraham in Gen. 17.17 and 18.11.

And if so, how and why? These are some of the questions prompted by the narrator's choice.

There are some obvious similarities between Abraham and Zechariah. They are both childless and they are both advanced in years.[1] But there are considerably more differences. Zechariah is a priest, Abraham was not; Abraham was the first in the line of childless OT figures to whom God gives offspring, Zechariah is the last; in Gen. 15.6 it is said of Abraham that he put his faith in God before he put his question,[2] but that is never said of Zechariah; Abraham's question comes in response to the promise of a land, Zechariah's in response to the promise of a son; Zechariah has prayed for a son,[3] but Abraham had not prayed for a land; and so on.[4] The parallel between the two figures is not as sure as the form of the question would suggest.

In fact, closer scrutiny shows that Zechariah's question, although almost identical in form, moves in a direction quite different from Abraham's question. Zechariah has seen the angel, and he has heard the promise. But this combination is not enough for him, since both vision and oracle require a faith which looks a risky proposition for a man of his years. Zechariah's question conceals a demand; and what he demands is a knowledge which might substitute for faith—and a knowledge, it seems, based not upon hearing but upon seeing, since what Zechariah demands is a sign.[5] This, then, is the first of the

1. For a more detailed indication of the way in which vv. 5-25 echo the Abraham stories of Genesis, see Aletti, *L'art de raconter*, p. 68.

2. The narrator says of Abraham: καὶ ἐπίστευσεν Αβραμ τῷ θεῷ καὶ ἐλογίσθη αὐτῷ εἰς δικαιοσύνην.

3. It is not wholly certain that εἰσηκούσθη ἡ δέησίς σου refers to Zechariah's personal prayer for a son or to some more public or liturgical prayer. But the use of the second person singular σου and the narrative's silence on the recitation of any liturgical prayer (save the prayer of ὁ λαός in v. 10) suggests that ἡ δέησις refers to Zechariah's own prayer for a son. See O'Fearghail, 'The Imitation of the Septuagint', p. 65.

4. Other differences are the following: Zechariah has his vision in the Temple, Abraham does not; the promise to Abraham is cast more in the form of a dialogue with God; the promise to Abraham is not just the promise of a single son, but of a vast progeny; the promise of a son to Abraham is linked to the promise of a land.

5. In the Aristotelian sense, what he demands is τεκμήριον rather than σημεῖον. According to Aristotle (*Rhetoric* 1.2.16-18), the difference is that where τεκμήριον is an infallible proof which leaves no room for doubt, σημεῖον is not. In Acts 1.3, the Lukan narrator adopts the Aristotelian language in referring to the appearances of the Risen Christ as τεκμήρια: οἷς καὶ παρέστησεν ἑαυτὸν ζῶντα

possible answers to the question, 'what kind of knowledge?', which the narrator introduces into the narrative. In order to recognize the moment of God's visitation, does one perhaps need an assured knowledge, based on sight, which might substitute for faith? A second point about the question is that it implies a failure of memory. Zechariah uses the words of Abraham, but forgets the biblical tradition which comes to birth in Abraham; and in that sense he fails to interpret rightly the signs of past fulfilment in a way which might enable him to understand and accept the new promise. Abraham was the first of the line of childless OT figures who are given offspring by divine intervention; Zechariah is the last. The question makes sense for Abraham, since the promise to him is a totally new event, a new and unforseeable beginning. But the promise of a son to Zechariah is not a totally new event, nor a new and unforseeable beginning. Scripture offers evidence of God's power to bring babes from barren wombs, and this is a moment of fulfilment rather than a new beginning. Zechariah's question implies that he sees himself as like Abraham, whereas his situation in time, as heir to the biblical witness, makes him quite different.

The question also implies that Zechariah knows the Scripture, since it implies the knowledge that Abraham was given a sign when he asked for it,[1] and that in one other OT annunciation scene a sign was given without being requested.[2] Yet as Aletti notes, 'if he knows the Scripture, he must know that the divine promise will be realized; but then there is no longer any reason for his question! The contradictory situation in which Zechariah finds himself could not be better expressed by the narrative'.[3] The puzzle is that he mouths the words of Abraham, but fails to remember the events of the biblical story which would answer the question he puts. He asks, 'By what?' (κατὰ τί;) when he has already the biblical evidence: there is the failure of memory. The narrator further underscores the contradictory nature

μετὰ τὸ παθεῖν αὐτὸν ἐν πολλοῖς τεκμηρίοις. But see too Lk. 11.16, 29 where σημεῖον occurs with the force of the Aristotelian τεκμήριον.

1. Gen. 15.9-21 reports the covenant ceremony which is the sign given to Abraham, but which also involves his descendants, including Zechariah.

2. See Judg. 13.9 where the angel appears a second time as a a sign, and Judg. 13.20 where the angel ascends to heaven in the flame of the burnt offering—a sign striking enough to have Manoah and his wife fall on their faces to the ground.

3. Aletti, *L'art de raconter*, p. 70.

of Zechariah's situation by presenting him as a man who has prayed for a son—presumably because he believes that God can still give him a son against all the odds—but who when faced with the heavenly promise fails to believe.[1]

A further point is that Zechariah fails to accept the reliability of the still anonymous messenger. In Genesis 15, it is God with whom Abraham treats, but here Zechariah must deal with an intermediary who may or may not be a reliable spokesman. In answer to the question 'By what?' (κατὰ τί;), the angel might well have replied, 'According to the promise I have just spoken and the sacred writings of which I am spokesman and interpreter'. But that is not enough for Zechariah, since he asks for something more than the angel's promise and the biblical witness. He seeks a sign which will demonstrate the intermediary's authority and reliability.

It appears, then, that despite their similar form the questions of Abraham and Zechariah move in quite different directions. The fact that the narrator begins to lay the epistemological ground of his narrative with a verbatim echo of Abraham's question suggests that a key question of the narrative is not only, 'how are we to recognize the divine visitation?', but more precisely, 'given Abraham as the archetype of right recognition, what (for us now) does the faith of Abraham look like?' Although the memory and echo of Abraham are ubiquitous in the episode, Abraham himself is never named.[2] He is everywhere but elided, since what matters for the narrator is that not Abraham but his faith appear, and that it be shown in the characters.

What has also emerged in Zechariah's reply is that he has been left free enough to baulk at faith and demand a knowledge which might substitute for it.[3] Faced with the heavenly irruption, the human being —it would seem at this stage—is not forced into submission, but is left

---

1.   O'Fearghail suggests that this 'incoherence' arises not from the narrator's desire to evoke the contradictory situation of the unbelieving Zechariah, but from Luke's less than wholly successful use of Gen. 15.8 and 18.11-12 ('Imitation of the Septuagint', pp. 65-66). Attention to narrative criteria avoids the need for such complex and speculative hypothesizing.

2.   Though he will be named quite conspicuously in both the Magnificat (1.55) and Benedictus (1.73). It is a question, then, of when Abraham is named and by whom.

3.   On the freedom of the human being before God in OT narrative, see the remarks of Sternberg, *Poetics*, p. 110, and with specific reference to the Lukan narrative see Aletti, *L'art de raconter*, pp. 205-209.

to decide freely how to respond. Gabriel's promise does not actively seek a response of any kind: he simply states what will happen. It is a question therefore of how open to what will happen the human being will show himself. This is the point at which freedom is to be exercised.

Gabriel's Judgment: Luke 1.19-20

Unwilling to believe the promise made by the angel, Zechariah has sought a sign which will give certainty. The question is how the heavenly intermediary will respond to the request, and how doubt will affect the implementation of the divine plan. What the narrator makes clear in vv. 19-20 is that the God whose plan transcends the laws of nature is also the God whose plan transcends human doubt. In doing so, he modulates in a new and important way his narration of the divine visitation;[1] and he does so in ways which will prove decisive for the entire Lukan narrative.[2]

God looks to the human being to accept his plan, but does not depend upon the human being for its implementation. Gabriel has stated what *will* happen, and he reiterates that assurance in v. 20. It is not as if Zechariah's unbelief threatens the divine plan in any way: it will happen. It is more a problem for Zechariah himself. He it is who must come to accept the plan now unfolding, a plan of which—despite himself—he is a vital part. He has freely chosen *not* to believe; and the question now is whether or not he will in time choose to believe. In the meantime, the divine plan will continue to unfold according to its dynamic of necessity. Gabriel's second speech, then, underlines the dynamic of promise-fulfilment and adds the new element of the dynamic of necessity.

The fact that the angel introduces himself and states his credentials with considerable éclat confirms the suspicion that lurking beneath the

---

1. In classical terms, Zechariah's unbelief amounts to peripateia. In his discussion of plot, Aristotle (*Poetics* 3.D.2) defines peripateia as an unexpected change of events or a surprising diversion which does not prevent the plot from reaching its goal, but which makes the attainment of the goal more complex. See F. Kermode's remarks on peripateia as a feature of 'every story of the least structural sophistication' in *The Sense of an Ending: Studies in the Theory of Fiction* (London and New York: Oxford University Press, 1967), p. 18.

2. Throughout Luke–Acts the divine plan not only will not be thwarted by human doubt and even outright rejection, but paradoxically will gain momentum in its trajectory because of doubt and rejection. What we have in this first episode, then, is a prolepsis of what will follow, as Aletti (*L'art de raconter*, p. 70) points out.

surface of Zechariah's question was doubt as to the authority and
reliability of the messenger.[1] This is Gabriel, fresh from the book of
Daniel, though speaking now in different accents.[2] No dubious angel
of the narrator's own devising, this is the great OT messenger who
comes not from the pen of the author but from the presence of God
himself; and it is he rather than the self-effacing narrator who not
only interprets but also evaluates Zechariah's question. For the first
but not the last time in the episode, the narrator leaves interpretation
to one of his characters. In choosing a figure familiar from the OT,
the narrator insists—in the light of Zechariah's failure of memory—
on the need to remember, and especially to remember the promise of
eschatological salvation which, according to the hermeneutic implied
in vv. 13-17, is the true meaning of the OT. But that it is the eschatological messenger from the book of Daniel also underlines the fact
that the promise of salvation is coming now to its fulfilment.

Once he introduces himself and assumes an identity of his own,
Gabriel also assumes a language of his own. He speaks now more personally than in vv. 13-17, using not the hieratic language of the OT
but a more spontaneous language adapted to meet the obstacle of
doubt. The oracle of vv. 13-17 was uttered under divine instructions,
as he himself makes clear in v. 19: 'I was sent to speak to you'
(ἀπεστάλην λαλῆσαι πρός σε). Again the divine passive occurs in
the description of what took place in heaven, that is, God's commissioning of Gabriel.[3] But what is clear is that the messenger, who until

---

1.   In the *Armenian Infancy Gospel*, Gabriel never introduces himself, and this
is because its version of Zechariah's question (3.7: 'How can I understand that?')
has not queried the angel's credentials in the same way. This is also why, in the
Armenian Infancy Gospel, Gabriel never mentions that he was sent from God: he has
no need to state the source of his authority.

2.   In his two appearances in the book of Daniel, Gabriel is the interpreter of
visions, and tends to speak in still loftier tones than he does in Luke 1, focusing in
Dan. 8.16-26 on the rise and fall of world empires, and in Dan. 9.21-27 on the
apocalyptic scenario of a Jerusalem rebuilt and destroyed and the coming of an
anointed prince. Though the sweep of his speech in Lk. 1.13-17 is grand enough, it
is less elevated and more personal, with its promise of a child to a childless couple;
and Gabriel is never as stern in the book of Daniel as he proves to be in Lk. 1.19-20.

3.   Unlike the OT narrator who describes the deliberations of the court of heaven
in texts such as Gen. 1.26; 3.22; 11.6-7, the Lukan narrator shows no interest
in narrating what happens in heaven. What passes between God and Gabriel
is implied, but never narrated. This is one of the reasons why Sternberg is

now has acted under divine instructions, begins to speak and act in his own right. He is a bearer of such authority that he has no need to refer back to God for new instructions to meet the new need. He even refers in v. 20 to the oracle as 'my words' (οἱ λόγοί μου), and also acts without reference to heaven by imposing silence on Zechariah.

A second more basic point is established in the reply; and it touches the heart of the epistemological question which the narrator has begun to treat. Where Zechariah has spoken in terms of knowledge (κατὰ τί γνώσομαι τοῦτο) Gabriel speaks of faith (ἀνθ' ὧν οὐκ ἐπίστευσας τοῖς λόγοις μου), and so denies Zechariah the right to a knowledge which might substitute for faith. The narrator makes it clear that the key to an understanding of what is required for the recognition of the divine visitation is faith—which prompts the further question, what exactly does faith involve? An answer to that question must wait; but for the moment the narrator asserts, via the heavenly intermediary, that to see faith as the matrix is to begin to understand what right recognition requires.

Zechariah has sought a sign which might confer an assured knowledge; and the sign he is given is the initially puzzling sign of silence until the fulfilment of the promise. The sign is both punitive and propaedeutic—both a judgment upon unbelief and an education for belief.[1] As punitive, it represents heaven's assessment of unbelief—the divine rejection of Zechariah's answer to the question, 'what kind of knowledge does the divine visitation require?' As propaedeutic, it refuses to meet Zechariah on his own ground, since it in no way confers a knowledge which averts the need for faith. It is a demonstration of the messenger's authority and reliability, and that is what Zechariah

right in describing the Lukan narration as 'earthly' (*Poetics*, p. 118)—though it is not one of the reasons prompting his description.

1. Not all agree that the sign is both punitive and propaedeutic. A. Plummer (*A Critical and Exegetical Commentary on the Gospel according to St. Luke* [New York: Charles Scribner's Sons, 1922], p. 17), H. Schürmann (*Das Lukasevangelium: Erster Teil: Kommentar zu Kap. 1,1-9,50* [Freiburg: Herder, 1969], p. 37), Gueuret (*L'engendrement*, pp. 53-54) and C.F. Evans (*Saint Luke* [London: SCM Press; Philadelphia: Trinity Press International, 1990], p. 152) think so. Marshall (*Gospel*, p. 61) and Fitzmyer (*Luke*, p. 328) see the sign as punitive, but see its second function as withholding the news of the revelation from ὁ λαός rather than leading Zechariah to faith. Brown (*Birth of the Messiah*, p. 280) and R. Laurentin (*Les Evangiles de l'Enfance: Vérité de Noël au-delà des mythes* [Paris: Desclée, 1982], p. 182) regard it as solely punitive.

has sought; but it is not one that confers the assured knowledge which he has presumed would be the result of the demonstration.

The silence is also a sign ensuring that the initiative does not pass to Zechariah, but remains firmly with heaven. Were Zechariah to sally forth from the sanctuary, armed with both the assured knowledge he has sought and a voice, the danger would be that he would rival heaven in the implementation and proclamation of the divine plan. The silence ensures that Zechariah retains his proper place in the narrative world and that for the time being heaven retains the initiative in both the implementation and proclamation of the divine plan. Zechariah clearly has his place in the plan, but as a collaborator rather than a rival of God; and that collaboration demands a faith at which Zechariah has baulked.

Though the sign is intended to lead Zechariah to faith, it in no way coerces or commands faith. Gabriel says simply that Zechariah will be silent until the promise is fulfilled; the narrator does not have him say that Zechariah will be silent until he believes. Once the child is conceived, born and named, Zechariah will be free to speak; and the question is, when he speaks, how well he will have read the signs of God's action, the first of which is given now in his silence.

Between the signs given and the salvation promised there lies a gap; and it is this gap that faith must traverse. Yet what Gabriel makes clear is that faith is not groundless. If knowledge can never substitute for faith, then neither does faith dispense with the need for knowledge. Faith is based upon knowledge of a kind—in particular a knowledge of God's fidelity to his promises in the past—but must move beyond it. Knowledge, though necessary, is never adequate.

Interpreting the Signs: Luke 1.21-25
The narrator leaves the sanctuary in v. 21, taking the readers with him and leaving Zechariah and Gabriel in the sanctuary.[1] Once again it is the People who enter the scene, reinforcing the sense that the

---

1.   The narrator gives no hint of Zechariah's reaction to Gabriel's second speech—either during it or at the end of it. The narration remains purely external. Compare again the *Armenian Infancy Gospel*, which after Gabriel has fallen silent has the now mute Zechariah prostrate himself before the altar beating his breast, lamenting and weeping bitterly (3.7). The Lukan narrator, however, is more interested in the reaction of ὁ λαός to Zechariah than in the reaction of Zechariah to Gabriel.

drama which has unfolded between Gabriel and Zechariah has wider ramifications. Once Zechariah does emerge, the People are shown no longer at prayer, but faced instead with a puzzling sign which calls for interpretation. The sign is the dumbstruck Zechariah; and the irony is that he who has sought a sign from the angel becomes himself a sign. Yet he is by no means a sign conferring assured knowledge of the kind he has sought.

Verse 21 makes it clear that the People have begun to suspect that something unusual has happened in the sanctuary: the question is, what and why? Even though in narrative time the exchange between Gabriel and Zechariah has been brief, it is the element of delay in story time which alerts the People to the fact that something is amiss.[1] When Zechariah emerges dumbstruck, we have the narrative's first sign of fulfilment. Despite himself and by the power of Gabriel's word, he becomes witness to a mysterious divine action. To Zechariah and the reader, at least, his wordlessness testifies to the power of the heavenly word. But for the People the situation is different, since they know far less than Zechariah and the reader. Left to themselves to interpret the sign of the silent Zechariah, they judge wrongly. They judge that he has been struck dumb because he has seen a vision, when in fact Zechariah has been struck dumb not because he has seen a vision, but because he has not believed Gabriel's promise. It is not what he has seen that is the problem, but what he has heard and refused to believe.

Still, the People recognize that there has been a revelation, even if they know nothing of the revelation's nature and purpose.[2] As the

---

1. The distinction between story time and narrative time relates to the Russian formalist distinction between *fabula and sjuzet* (or, as Chatman has it, between story and discourse) and is a commonplace of narratology. However, the terminology is a little confusing. Chatman speaks of story time and discourse time, Rimmon-Kenan of story time and text time, others of narrated time and narrating time, or *erzählte Zeit* and *Erzählzeit*. This study will adhere to Genette's story time and narrative time. For different though related treatments of the question, see Genette's long and sophisticated study in *Narrative Discourse*, pp. 33-160 (well summarized and explained by Rimmon-Kenan, *Narrative Fiction*, pp. 43-58), and Chatman, *Story and Discourse*, pp. 62-84. On the relationship between Genette and Chatman, see Culpepper, *Anatomy of the Fourth Gospel*, p. 53 n. 2.

2. Aletti rightly sees the reaction of ὁ λαός as emblematic of the entire Lukan narrative. He writes: 'Luc n'aurait pu mieux trouver pour indiquer la nature de son récit: non point fiction ou mensonge, mais véridiction, au sens déjà énoncé, puisque

Lukan narrative unfolds, the narrator will lead 'the whole multitude of the People' to a recognition of the revelation's nature and purpose, and will lead the knowing readers to follow their coming to knowledge and to either belief or unbelief on the basis of what they come to know of the nature and purpose of the revelation. It is in this sense that the narrative is 'doublement gnoséologique'.[1] Readers and characters journey together, but in different modes.

The People judge on the basis of what they see now (the dumb priest and the signs he makes[2]) and know of the past (that visions in the sanctuary, if not an everyday event, were not unknown);[3] but they need to hear a word of interpretation. Until they do, they do not have knowledge enough to serve as a basis for faith. They are left in the realm of guesswork until, knowing more, they might have a basis from which they might decide for either belief or unbelief. Where Zechariah knew enough, but in his demand to know more refused to believe, the People do not yet know enough to make faith a possibility.

In narrating the response of the People to the sight of the dumb Zechariah, the narrator modulates his treatment of the relationship between knowledge and faith. Again, it is no accident that in the report of their response we find a compound form of the verb 'to know' (ἐπέγνωσαν)—the same verb we found in 1:18. They know without really knowing: theirs is a seeming knowledge. It is a question of knowledge, but more especially a question of what kind of knowledge.

After v. 23, Zechariah disappears from the narrative, and Elizabeth, who has been only a name until now, moves to centre stage. Her pregnancy is the narrative's second sign of fulfilment, with Gabriel

---

les personnages du récit primaire eux-mêmes vont tous, et dès le premier épisode, reconnaître qu'il y a eu intervention divine' (*L'art de raconter*, p. 67).

1. Aletti, *L'art de reconter*, pp. 79-80.

2. It is hard to know exactly what διανεύων connotes. It can mean either to nod with the head or to signal with the hands, but the second seems more likely in this context, with Zechariah seeking to explain with gesture what he cannot explain with speech. As a manual sign that testifies to his powerlessness before the power of heaven, it may well be intended as an ironic comment on the blessing which Zechariah was supposed to offer after emerging from the sanctuary. If the blessing involved both speech and gesture (on which see above), then Zechariah fails on both counts: he cannot speak and his gesture is not a gesture of blessing but an attempt to explain why he cannot speak.

3. There was at least the one occasion recorded by Josephus (*Ant.* 13.10.3) where the High Priest John Hyrcanus had a vision during the incense offering.

again shown to be as good as his word. The question is again how well Elizabeth will interpret the sign of her own pregnancy. Unlike Zechariah, she is not asked to believe a promise; like the People, she is faced with a *fait accompli* which calls for interpretation. The narrator remains silent on the score of Elizabeth's reaction to the sight of her speechless husband, since that would shift the focus back to Zechariah at a point where the narrator wants to move instead to Elizabeth. Nor is there any report of an exchange between Zechariah and Elizabeth; and the reader cannot presume that Zechariah has somehow communicated everything to her.[1] In the task of interpretation, then, the narrator leaves Elizabeth to her own devices. As it turns out, her words in v. 25 are a right, if incomplete reading of the sign of her pregnancy: God has intervened. Without the aid of either a heavenly revelation or a word from her husband, Elizabeth comes to the recognition that this is God's work. She interprets the sign aright; and that she is made to do so in language reminiscent of OT women suggests that the ground of her interpretation of the present sign is a remembering of what God has done in the past.[2]

In having her proclaim the action of God in her life, the narrator again leaves interpretation to his character, and in a way which underscores the freedom of her response. Elizabeth speaks for herself. The narrator chooses the same ploy in having Elizabeth refer to her sterility as 'my reproach' (ὄνειδός μου), where in v. 7 he had mentioned Elizabeth's sterility with no hint of interpretation and in v. 18 he had Zechariah mention Elizabeth's sterility without interpretation of the kind she now offers.

It is the same decision to leave interpretation to his characters which leads the narrator to say nothing of any communication between Zechariah and Elizabeth, nor of any divine intervention to enable her conception. In v. 24 the narrator mentions that Elizabeth conceives, but makes no mention of God. She it is, rather than Zechariah or the narrator, who interprets the fact of her pregnancy.

Elizabeth reads rightly the signs of God's action, but there is still a

---

1. As does, for example, N. Geldenhuys, *A Commentary on the Gospel of Luke: The English Text with Introduction, Exposition and Notes* (Grand Rapids: Eerdmans, 1951), p. 69.
2. Elizabeth is made to sound very like similar OT women—Sarah (Gen. 21.6) and Rachel (Gen. 30.23) in particular—which suggests that, unlike her husband, Elizabeth rightly interprets the sign of her pregnancy because she remembers aright.

self-absorbed quality in her words, as if God has intervened primarily to vindicate her; and it is this which makes her reading incomplete. She extols God 'because thus he has done for *me*' (ὅτι οὕτως μοι πεποίηκεν); and she refers to '*my* reproach' (ὄνειδός μου), with the first person singular pronoun sounding again. The sense of self-absorption is conveyed not only by the words the narrator puts in her mouth, but also by her concealment. Locked by choice in a private world, Elizabeth gives no indication of having any comprehension of the wider, more public implications of her pregnancy, that is, that her child will prepare the way of the Lord. Elizabeth recognizes the hand of God in what has happened, but she needs to know more if she is to come to the full comprehension which makes mature interpretation possible.

A second reason why the narrator has Elizabeth hide for five months is that again, in the implementation and proclamation of the plan, heaven may retain the initiative.[1] Any character who may threaten to wrest the initiative from heaven is elided in one way or another—Zechariah is struck dumb and Elizabeth is made to hide. At that point, the revelation is neither audible nor visible; and it cannot be made audible or visible unless God intervenes once more. The time will come when the initiative will pass to human characters, but for the moment it is heaven that retains the initiative.

By the end of 1.5-25, the stage is clear and God is left in control, working single-mindedly but in separate arenas for the time being. In the silence of Zechariah and the concealment of Elizabeth, heaven decides to remain hidden for the time being. God is therefore both revealed and concealed; but here as throughout the infancy narrative it is he who controls the interplay of revelation and concealment.

Conclusion

By having heaven trigger the action in the form of the angelic announcement, the narrator shows that God has the initiative; and in

---

1. Aletti (*L'art de raconter*, pp. 34-35) suggests that Elizabeth's silence has 'des conséquences importantes au niveau de la véridiction'. He explains that Elizabeth's concealment ensures that Mary, if she comes to know of Elizabeth's condition, can have come to the knowledge only through revelation—as Elizabeth will realize as soon as she sees Mary. He concludes: 'Ces cinq mois sont donc essentiels au propos du narrateur: grâce à ce long silence, les voies par lesquelles la bonne nouvelle se transmet n'en apparaîtront que plus merveilleuses et vraies'.

having Gabriel speak the promise and then recounting the beginning of fulfilment, the narrator shows how God exercises the initiative. From the start, the divine visitation is seen to have a dynamic of promise-fulfilment: God first announces what he will do and then does it. This is shown to be true not only in the Lukan narrative or by narratorial fiat, but also in the whole of Scripture. As the narrative sees it, this is the way God has always worked. Heaven also offers a clue as to how to interpret the new promise and the signs of its fulfilment: first, look backwards and read aright the signs of past fulfilment, and secondly, make the leap of faith from the basis of that knowledge.

In having Gabriel insist that the divine plan will unfold as promised despite Zechariah's failure, the narrator has shown how the divine plan is not thwarted by human doubt. It has its own dynamic of necessity. In that sense, God is shown to be one who seeks human acceptance of his plan, but does not depend upon it. The narrator has left Zechariah free enough to baulk at such a response, to disbelieve the divine promise; and he has left Elizabeth free enough to read rightly (if incompletely) the sign of her pregnancy. Yet for all the freedom granted the characters, they are not wholly free. The dynamic of necessity in God's action creates an interplay of divine necessity and human freedom which will remain decisive throughout both the infancy narrative and the Lukan narrative as a whole.

In beginning his narration of the divine visitation, the narrator has set the scene in the religious world of Judaism by focusing on the piety of the characters, by constant reference back to the world of the OT in a way that gives the whole episode the flavour and atmosphere of the OT, and by setting the bulk of the action in the Temple. This makes it clear that God's action comes from within Judaism. Yet by having Gabriel appear unexpectedly at the moment when the rite of incense-burning should have been performed and by deciding not to narrate the rite itself, the narrator has made the divine visitation disruptive in a way which shows how God's action moves beyond the Temple cult. A further paradox is that the pious priest fails to believe: he who is a most likely candidate for faith finds faith beyond him.

In having Gabriel reject Zechariah's demand for a knowledge which might substitute for faith and insist upon the need for a faith which is based upon knowledge but which surpasses it, the narrator has established that human recognition of the divine visitation (understood as promise) demands not a knowledge which might substitute for faith, but a faith which is based upon knowledge—especially knowledge of what God has done in the past (that is, right remembering of promises fulfilled).

In the People and Elizabeth, the narrator has introduced into the narrative the element of interpretation of the signs which appear once the process of fulfilment begins, as it does embryonically in this first episode. Just as faith corresponds to the divine visitation understood as promise, right interpretation of the signs corresponds to the divine visitation understood as fulfilment. The two are parts of a single process.

The narrator has also laid what look to be some of the ground rules of the rhetorical transaction. Among these is a narratorial discretion which prefers to pass the word—especially at key moments of evaluation or interpretation—to his characters. Another is the knowledge gap between reader and characters. In Perry's terms of the interplay between primacy and recency effect, it remains to be seen whether ground rules such as these and the rudiments of a vision of divine visitation and human recognition offered by the narrator in this first episode will be either confirmed or modified. Either way, it will be a question of how this is to happen.

Chapter 3

EXPLORING FAITH IN LUKE 1.26-38

Continuing a Narrative

At the threshold of the second episode, the readers have questions. They know something of the *what* of the narrative, but little enough of the *how*. They know that God wants a people prepared for his eschatological intervention and that the son of Zechariah and Elizabeth is the one appointed to the task; but what the precise shape of God's intervention might be—how it will happen—is unclear. Similarly, the readers know that God's promise requires faith, but they know little enough of what the precise contours of faith might be. In narrating a story of doubt, the first episode has established a basic relationship between knowledge and faith; but the readers need to know more of what faith involves, how it happens. At the same time, the readers know more than any of the characters as the episode begins; and so, while learning more of the *how*, they are well positioned to follow the responses of the characters to the *what* as they appear on the stage of the narrative.

Having brought the readers to that point, the narrator decides to leave the story of the first episode and to begin instead a story which, like the first episode, conforms well enough to the pattern of OT annunciations of birth. At first glance, the two episodes seem very similar, but it remains to be seen whether the similarity is superficial (as with the questions of Abraham and Zechariah) or more thoroughgoing.[1]

The narrator again has heaven trigger the action by the arrival and

1. There is a range of opinion on this. Fitzmyer for instance claims that '[t]he second episode. . . is parallel to the first' (*Luke*, p. 334), and L. Legrand by contrast claims that '[l]e parallélisme de composition n'est que superficiel. Les structures narratives sont différentes' (*L'annonce à Marie [Lc 1,26-38]: Une apocalypse aux origines de l'Evangile* [Paris: Cerf, 1981], p. 75).

announcement of Gabriel—thus reinforcing the dynamic of promise-fulfilment established in the first episode. But there are significant differences of setting of the action, composition of the oracle and characterization of both angel and addressee. Therefore, we are dealing with a technique not of repetition but of reprise; the narrator resumes elements of the previous episode but modulates them by means of variation and addition at times subtle, at other times less so.

In vv. 26-38 the narrator explores the faith upon which Gabriel has insisted in the previous episode. In that sense, the second episode develops the epistemology of the first episode in decisive ways; and it does so by contrasting Zechariah and Mary, having the two characters meet the same challenge quite differently.

The Initiative of Heaven: Luke 1.26-29

Gabriel Again: Luke 1.26-27

In this episode, the narrator begins not by introducing the human characters who will enter the scene, but by plunging immediately into the narration of the heavenly initiative: God does not so much enter a story as make a story. As Legrand notes: 'For the annunciation to Mary, it is heaven, not the parents, which is the point of departure'.[1] The narrator again has God work through Gabriel, who provides the link not only with heaven, but also with the previous episode and the OT, although now there is not the same evocation of the biblical past. In this episode, there is the sense of a new beginning rather than the fulfilment of a past stretching back to Abraham.

In the first episode Gabriel did not name himself until v. 19; but now the narrator names him in v. 26, making a strong and immediate link with the preceding episode. For all that the narrative moves ahead in time, moves elsewhere in space and introduces a new character in Mary, there is a unity of action—if not at the level of human circumstance, then at least at the level of God's plan. Gabriel is named not simply as 'Gabriel', but as 'the angel Gabriel'. He is introduced to the reader not only in terms of his person, but also in terms of his role.

---

1.   Legrand, *L'annonce*, p. 71. In his study of the differences between the first and second episodes (*L'annonce*, pp. 67-87), Legrand observes rightly that where the first episode is essentially 'hagiographique' (with a 'code horizontal'), the second episode is essentially 'apocalyptique' (with a 'code vertical'). This suggests that the two episodes may not be as symmetrical as they seem.

Referring to him as 'the angel' the narrator insists on his link with the God who has sent 'him'. This will remain so throughout the episode with Gabriel referred to by the narrator as 'the angel' in vv. 30, 34, 35, 38. As the narrator sees it, Gabriel is important not in himself, but as servant of the God whose messenger he is.

In another way the narrator displaces Gabriel from the central position he held in the first episode. There the movement of Zechariah was reported, with Gabriel the unmoving fulcrum of the narrative. In vv. 26-38, however, Gabriel's movements are reported—in v. 28 we have 'he came' (εἰσελθών) and in v. 38 'he departed' (ἀπῆλθεν); and it is Mary who becomes the unmoving fulcrum of the narrative in a way that was not true of Zechariah in the first episode.

The narrator also names God immediately and explicitly as prime mover: 'the angel Gabriel was sent from God' (ἀπεστάλη ὁ ἄγγελος Γαβριὴλ ἀπὸ τοῦ θεοῦ).[1] Where in vv. 5-12 God was introduced in the context of Jewish religion, now he moves outside that context in a way that makes his action more direct, less mediated, and the sense of his initiative stronger.

Before we are told to whom Gabriel has been sent, we are told where. Now we have not the sacral space of the Temple but far-flung Nazareth, which is nowhere mentioned in the OT. This strengthens the sense of a new beginning in the second episode. If Gabriel has been displaced from the centre in this episode, then so too have Jerusalem and the Temple, as God himself moves more on the margin. Once we know that it is to Nazareth that Gabriel has been sent, the spatial references evaporate. Nothing is said of where exactly Gabriel and Mary meet, which seems odd in a narrative that has been so detailed in its spatial references, even to the point of designating on which side of the altar the angel was standing (v. 11).[2] But in v. 28 we are told simply that Gabriel went 'to *her*' (πρὸς αὐτήν). The spatial references give way to a personal reference. The goal of the divine action is not a place but a person.

---

1. There is the question of whether ἀπο or ὑπο should be read in v. 26. ὑπο is attractive, since it gives a more energetic sense of the divine initiative and has fair manuscript support (A C D θ 053 𝔐). But the weight of manuscript evidence supports the reading of ὑπο (ℵ B L W Θ 0130 f¹.(13) 565 700 892 1241pc).

2. Compare again the *Protoevangelium of James* (11.2) which has Mary, having returned to her home and put down the water-jar, sitting on a stool sewing the purple stuff she has been working.

The enigmatic character of God's initiative becomes clearer still when we learn to whom Gabriel has been sent. In the first episode, Gabriel appeared to a character made venerable by his piety, his age and his office (and therefore lineage). Now, however, Gabriel is sent to a young woman, unmarried if betrothed, of whose lineage and piety nothing is said.[1] Nor is there any hint that Mary takes the initiative as there was with Zechariah in vv. 5-25, where the divine action was presented as a response to his prayer. But the narrator says nothing of what Mary is doing when Gabriel enters.[2] Where Zechariah, if alone in the sanctuary, is still surrounded by the People at prayer, Mary is presented as physically alone. As Legrand notes, 'the narrative discourse on Mary is reduced to a minimum'.[3]

Mary is not named immediately, but is referred to twice by the narrator as 'a virgin' (παρθένος) to prepare for what is to come in vv. 34-35.[4] Joseph too is mentioned, but only as a name and in terms of his status as a Davidide (ἐξ οἴκου Δαυίδ); and he will play no role

---

1.   Dissatisfied with such elliptical narration, both popular piety and various Christian liturgical calendars have turned to the *Protoevangelium of James* (1.1; 2.1) where the figures of Joachim and Anne appear as Mary's parents. Various commentators through the ages have also sought to confer Davidic lineage on Mary. The *Protoevangelium of James*, Ignatius of Antioch, Justin Martyr and Origen all have Mary a Davidide. This is partly because of the ambiguity of v. 27, partly because the commentators wanted Jesus to have real rather than apparent Davidic descent, and partly because they wanted to give Mary some lineage rather than leave her as the narrator does with none at all—though Fitzmyer notes that 'from 1.5, 36 one could conclude that she was of Aaronic lineage' (*Luke*, p. 344). On the score of Mary's piety, J.T. Carroll is right in noting that where the piety of Zechariah and Elizabeth is told to the reader, the quite different piety of Mary is shown as the episode unfolds (*Response to the End of History: Eschatology and Salvation in Luke–Acts* [Atlanta: Scholars Press, 1988], p. 41 n. 16).

2.   Compare the *Protoevangelium of James* (11.1-2) which has Mary first hear a mysterious voice as she goes to draw water (presumably at the well), and then finally has the angel appear once she has returned to her house and is sitting on a stool.

3.   Legrand, *L'annonce*, p. 73.

4.   Where in Mt. 1.22-23 the reference to Isa. 7.14 is explicit, here in Luke it is not. The repetition of παρθένος (which the LXX uses to translate the less specific MT עלמה) and other verbal links make it possible, though not certain. Laurentin (*Structure*, p. 72), Schürmann (*Lukasevangelium*, pp. 62-63) and Marshall (*Gospel*, p. 64) claim that it is probable that the Lukan text has been composed in dependence upon the Isaian text—a claim vigorously rejected by J.A. Fitzmyer, 'The Virginal Conception of Jesus in the New Testament', *TS* 34 (1973) p. 568 n. 9.

at all in the episode. In these first verses, then, three characters are introduced, all of them in terms of an identity linking the character to God's plan. Gabriel is introduced as 'the angel'; Mary as 'a virgin'; and Joseph as 'of the house of David'.

An Ambiguous Greeting: Luke 1.28

In the first episode, the narrator had Gabriel at first stand silent in the sanctuary, but now he has him begin with the greeting: 'Hail, O graced one, the Lord is with you' (χαῖρε κεχαριτωμένη, ὁ κύριος μετὰ σοῦ). The greeting is ambiguous because it is not immediately obvious what either 'Hail, O graced one' (χαῖρε κεχαριτωμένη) or 'the Lord is with you' (ὁ κύριος μετὰ σοῦ) might mean.[1] How has she been graced? In what way and to what effect is the Lord with her? The greeting states the 'what', but says nothing of the 'how'. God is astir, but the purpose of his stirring remains veiled behind the words of his messenger, who uses another divine passive in referring to God's gracing of Mary.

Though greeted as 'graced one' (κεχαριτωμένη), Mary herself is not named by Gabriel. She is greeted not so much in her own right, but in terms of what God has done to her, in a way that paradoxically focuses on both God and her.[2] Nor does Gabriel make any attempt to

---

1. Evidence of this is the diversity of opinion among scholars. On χαῖρε, some (for example Fitzmyer, *Luke*, pp. 344-45; Marshall, *Gospel*, p. 65) claim that it is best understood as the standard Greek salutation and should therefore be translated as 'Hail!' or something similar. Others (for example S. Lyonnet, 'χαῖρε κεκαριτωμένη', *Bib* 20 [1939], pp. 131-41; Laurentin, *Structure*, pp. 64-71) argue for a more theologically charged sense, and for a literal translation ('Rejoice!'), which would suggest a link with the OT Daughter of Zion (see especially Zeph. 3.14). On κεχαριτωηένη, some have argued that it should be understood as referring to Mary's future role as mother of the messiah (for example Fitzmyer, *Luke*, pp. 345-46), while others (for example de la Potterie, 'κεχαριτωμένη en Lc 1.28: Etude philologique', *Bib* 68 (1987), pp. 357-82, and, 'κεχαριτωμένη en Lc 1.28: Etude philologique et théologique', *Bib* 68 (1987), pp. 480-508) see it as referring rather to a pre-existing state of grace in Mary herself, with de la Potterie favouring the translation, 'Rejoice to have been transformed by grace'. From a narrative point of view, it is less a question of trying to decide what exactly the greeting might mean than of trying to explain the function of the greeting's ambiguity.

2. See too the textual variant (A C D Θ 053.0135 f[13] 𝔐 latt sy[ph]bo[mss]) which imports Elizabeth's words from v. 42 (εὐλογημένη σὺ ἐν γυναιξίν) as a way of dealing with a text judged too elliptical and wanting therefore to focus more on Mary

introduce himself. In the first episode, Gabriel introduced himself to
Zechariah once his credentials were questioned. If Gabriel never
introduces himself to Mary in this episode, it is because she never
questions either his reliability or authority. Secondly, by deciding not
to have Gabriel introduce himself the narrator makes it clear that
Mary does not need to know the messenger's identity in order to
submit to the divine plan. Her faith will have another basis.

The Reaction of Mary: Luke 1.29

With its reference to the gracing of Mary by God, the greeting
offered the first piece of more than purely external narration in her
regard. But in v. 29 we are given for the first time an inside view
which focuses not on what God has done or will do to Mary, but how
she reacts to what she hears. At first, v. 29 seems very like v. 12,
again a standard element of the OT annunciation scheme; and linguis-
tically there is the link between ἐταράχθη ('he was alarmed') in v. 12
and διεταράχθη ('she was very alarmed') in v. 29, the compound
adding intensity without changing the sense.[1]

Yet the similarities become less stable upon closer scrutiny. First,
Zechariah was upset by what he saw, and Mary is upset by what she
hears ('she was very alarmed by the utterance' [ἡ δὲ ἐπὶ τῷ λόγῳ
διεταράχθη]).[2] Throughout the episode, there is very little visual
detail—much less than in vv. 5-25. We are, for example, told nothing
of where exactly the meeting took place, of what Mary was doing
when Gabriel arrived, and there is no suggestion that Mary ever sees
Gabriel.[3] In a story of doubt, the narration was in a visual mode, with
Zechariah startled by the vision, demanding a sign, and becoming

---

and her privilege than on God and his grace as the narrator does.

1. On the change of nuance, see Plummer, *Critical Commentary*, p. 22, and
Brown, *Birth of the Messiah*, p. 288.

2. Some manuscripts (for example A C Y 053. 0135) add ἰδοῦσα at this point
in order to secure the parallel with v. 11. The Vulgate has its own addition, 'Quae
cum audisset', which is closer to the mark than the other.

3. Were it not for the reference to his coming (εἰσελθών) and going
(ἀπῆλθεν), there would be nothing in the episode to suggest that Gabriel was more
than a voice. Compare too the *Book of the Birth of Mary* (9.2) which in its account
of the Annunciation reads: 'The Virgin, who was well acquainted with angelic faces
and accustomed to celestial light, was not alarmed by the vision of the angel nor
astonished by the immense light'.

himself a wordless sign strongly visualized in the narrative.[1] Now in a story of faith the narration moves into an aural mode. In v. 29 Mary is upset by what she hears; and in vv. 34 and 38 she is heard without being visualized, a sound but not a sight.[2] After v. 18, we see Zechariah, but do not hear him; in v. 38, we hear Mary but do not see her.

Secondly, the report of her reaction is less stereotyped. Where v. 12 mentioned the fear which is the standard OT reaction of the human being to the irruption of heaven ('fear fell upon him' [φόβος ἐπέπεσεν ἐπ' αὐτόν]), v. 29 refers instead to puzzlement ('she wondered what this greeting might mean' [διελογίζετο ποταπὸς εἴη ὁ ἀσπασμὸς οὗτος]).[3] This suggests that Mary's problem is not the apparition (as it was for Zechariah), but the greeting and what it means.[4] As Legrand notes, Mary's reaction is 'less a reaction to a theophany than a need for clarification'.[5] In that sense, v. 29 offers a more penetrating view of Mary than did v. 12 of Zechariah.

Narrating the Promise: Luke 1.30-34

Announcement and Interpretation: Luke 1.30-33
The beginning of an answer to Mary's implied question comes as soon as Gabriel resumes speaking. The shape of the divine grace

1. Zechariah's exit from the sanctuary is strongly visualised. There is first in v. 21 the detail of the waiting λαός, and then in v. 22 his appearance, his dumbness and his signing are described.

2. There is, for example, no indication of Mary's posture, gesture or facial expression, none of the visual detail supplied (necessarily) by the many painters of the scene. Compare the *Book of the Birth of Mary* (9.4) which has Mary extend her arms and raise her eyes to heaven before she speaks her word of submission.

3. The imperfect διελογίζετο is unusual in the narrative context which does not give Mary any time for prolonged pondering. What it suggests is that Mary's inner questioning was something more than a spontaneous and uncontrolled reaction, and in that sense different from Zechariah's reaction in v. 12.

4. Mary is not shown as troubled by the heavenly messenger as was Zechariah: it is the greeting rather than the messenger that alarms her (ἐπὶ τῷ λόγῳ διεταράχθη). Nor is she shown as troubled by the circumstances of the apparition, that an angel should appear in such unlikely circumstances, or even that the (apparently) male Gabriel should greet a young unmarried woman in such terms (as suggested by J. Neyrey, 'Maid and Mother in Art and Literature', *BTB* 20.2 [1990], pp. 65-75).

5. Legrand, *L'annonce*, p. 74.

proclaimed in the vocative κεχαριτωμένη ('O graced one') emerges; and as it does Mary receives her own name from Gabriel. The shape of the divine visitation announced in the oracle of vv. 13-17 becomes clearer: through the Davidic messiah God will visit the people prepared by John. In vv. 13-17, nothing was said of the Davidic messiah as the one through whom God would visit his people; but now that is made clear.[1] As in vv. 13-17, Gabriel announces a birth and then offers an interpretation of it framed in language drawn from the Scripture: understanding, we see again, comes from looking backwards.[2]

In the way the Davidic messiah's coming is announced there is nothing exceptional, even if the choice of a woman of undistinguished provenance as mother seems odd. The announcement is couched in traditional language,[3] and Mary has already been introduced as a woman betrothed to a Davidide. There is nothing, then, to suggest that a Davidic messiah matching customary expectation will not be born in the usual way.[4]

---

1.   Not only is it made clear that God will intervene through a messiah, but also that the messiah will be Davidic. Davidic messianism did not exhaust the range of Jewish messianic expectation. As well as the royal messianism which found expression in the hope of a triumphant fulfilment—for the most part political—of the promise made to the long gone Davidic dynasty, there was the sacerdotal messianism found in the apocryphal literature and in the Qumran texts, as well as figures such as the Servant of YHWH and the Son of Man, neither of which is strictly messianic. It is also true that Jewish understandings of salvation were not coextensive with Jewish messianism. For a concise treatment of a most complex question, see E. Rivkin, 'Messiah, Jewish', *IDBSup*, pp. 588-91.

2.   In this episode, however, Gabriel's oracle does not draw on all elements of Scripture in the way his oracle in vv. 13-17 did. This is for reasons of narrative economy, since the cento-like composition of vv. 13-17 not only stated the prophecy of John's birth, but also implied the coming of ὁ κύριος—a prophecy which is specified now in the second episode. What matters now is not that Gabriel repeat the hermeneutical performance of vv. 13-17, but that human beings accept its implications and follow its trajectory.

3.   On the links between vv. 32-33 and 2 Samuel 7, see Brown, *Birth of the Messiah*, pp. 310-11, where he claims that what Luke offers is a 'free interpretation' of the OT passage. See too Laurentin, *Structure*, pp. 71-72, where he notes two differences between the texts: first, Luke omits the reference to the iniquity of the messiah (2 Sam. 7.14b), and secondly he changes the order, mentioning divine filiation first.

4.   For all the diversity of Jewish messianic expectation, it was never believed or suggested that the messiah—Davidic or otherwise—would be born in any other than

In contrast to what was said of Zechariah, nothing is said of Mary's desire to be mother of the Davidic messiah nor of any prayer on her part. Zechariah's prayer signalled a disappointed expectation, but in Mary's case there is no hint of disappointment. As a betrothed woman, she is geared to the future—to an imminent marriage and presumably to children as its fruit. As a childless spouse, however, Zechariah was more geared to the past, looking more to what might or should have been than to what will be.

That nothing is said of any desire or prayer on Mary's part leaves the initiative firmly with heaven. This is emphasized further by the three references to God in vv. 30-33. In v. 30, Gabriel specifies what was not said in κεχαριτωμένη, that Mary has found favour with God (χάριν παρὰ τῷ θεῷ); and in v. 32 it is said of Jesus that he will be called 'son of the Most High' (υἱὸς ὑψίστου) and that 'the Lord God' (κύριος ὁ θεός) will give him the throne of David. God is named in three different ways to ensure that he appears as prime mover.

In the action described by the oracle, Jesus remains passive until v. 33. In vv. 30-31, Mary is the subject of the five verbs (φοβοῦ, εὗρες, συλλήμψῃ, τέξῃ, καλέσεις); and in v. 32, it is God who will give Jesus the throne of David and unspecified others who will call him 'son of the Most High'. Apart from the vague 'this one will be great' (οὗτος ἔσται μέγας) in v. 32, Jesus becomes subject only in v. 33 with the reference to his rule (βασιλεύσει). The revelation may be about Jesus, but Mary and God are the real protagonists of the action described by the oracle. The figure of the Davidic messiah emerges from the shadows, and Gabriel even insists upon the name Jesus for reasons he does not specify, but for the moment it is not the Davidic messiah who has the initiative: much has to happen before that will be so. God has taken the initiative in the approach to Mary; she will take the initiative in conceiving, giving birth to and naming Jesus;[1] once that has happened, God will again intervene to give Jesus the throne of David; and only then will Jesus assume the initiative as king.[2]

---

the normal way. As Brown notes, 'there was nothing in Jewish expectation to suggest that the Davidic Messiah would be God's Son in the sense of having been conceived without a male parent' (*Birth of the Messiah*, p. 312).

1. Joseph is nowhere mentioned by Gabriel.

2. This is why Gabriel proclaims the future kingship of Jesus, but does not actually *name* him king. That will come later in the Third Gospel, when Jesus will be named king not by heaven but by το τὸ πλῆθος τῶν μαθητῶν χαίροντες αἰνεῖν

Throughout the oracle, there is no description of Jesus' mode of life nor any detail of what shape his endless reign might take. This is in contrast to vv. 13-17 where Gabriel gave detail enough of John's mode of life and the shape of his ministry. As Legrand has it: 'John will be great because of what he does, Jesus because of what he is. John is defined by his action. Jesus is the ultimate act of God, resuming and bringing to an end all human action'.[1] Gabriel has announced the 'what' of Jesus' role and identity but has said nothing of the 'how', so that for the reader the question becomes, 'how will this happen?'

The Need to Know More: Luke 1.34

Given her betrothal to the Davidide Joseph, Mary and the reader might both expect that the messiah will be born in the course of the coming marriage.[2] This is why Mary's question in v. 34 comes as a surprise, since it implies an assumption on her part that the child is to be born before she comes to be with Joseph as wife, though there is nothing obvious in what Gabriel has said which might have prompted such an assumption.[3]

τὸν θεὸν as he enters Jerusalem (19.37-38). Gabriel proclaims the kingship of Jesus in this first chapter, and the question is how the characters will come to recognize his kingship. On the way the narrative builds to the point of recognition and the naming which recognition enables, see Aletti, *L'art de raconter*, pp. 210-13.

1. Legrand, *L'annonce*, p. 78.
2. See the remarks of Brown, *Birth of the Messiah*, pp. 123-24, on the meaning of betrothal in first-century Judaea and Galilee.
3. It has therefore been proposed that v. 34 be omitted on textual grounds (see H. Vogels, 'Zur Textgeschichte von Lc 1,34ff.', *ZNW* 43 [1950–51], pp. 256-60). But as the refutation by B. Brinkmann ('Die Jungfrauengeburt und das Lukasevangelium', *Bib* 34 [1953], pp. 327-32) points out, the textual grounds for such a manoeuvre are flimsy, with the question omitted only by OL ms. b, where the omission is explicable on grounds other than fidelity to an authentic text (see Brown, *Birth of the Messiah*, p. 289). Others, such as A. von Harnack ('Zu Lk 1,34-35', *ZNW* 2 [1901], pp. 53-57) have argued against the unitary character of vv. 28-37, claiming that vv. 34-35 are a later addition to a story which has more coherence without them. R. Bultmann (*The History of the Synoptic Tradition* [trans. J. Marsh; Oxford: Basil Blackwell, 1963], p. 295) extends the addition to v. 37, claiming that 'Mary's question in v. 34 is absurd for a bride'. Other less drastic solutions are: (1) that Mary had taken a vow of virginity (Gregory of Nyssa, *Or. in Diem Nat. Dom.*; Augustine, *De Sancta Virg.* 4.4; Laurentin, *Structure*, pp. 176-88); (2) that Mary had not yet reached puberty (G. Vermes, *Jesus the Jew* [London: Collins, 1973], pp. 218-22; and (3) that Mary realized that Gabriel was referring to a virginal

The question may seem odd, but the oracle itself has been odd in several ways. If the child is to be born in the course of the marriage, why then has Gabriel made no mention of Joseph? Why has he made the announcement to Mary rather than Joseph who is, after all, the Davidide? And why to a woman who is betrothed but not yet married? Scripture may give evidence of annunciations to women,[1] but there is no precedent for an annunciation to an unwed virgin. In the sense of there being no precedent, Mary is more like Abraham, even though the explicit evocation of the patriarch is nowhere to be found in the episode.[2] It is not that the promise of vv. 30-33 is strange; what is strange is that it should be made to Mary. Yet however odd the oracle, it has not been unusual enough to prompt the presumption that she will conceive before marriage.

Rejecting attempts to explain the question in terms of Mary's psychology,[3] a growing number of critics have argued for a literary solution which reads the question as a device on the part of the narrator to prompt the climactic christological revelation of v. 35.[4] But

conception (perhaps) because of her knowledge of Isa. 7.14 (J.-P. Audet, 'L'annonce à Marie', *RB* 63 [1956], pp. 346-74; Geldenhuys, *Commentary*, p. 80). The narrative itself offers no support to any of these proposed solutions. For a fuller presentation and assessment of critical opinion, see Legrand, *L'annonce*, pp. 236-41, and Brown, *Birth of the Messiah*, pp. 303-309.

1. As it does in the case of Hagar in Gen. 16.11 and Samson's mother in Judg. 13.3.

2. See the parallel drawn by H. Räisänen (*Die Mutter Jesu im Neuen Testament* [Helsinki: Suomalainen Tiedeakademia, 1969], pp. 104-106) between Mary's faith in this episode and the faith of Abraham in Romans 4.

3. Examples of psychologizing attempts to solve the problem are the following: (1) Mary was so astonished by the oracle that she did not know what she was saying (cited by Räisänen, *Mutter Jesu*, p. 94); (2) Mary had made a vow of perpetual virginity (on which see Brown, *Birth of the Messiah*, pp. 303-306); (3) Mary took the angel to mean that she was to conceive immediately or that she was already pregnant; (4) Mary knew the prophets well enough (especially Isa. 7.14) to know that the mother of the messiah was to be a virgin. See too the protracted dialogue between Gabriel and Mary in the *Armenian Infancy Gospel* (5.1-8), which has Mary protesting repeatedly in an attempt by the narrator to lay bare her psychology in a way the Lukan narrator does not.

4. The first to propose a solution of this kind seems to have been J. Gewiess ('Die Marienfrage, Lk 1,34', *BZ* 5 [1961], pp. 221-54), though much earlier A. Loisy (*L'Evangile selon Luc* [Paris: E. Nourry, 1924], p. 89) had noted that 'rien ne faisait prévoir cette difficulté, qui, dans l'économie actuelle de la narration,

why does the narrator choose this particular device in order to introduce the climactic revelation of v. 35? Why insert a question when it
would have been simpler to have Gabriel move uninterrupted from v.
33 to v. 35 inserting a simple γάρ ('for') rather than the question?[1]
Accepting that the question is a literary device, there is still the need
to press more closely the question, what kind of literary device?

One thing is clear: Mary needs to know more if the comparison
with Zechariah's unbelief and Mary's eventual belief is to work con-
vincingly. For the strategy to succeed, the narrator must bring them
to different decisions on the basis of the same knowledge. There can
be no privileging of one character over the other. In a number of
ways, Gabriel's speeches to Zechariah and Mary are similar. Both
characters are told what is to happen (a son will be born to them);
both are told who this son will be (precursor and messiah) and therefore why this is to happen; neither is told when the birth will be. To
this point, Zechariah and Mary are on an equal footing.

There is however one further point revealed to Zechariah but not to
Mary—and that is how this is to happen. In v. 13, Zechariah is told
that 'your wife Elizabeth will bear you a son' (ἡ γυνή σου 'Ελισάβετ
γεννήσει υἱόν σοι): John will be born by divine intervention, but in
the normal way nonetheless.[2] In vv. 30-33, however, Gabriel says
nothing of how the conception and birth will happen and makes no
mention of Joseph. This means that at the end of v. 33, Mary knows
less than Zechariah, and so does not have the same basis for a decision
either to believe or disbelieve. She needs more knowledge, not to
avert the need for faith, but to enable faith. Gabriel must say more if

---

sert uniquement à introduire la déclaration de l'ange touchant la conception virginale'.
More recently, Brown has claimed that 'Mary is a spokeswoman for Luke's
christological message even as Gabriel is a spokesman; and between them they fill in
the picture of the messiah's conception as God's Son' (*Birth of the Messiah*,
p. 308). Legrand follows suit with his remark that 'la question ne fait pas rebondir
l'intrigue; elle introduit une mise au point de la révélation' (*L'annonce*, p. 78); and
Schürmann ascribes to the question 'eine schriftstellerische Funktion' (*Lukasevangelium*, p. 49).

1.   So Marshall, *Gospel*, p. 70.
2.   It is not said explicitly that Zechariah had intercourse with Elizabeth, as it is
of Abraham and Hagar in Gen. 16.4, though not of Abraham and Sarah where it
only implied in Gen. 21.2. Here too it is implied in v. 13 (with the juxtaposition of
'Ελισάβετ and σοι) and in v. 24 where Elizabeth conceives only after Zechariah has
returned from Temple service.

Mary is to come to the same point of knowledge as Zechariah. Because she knows less than Zechariah, hers is the voice not of doubt but of puzzlement. To say that, however, leaves unanswered the question of why the narrator chooses to insert Mary's question rather than have Gabriel continue the oracle uninterrupted.

The insertion of the question at v. 34 wins two advantages for the narrator. First, it insinuates into the narrative a sense of collaboration between Gabriel and Mary in the unfolding of revelation—which contrasts with the sense of confrontation between Gabriel and Zechariah in the first episode. On the one hand, the narrator has Mary seem wholly passive before the divine initiative; but on the other, she appears as a collaborator in the unfolding of revelation. This paradoxical blend of the passive and active in Mary will appear still more clearly in v. 38; but what emerges climactically there is already present here.

Secondly, it serves as a technique of emphasis, with Mary focusing on what seems to be the insurmountable obstacle to the divine initiative in order that the proclamation of v. 35 will be all the more powerful. This is like the rhetoric of divine glorification in OT narrative, where the difficulty of a proposed divine action is emphasized in order that its successful performance will redound all the more to God's glory.[1] The greater the difficulty, the greater the glory for God. In that sense here, Mary's focusing on her own virginity is a way of focusing on God; and again the self-effacing narrator prefers to have one of his characters do the focusing.

From a consideration of the question as narrative strategy we turn now to a comparison with the question of Zechariah at the level of form and meaning. There is no agreement among the critics as to whether the two questions are identical, similar or totally unalike. Harnack suggests that to hear the voice of doubt in the question of Zechariah and not in the question of Mary amounts to 'sophistische Künste';[2] and Brown remarks more soberly that Zechariah's question 'is not noticeably different from the objection Mary will pose in 1:34'.[3] Others however see the difference as crucial.[4] Even if it is

---

1. On this, see Sternberg, *Poetics*, pp. 112-15, where he notes that 'the less credible the marvel before the fact the more impressive its performance' (p. 113).

2. Harnack, 'Zu Lk 1:34-35', p. 56.

3. Brown, *Birth of the Messiah*, p. 280.

4. See, for example, Legrand, *L'annonce*, p. 78; Meynet, *Quelle est donc cette parole?*, p. 154. Among older commentators, F. Godet claims that 'la question de

crucial, the difference is not immediately evident—to the point where one wonders why the narrator would decide to include in the narrative two questions which seem at first glance so similar but which closer scrutiny shows to be dissimilar. Are we perhaps looking at another example of the technique first met in v. 18, where although Zechariah's question was made to seem very like Abraham's in Gen. 15.8 the two questions turned out to be quite different?

The first and most obvious difference between the two questions is their form. Where Zechariah asks, 'by what shall I know this?' (κατὰ τί γνώσομαι τοῦτο), and goes on to mention his and Elizabeth's age, Mary asks, 'how will this be?' (πῶς ἔσται τοῦτο), and goes on to mention her virginity. For all their similarity, the difference between the two questions is more than superficial:

1. Mary does not focus immediately upon herself, but upon τοῦτο ('this'), understood as heaven's initiative. This is in contrast with Zechariah who began by stressing his own need to know.

2. The question asks not whether, but how—which presumes that what the angel has said will happen, with ἔσται understood best and most simply as a future: what is promised will happen, and the question is how in the circumstances.[1]

3. Mary questions her own credentials ('I do not know man' [ἄνδρα οὐ γινώσκω]) rather than the messenger's credentials. She states a lack in herself rather than imply any lack on heaven's part.

Marie n'exprime pas le doute...Cette question est l'expression légitime de l'étonnement d'une conscience pure' (*Commentaire sur l'Evangile de saint Luc* [2 vols; Paris: Librairie Fischbacher, 1888–89], p. 113).

1. J. Bauer ('πῶς in der Griechischen Bibel', *NovT* 2 [1957], pp. 81-89) claims that followed by a future as it is here πῶς has the force of a negation with the form of a rhetorical question, and that a genuine question would demand the subjunctive. He cites a range of NT examples in support of the claim (Mk 3.23; 4.13; Mt. 7.4; 12.29; Lk. 6.42; Jn 3.4, 9; 6.52; 9.16; Rom. 3.6; 6.2; 8.32; 1 Jn 4.20), and claims also that the usage is found in the LXX. But the phenomenon is not as widespread or clearcut as Bauer suggests, with some of his examples (e.g. Mt. 7.4) read as genuine questions with no great difficulty, and a text such as 1 Cor. 15.35 offering πῶς + subjunctive in what is certainly a question.

4. Rather than demanding to see, Mary simply states her inability to see. Hers is a statement of powerlessness rather than an attempt to seize a knowledge which might give her the initiative.
5. Zechariah's question implied a failure of memory, where Mary's implies the memory that all other annunciations have been made to married people.[1]

If the form of the questions seems similar, then there is also a point of contact in the language, with the key verb 'to know' (γινώσκω) found in both, albeit in quite divergent senses. In Zechariah's question, it refers to the assured knowledge that he seeks; and in Mary's question, it has the sexual connotation familiar from the OT.[2] But for all the differences of meaning, the narrator plays on the word as a way of modulating the epistemology of the narrative and leading the reader further towards an understanding of what kind of knowledge is required for recognition of the moment of God's visitation. On the score of carnal knowledge, Mary is not qualified to play the role assigned to her in the divine plan. But that is not the kind of knowledge required. The knowledge to which her question gives voice is a knowledge of her own powerlessness; and that, it seems, is part of the knowledge required.

We are now in a position to decide whether the two questions—and by further implication the two episodes—are parallel or not. A study of the differences between v. 18 and v. 34 suggests that Mary's question is not the dramatic equivalent to Zechariah's question in the first episode. Her question is not a moment of decision in the way that Zechariah's is. She is on the way to a decision which will find voice only in v. 38, and part of her journey to that point is a puzzlement which is not the same as doubt. The different narrative function of the two questions means that the first two episodes, for all that they are superficially similar, are not parallel.

Yet the further question is why the narrator wants to create the

1. Gabriel's oracle presumes a knowledge of Scripture on Mary's part. It presumes she knows not only who God is, but also that she knows of the divine promise to David and his dynasty, and how this relates to the house of Jacob. Gabriel makes no attempt to explain any of these things, and Mary asks no questions about them. The narrator will amplify the sense of Mary's knowledge of the Scripture in the Magnificat.

2. See, for instance, texts such as Gen. 4.1, 17, 25; Num. 31.18; Judg. 21.12.

impression of similarity at one level only then to subvert it at another. If there is a convergence between the stories of Zechariah and Mary, then it is not to be found on the surface of the stories. One must go beyond the surface to a point where the two stories are divergent. But there is a further step to a final point where the true convergence of the two stories is discovered—a convergence rooted in the divine plan, which itself is not to be sought on the surface. All of this has implications for an understanding of the kind of vision required for recognition of the moment of God's visitation.

Submitting to Power: Luke 1.35-38

The Power of the Most High: Luke 1.35

If the oracle of vv. 30-33 was in some ways strange, the oracle of v. 35 is quite extraordinary. Gabriel moves beyond all precedent to tell Mary that she will conceive the Davidic messiah by direct divine intervention. The evocation of the past dwindles as the narrator brings the narrative to a point of radical newness.[1] Because Mary needs to know more in order to decide, Gabriel tells her more; because she has not questioned his authority or reliability, Gabriel says nothing of himself;[2] because hers is the voice not of doubt but of puzzlement, Gabriel responds more graciously, less imperiously than in vv. 19-20.

For the second time, Gabriel mentions the Holy Spirit. The first

---

1.   The evocation of the past does not, however, vanish altogether. Brown (*Birth of the Messiah*, pp. 314-15) notes the echo of Gen. 1.2 where the Spirit of God hovers over the waters of chaos at the dawn of creation, noting that '[t]he earth was void and without form when that Spirit appeared; just so Mary's womb was a void', and further that if in the annunciation of John's birth 'there was a reminder of the evil to be faced ('the disobedient' in 1.17d), here the message is entirely positive, reflecting the word of the creator God who made everything good'. The verb ἐπισκιάσει also recalls the overshadowing of the divine presence in various forms and situations in different OT texts (see Brown, *Birth of the Messiah*, p. 327), but that does not oblige an understanding of Mary here as either the new Tabernacle or Ark of the Covenant as if containing the divine presence (on which see Laurentin, *Structure*, pp. 73-74; 159-61). The OT references are too various and the Lukan use of the OT in general too allusive to allow for any absolute certainty in the matter; but the emphasis in v. 35 is upon the overshadowing of Mary by God (to conceive the messiah) rather than the presence of God within Mary (in the form of the messiah), as an understanding of her as new Tabernacle or new Ark implies.

2.   Again the narrator styles him simply ὁ ἄγγελος.

time was in v. 15, where it was said of John that 'he will be filled with the Holy Spirit from his mother's womb' (πνεύματος ἁγίου πλησθήσεται ἔτι ἐκ κοιλίας μητρὸς αὐτοῦ). But now there is a difference. In the case of John, the Holy Spirit would help him to fulfil his allotted task, but in the case of Jesus the action of the Holy Spirit is presented more radically. The Holy Spirit will fill John once he is conceived, but Jesus will be conceived by the action of the Spirit. In the case of John, the Spirit assists; in the case of Jesus, the Spirit enables.[1]

This might suggest that the focus falls upon Jesus, but that is not how the narrator has it. The parallelism of v. 35 focuses firmly upon heaven (πνεῦμα ἅγιον; δύναμις ὑψίστου) and Mary (σε; σοι). As throughout the episode, the movement is from God to Mary, with the downward thrust from heaven to earth captured by the threefold use of ἐπί- (ἐπελεύσεται, ἐπί, ἐπισκιάσει), leaving a sense of Mary at this point as wholly passive. The references to God are oblique, with the emphasis more on his communication (πνεῦμα and δύναμις) than on God himself. Jesus is not mentioned by name, but by the elliptical 'the holy one to be born' (τὸ γεννώμενον ἅγιον).[2] Again he is more acted upon than acting, with the verbal forms (γεννώμενον and κληθήσεται) both passive, and with the stress falling not upon Jesus himself but upon his relationship to God (υἱὸς θεοῦ) and therefore upon God's action in generating him.

Then at a point where the reader might expect Gabriel to say more of Jesus in the way he said more of John in vv. 15-17, Gabriel turns

---

1. On which see Legrand, *L'annonce*, 79.

2. The difficulty here is to decide whether the neuter ἅγιον modifies the subject (τὸ γεννώμενον) or is a predicate (and hence to be read in conjunction with υἱὸς θεοῦ). Brown (*Birth of the Messiah*, pp. 291-92) opts for it as a predicate, suggesting that two predicates in v. 35 better matches the two predicates in v. 32a (μέγας and υἱὸς ὑψίστου) and that 'the logic of vs. 35 favors the child being called holy, since the Holy Spirit comes upon Mary'. Fitzmyer (*Luke*, pp. 351-52) prefers to read it as the predicate of a verbless clause (i.e. 'will be holy; he will be called Son of God'; and he notes further the remark of C.F.D. Moule (*An Idiom-Book of New Testament Greek* [Cambridge: Cambridge University Press, 1953], p. 107) that it would be most irregular were ἅγιον to modify γεννώμενον. Yet to understand it in that way makes a verbal link between πνεῦμα ἅγιον and το γεννώμενον ἅγιον which insists upon the most irregular and radical relationship between the Holy Spirit and Jesus. I would therefore read ἅγιον as modifying γεννώμενον, without denying the solid reasons for other readings.

instead to the pregnant Elizabeth in v. 36. This serves the narrator's purpose of focusing upon God as powerful enough to do what seems even less likely than the bringing of a child from a barren womb. If the beginning of right knowledge is a knowledge of one's own powerlessness (as has emerged in Mary's question), then its completion is a knowledge of God's power (as emerges in Gabriel's answer).

The Unseen Sign of God's Power: Luke 1.36-37

The narrator's switch from Jesus to the pregnant Elizabeth serves the very practical purpose of linking the episode with the first and third episodes. Yet there is more to the manoeuvre than this, since the real shift of focus is not from Jesus to Elizabeth, but from Jesus via Elizabeth to God whose power Gabriel proclaims in the climactic v. 37. Elizabeth is not introduced for her own sake nor in her own right; nothing, for example, is said to Mary of the circumstances of Elizabeth's pregnancy. It is not the personal story of Zechariah and Elizabeth which interests either the narrator or Gabriel at this point, but Elizabeth as sign of God's power. Despite her concealment, she becomes a public witness to the power of God to do what by any ordinary reckoning seems impossible. In this, she is like her husband who, despite himself, became a wordless sign of the divine action in v. 22.

As an echo of the OT, Elizabeth witnesses to God's power revealed through the biblical story; as a woman of the present time, she witnesses to God's power as not solely a thing of the past; and as a kinswoman of Mary, she witnesses to the divine power as mysterious, but not distant.[1] Gabriel's proclamation of the power of God in vv. 36-37 is heaven's answer to Mary's statement of her own powerlessness in v. 34. The power of God empowers the powerless; and the hidden Elizabeth is made a sign of that.[2]

---

1. It is not immediately clear why the narrator saves this piece of information until now, when he might as easily have begun by introducing Mary not only as Joseph's betrothed, but also as Elizabeth's kinswoman. Yet to have mentioned Elizabeth earlier would have worked against the very concentrated focalization on Mary in the early verses; and to introduce Elizabeth at this point allows the narrator to expand his focus in a way that looks away from both Mary and Jesus to God who is the prime mover. For both Mary and the reader there is a surprise. For Mary, the surprise is that Elizabeth is pregnant; but for the reader, it is that the two women are related.

2. The active verb συνείληφεν (with Elizabeth the subject) and the passive participle καλουμένῃ (where she is the object) suggest the empowerment of Elizabeth.

If Elizabeth is a sign, then she is a sign about whom Mary hears but whom she does not see. Mary must therefore take it on Gabriel's word, accepting the messenger's reliability and authority in a way that was beyond Zechariah. The sign proclaimed to Mary is very different from the sign requested by Zechariah: where he requested a sign which might confer certain knowledge, she is told of a sign which demands faith.

Mary must make the leap from the known to the unknown, since a conception in old age by normal means cannot be thought of in the same way as a virginal conception by an unmarried woman. On the one hand, we have the belated fulfilment of a lifelong desire, which means the removal of social stigma. On the other, we have the totally unheard of approach of God to a woman who has not sought the pregnancy nor even dreamed of its possibility. A knowledge of the biblical witness might well have assured Mary that old and barren women do conceive by God's power; but there was nothing in Scripture which might have encouraged her to make the leap to faith in a virginal conception of the Davidic messiah.[1] Where Zechariah has been asked to believe that God will do again what he has done before, Mary is asked to believe that God will do what he has never done before. She is given no more than Zechariah, but she is asked to believe a good deal more.

The Submission of Mary: Luke 1.38
When Mary speaks her submission, the narrative finds its dramatic equivalent to Zechariah's question of v. 18. On the basis of the same knowledge, she comes to a different decision. What Gabriel has said in vv. 35-37 should, one would think, prompt many more questions than his less startling words in vv. 30-33 which drew from Mary the question of v. 34. Yet where his earlier words drew a question, his words now draw from Mary a statement of acceptance.

Her word of acceptance is threefold. It is a word about God, about his messenger and about herself. It is an acceptance of Gabriel's claim of divine omnipotence in v. 37 ('nothing is impossible for God' [οὐκ

She becomes the subject rather than the object, but only because of what God has done for her.

1. This presumes that Isa. 7.14 was not understood at the time as referring to the manner of the child's conception, on which see Brown, *Birth of the Messiah*, pp. 145-49.

ἀδυνατήσει παρὰ τοῦ θεοῦ πᾶν ῥῆμα]); it is an acceptance of the messenger's reliability and authority ('let it be done to me according to your word' [γένοιτό μοι κατὰ τὸ ῥῆμά σου]);[1] and it is an acceptance of her own status as servant of the omnipotent God ('behold the servant of the Lord' [ἰδοὺ ἡ δούλη κυρίου]). In its threefold aspect, it is a fundamental statement about the contours of faith, and hence a key moment in the setting of the epistemological ground of the narrative. Where Zechariah had seen himself as beneficiary of the divine plan, Mary sees herself as its servant; where Zechariah had sought the initiative, Mary surrenders; where Zechariah had queried the messenger's authority and reliability, Mary does not; where Zechariah sought knowledge instead of faith, Mary believes on the basis of what she knows.

Her response is paradoxical in the way it blends the active and passive. On the one hand, the narrator has presented Mary throughout the episode as wholly passive before the divine initiative—and never more so than now. Yet her question in v. 34 has made her an active collaborator in the unfolding of the revelation; and now even more, her response makes her sound like a collaborator in the unfolding of the divine plan. As Legrand remarks: 'The fiat of Mary is less passive than it seems: implicitly it contains all the exertions of a servant'.[2]

The presence of heaven is paradoxical too, because Gabriel, after proclaiming the boundless power of God, does not depart imperiously. Instead, the narrator has him wait for Mary's reply, which sounds like the acceptance of an invitation, when nothing that Gabriel has said has suggested an invitation.[3] He has announced that something

---

1.   Earlier it was Gabriel who referred to the oracle of vv. 13-17 as οἱ λόγοί μου at a point where his authority and reliability were questioned. Now it is Mary who refers to the oracle of vv. 30-33, 35 as τὸ ῥῆμά σου. She has recognized what Gabriel had to state explicitly to Zechariah.

2.   Legrand, *L'annonce*, p. 82.

3.   Mary replies as if accepting an offer of marriage, though there has been no suggestion whatever of ἱερός γάμος and the narrative will leave no doubt that Mary and Joseph go ahead with plans. The narrator carefully and consistently excludes any hint of sexual rapport between God and Mary. Unsuccessful attempts have been made to interpret ἐπισκιάσει in a sexual sense from the rabbinic background (for example D. Daube, 'Evangelisten und Rabbinen', *ZNW* 48 [1957], pp. 119-20), and from a pagan mystery-cult background (for example H. Leisegang, *Pneuma Hagion* [Leipzig: Hinrichs, 1922], pp. 25-33). See the refutation by M. Dibelius, 'Jungfrauensohn und Krippenkind: Untersuchungen zur Geburtsgeschichte Jesu im

will happen. All powerful heaven waits on the human being's reply. Once the reply is given, the narrator has Gabriel depart wordlessly in v. 38, leaving the last word to Mary; and we are told that the still anonymous 'angel' departs 'from her' (ἀπ' αὐτῆς), leaving the focus on Mary.

A final point about this strikingly elliptical narrative is that it says nothing of the conception of Jesus.[1] The question then is why the narrator chooses to shroud the moment of conception in such uncertainty, when at other points he is so precise—as he was in reporting the conception of John in v. 24. Some have suggested that it is for reasons of delicacy on a matter calling for the greatest of tact, of which the Lukan narrator is an acknowledged master. Yet this is less than wholly satisfying.[2] An answer must be sought at the level of narrative strategy.

The decision to say nothing of the conception is one of the ways in which the narrator focuses not so much on the figure of Jesus as on the figures of God as prime heavenly mover and Mary as prime human collaborator. In that sense, the narrator's twin interest at this point is theological and epistemological. The focus of the narrative is not the meeting of God and Mary in the physical conception of Jesus, but the meeting of God and Mary in the faith which comes to birth in

Lukas-Evangelium', in G. Bornkamm (ed.), *Botschaft und Geschichte: Gesammelte Aufsätze von Martin Dibelius* (Tübingen: Mohr, 1953), pp. 19-22.

1.   We cannot therefore assume that Mary conceives as soon as she speaks her word of submission, as does the *Armenian Infancy Gospel* (5.9), which has Mary conceive (*per aurem*) while she is actually speaking. It has been argued that underlying the Greek future συλλήμψῃ in v. 31 there lies a Semitic original הרה referring to a present action—with the implication that Mary conceives as soon as Gabriel speaks. G. Graystone (*Virgin of All Virgins: An Interpretation of Lk 1:34* [Rome: Tipografia Pio X, 1968], pp. 89-93) refers to attempts to read the Greek future with a past sense. But this would make an already-pregnant Mary's word of acceptance in v. 38 irrelevant. See too the earlier attempts of Loisy (*Evangile*, p. 92) and Dibelius ('Jungfrauensohn', pp. 5-6) to answer the question.

2.   Plummer (*Critical Commentary*, p. 26) contrasts the delicacy of the Lukan account with what he calls 'the gross offences against taste, decency, even morality' of the apocryphal gospels, and then makes his own the lyrical trope of Godet (*Commentaire*, p. 128): 'Quelle dignité! quelle pureté! quelle simplicité! quelle délicatesse dans tout ce dialogue!' However true this might be, it does not answer the question, 'why?'

v. 38. Restraint therefore on the part of the narrator serves focalization in the narrative.[1]

Conclusion

In this as in the first episode heaven triggers the action, though now more vigorously and obviously as the narrator has God send Gabriel immediately rather than wait for some time as he did in vv. 5-25. Gabriel's announcement of a new divine promise reinforces the dynamic of promise fulfilment established in the first episode. It also reinforces the insistence that there is a need to look to the past in order to understand present and future.

At the same time, there are significant differences of setting of the action, composition of the oracle and characterization of both angel and addressee. The setting is no longer religious; it is more marginal than central, with the emphasis more on the person than the place. The oracle, though again couched in biblical language, is not this time composed in cento-like style.

Though Gabriel appears again, the characterization of him is different. He is now the one who does the moving; at no stage does he introduce himself; after v. 26, the narrator styles him simply as 'the angel'; he is a more courteous, less imposing figure than earlier, prepared to greet Mary graciously and wait for her reply before departing wordlessly himself. The different characterization of Gabriel is tied to a different narration of the divine visitation, which in many ways seems similar to the first episode, but which is different in ways both subtle and important.

The characterization of Mary is also different from anything found in the first episode. She is young and betrothed, and nothing is said of her piety nor of her desire to be mother of the messiah. The narrator also focuses on the figure of Mary with a concentration not found in the first episode. She is the one human character to appear; Gabriel moves to her, leaving her the unmoving fulcrum of the episode; she is made a collaborator in the unfolding of the revelation; and Gabriel awaits her word.

The narrator has Gabriel proclaim the 'what' of Jesus' role and identity as Davidic messiah and Son of God, but nothing of the 'how'.

---

1.   On this, see the brief but enlightening remarks of Legrand, *L'annonce*, p. 83.

For the reader and for Mary, then, the question of 'how' emerges: what will it mean in concrete terms for Jesus to be Davidic messiah and Son of God? This is a question which will be answered only in the course of the infancy narrative and indeed of the entire Lukan narrative.

On the level of human recognition of the divine visitation, the narrator has revealed a good deal more of the 'how'. Having established in the first episode that faith is required by the divine promise, the narrator in this episode offers a fuller dramatization of faith. In that sense, the second episode develops the epistemology of the first episode in important ways. It does so by contrasting Zechariah and Mary, having the two characters meet the same challenge quite differently. On the basis of the same knowledge given to Zechariah, Mary comes to the opposite decision: she chooses to believe.

This means that it is Mary's word of faith in v. 38 rather than her question in v. 34 which is the dramatic equivalent of Zechariah's question in v. 18. Mary's question in v. 34 is not the same as Zechariah's in v. 18, because her question is not a moment of decision in the way that his is. She is on the way to a decision which will find voice only in v. 38, and part of her journey to that point is a puzzlement which is not the same as doubt. The different narrative function of the two questions means that the first two episodes, for all that they are superficially similar, are not parallel, that they do not sit together as neatly or as statically as the image of a diptych suggests. Another way in which this is true is that where the first episode introduced both faith in the promise and interpretation of the signs of fulfilment, the second episode has focused exclusively upon faith in the promise. It is focused more narrowly and intensely.

For all their asymmetries, the first two episodes work together to form the ground of the Lukan narrative, establishing the rudiments of the narrative's vision of both the divine visitation and human recognition of it. In a real sense, the readers now know the 'what' of the entire Lukan narrative: God will intervene eschatologically through a divine messiah whose reign will last forever. But they also know a good deal more of the 'how' than they did at the end of the first episode. They know that the messiah will be Davidic, that his name will be Jesus, that Mary will be his mother, and that John will be a key figure in preparing for his coming. Moreover, the readers know that faith is demanded by God's promise and that the signs of fulfilment demand right interpretation; and if they know little enough at this stage of the 'how' of right interpretation of the signs, they know a good deal of the 'how' of faith.

Yet at this early stage of the narrative every answer to the question 'how?' generates more questions for the readers. What kind of Davidic messiah will Jesus prove to be? What will it mean for him to be Son of God? What kind of journey opens before the believer once the word of submission has been spoken? It is this third question in particular that opens the door to the following episode and leads the readers into the hills of Judah.

Chapter 4

THE MEETING OF FAITH AND INTERPRETATION IN LUKE 1.39-56

Between Human Characters

After the exceptional weight of the first two episodes, the narrative of vv. 39-56 seems almost an intermezzo—a moment in which readers and characters may catch their breath before launching into the stories of fulfilment which follow. LaVerdiere speaks of it as 'a supplement',[1] and Brown as 'an epilogue'.[2] Yet from a narrative viewpoint, for all that it may seem to be an intermezzo, supplement or epilogue, the episode has more narrative weight than descriptions of that kind imply.[3]

The narrative function of the episode is to stage a meeting of faith and interpretation, and it does so in a way that shows how faith in the promise and interpretation of the signs are intimately related—as intimately related as promise and fulfilment in the action of God.

An important element of the episode is the completion of the profile of faith, the rudiments of which were given in the first two episodes.[4]

1. E. LaVerdiere, *Luke* (Dublin: Veritas Publications, 1984), p. 22.
2. Brown, *Birth of the Messiah*, p. 252.
3. Brown notes further that 'while the scene fits Luke's thought, it creates a certain awkwardness in what seems to be a carefully balanced structure' (*Birth of the Messiah*, p. 339). By 'carefully balanced structure', he means the John–Jesus 'parallelism'. That there is a parallelism of some kind is clear, but to make it a keystone of interpretation can obscure the narrative weight and function of an episode such as this and create the impression of 'awkwardness'. A narrative approach calls for less attention to the spatial disposition of the narrative (that is, 'structure' in the sense of a parallelism) and more attention to its sequential flow. Attention of that kind reveals a narrative that is carefully balanced in other ways and dispels the impression of awkwardness.
4. Some would see the link between this and the preceding episode as so close that they would read 1.26-56 as a narrative unit. So, for instance, R. Meynet, 'Dieu donne son nom à Jésus: Analyse rhétorique de Lc 1,26-56 et de 1 Sam 2,1-10', *Bib* 66 (1985), pp. 39-72.

Now the narrator turns to the ground and effects of faith. For the first time in the infancy narrative, the initiative passes to a human character, and more precisely to a believer. Faith therefore appears for the first time as the engine of the plot: it makes the story and helps stir the act of interpretation which the episode will recount. This means that 'the stress on cognition rather than action'[1] is complete in an episode wholly concerned with the explication of faith and interpretation as the response required by God's promise and its fulfilment.

The Believer as Prime Mover: Luke 1.39-42a

The Coming of Mary: Luke 1.39-40

Verse 38 had left the focus on Mary, and this remains so in v. 39 as the narrator has her journeying to Judah. Mary is again alone, with no mention of Joseph, who was a name in the previous episode but vanishes completely in this episode. In vv. 26-38, Mary was the unmoving fulcrum of the narrative; but now she is the one who moves, her movement stressed by the first word of the episode, 'rising' (ἀναστᾶσα), which is the first of three verbs of motion used to describe her (ἀναστᾶσα, ἐπορεύθη, εἰσῆλθεν).[2] Not only are we are told in v. 39 that Mary goes 'to the hill-country' (εἰς τὴν ὀρεινήν) 'to a city of Judah' (εἰς πόλιν Ἰούδα) 'into the house of Zechariah' (εἰς τὸν οἶκον Ζαχαρίου), but also that she returns 'to her own house' (εἰς τὸν οἶκον αὐτῆς) in v. 56. As with Gabriel in the preceding episode, it is her coming and going which are narrated. Yet where in vv. 26-38 the effect was to focus upon Mary as the centre of the narrative, here the effect is different. Although the motionless Elizabeth is the goal of her journey, it is Mary who becomes increasingly the focus of the narrative—at least until v. 46. Once she arrives, neither Mary nor Elizabeth is reported as moving. The only

---

1. See Aletti, *L'art de raconter*, p. 37, where he notes 'une dominance du cognitif sur le factitif'.
2. ἀναστᾶσα is a decidedly Lukan word, occurring in the participial form 36 times in Luke–Acts and only 9 times in the rest of the NT. The pleonastic use with another verb is an example of LXX style (see J. Hawkins, *Horae Synopticae* [Oxford: Clarendon Press, 1909], pp. 35-36; Fitzmyer, *Luke*, pp. 114, 362). Laurentin (*Les Evangiles*, 197) gives the word a symbolic charge, linking it to the resurrection, but that claims too much for a common Lukan (and LXX) expression, which denotes inception (see Fitzmyer, *Luke*, p. 362).

movement narrated is the leap of the child in the womb; and this serves to highlight Mary in the way the narration of Gabriel's movement has in the previous episode. Mary may not be the unmoving fulcrum of the narration she was in the previous episode, but she is its focus nonetheless.

The narration remains external, with the narrator saying nothing of why Mary goes.[1] We are told when she goes (ἐν ταῖς ἡμέραις ταύταις) and how (μετὰ σπουδῆς),[2] and it is implied that she goes freely, with nothing said of any command or compulsion. But the question of why she goes remains unanswered. Attempts to plumb Mary's motivation here are as doomed as they are at other points where the narrator denies the reader any inside view of the characters.[3] In v. 36, he has mentioned that the two women are blood-relatives in

1. Various attempts have been made to plumb Mary's psychology at this point (for example: she goes lest the neighbours in Nazareth come to know of her pregnancy; because Joseph, having discovered her pregnancy, was going to put her away; because she needs to speak to someone who will understand her extraordinary situation), but the text offers no basis for speculation of this kind. On grounds other than the strictly psychological, it is possible that Mary goes on her journey: (1) in obedience to Gabriel; (2) to verify the extraordinary declaration of Gabriel: she needs to see for herself; (3) because she is overjoyed at Elizabeth's good news; (4) because she wants to share her own good news with Elizabeth; (5) because she wants to help Elizabeth in the last stages of pregnancy. Yet there are problems with all of these. Gabriel does not issue a command. Nor is there any suggestion that Mary doubts what Gabriel has said of Elizabeth. Mary may be overjoyed that Elizabeth is pregnant, but once she arrives at the house of Zechariah she says nothing of either her own or Elizabeth's pregnancy. Once they meet, the two women do not exchange their remarkable stories. And finally, although the narrator tells us that Mary stayed three months with Elizabeth and presumably in that time offered some assistance, there is nothing in the narrative to suggest that this was why she went. The narrator shrouds her motivation in silence in order to focus not upon Mary personally, but upon her as servant of the divine plan. Elision here serves focus in the narrative.

2. Different suggestions have been made as to why the narrator has Mary go μετὰ σπουδῆς (e.g. Mary was understandably eager; she was overjoyed; it is the proper reaction to a divine sign). But, from a narrative point of view, the report serves both to evoke the growing pace at which the divine plan is now unfolding and to unclutter the narrative (of details of her journey) and so focus not upon Mary's personal story, but upon what awaits her in the hills of Judah.

3. Other points where the narrator gives no hint of the characters' inner world are Zechariah's reaction to Gabriel's stern words in vv. 19-20, Elizabeth's decision to hide in v. 24, and Mary's reaction to Gabriel's extraordinary speech in vv. 35-37.

order to provide a motive for the journey.[1] At the level of external circumstance, that is enough. The question, then, is not why Mary goes, but why the narrator wants the two women to meet. Narrative strategy matters more than the psychology of the character.

One reason for the narrator's decision can be given immediately: he wants to have faith trigger the action for the first time. In the first two episodes it was heaven's initiative that set the action in motion; now it is the human response to heaven's initiative, that is, faith. For that to happen, Mary has to do something; and it is no coincidence that what she does is visit the only character who to this point has read the signs of fulfilment successfully if incompletely. The narrator has Mary go, therefore, because he wants to show how faith in the promise makes the story; and he has her go to Elizabeth because he wants to show how a vital part of that story is a more secure and ample interpretation of the signs of God's action.

A second point on which the narrative remains silent is the pregnancy of Mary. It is usually assumed that Mary is already pregnant,[2] and there are possible hints in the narrative that this is so. Elizabeth acclaims Mary in v. 43 as 'the mother of my lord' (ἡ μήτηρ τοῦ κυρίου μου), though that is more important for what it says about Elizabeth's response than Mary's condition, and it could be taken as referring to the future. In v. 49 Mary announces that 'he who is mighty has done great things for me' (ἐποίησέν μοι μεγάλα ὁ δυνατός), but this again might be read as referring to the promise rather than the pregnancy. These are possible hints and no more. The narrator in fact says nothing which allows a conclusive judgment that Mary goes already pregnant to visit Elizabeth.[3]

---

1.   From a narrative point of view, the question is not whether Elizabeth and Mary were in fact blood relatives. Whether they were or not, the narrative question is why the narrator chooses to include the information (whether factual or not) in the narrative at v. 36. As always in a narrative critical context, the important question concerns not history 'as it actually happened', but the choices of the narrator.

2.   Underlying the assumption at times is the sense that the narrative is better balanced if the two women meet carrying their two sons in the womb, so that the women may greet each other and the sons greet each other. But this is not how the narrator has it in this episode, as will emerge in the analysis. The attempt to force the symmetry of the narrative can lead to assumptions that are hard to justify on the basis of the narrative itself.

3.   As F. Spitta noted long ago: 'von der Gegenwart des noch ungeborenen Messias ist nirgends eine Andeutung' ('Die chronologische Notizen und die Hymnen

From a narrative point of view, the question is why the narrator continues to treat the question of the conception of Jesus so elliptically. The effect of the manoeuvre is to continue the elision of Jesus, which may seem odd in an episode of which Bovon, for instance, claims that 'the accent of the scene is on Jesus'.[1] The truth of Bovon's claim needs to be tested; but even now the suspicion is that it may not be Jesus upon whom the accent of the narration falls. We cannot even be sure if he is there or not.[2] This suggests that the accent of the narration falls instead upon God and Mary.

Mary as Sign: Luke 1.41-42a

Once Mary's greeting is reported at the end of v. 40, the narrative moves into a strongly aural mode which will dominate the episode. It is the greeting that stirs the action, and throughout the episode the narrator will suppress visual detail as he did in the previous episode. There is no mention of physical contact between the women;[3] there is no mention of them even seeing one another; and the dumbstruck Zechariah is nowhere to be seen. The characters are heard but not visualized, with description reduced to a bare minimum. This decision to move into an aural mode in narrating faith and its consequences suggests that in the response of faith what is heard matters more for

in Lc 1 u. 2', *ZNW* 7 [1906], pp. 282-83). Of Elizabeth's words in vv. 42-43 he remarks: 'Dass Maria vom Schriftsteller damals bereits als schwanger vorgestellt worden sei, ist . . . aus diesen Worten keinesfalls zu gewinnen' (p. 284). Spitta's article, which runs from pp. 281-317, is (to my knowledge) a lone attempt to argue that Mary is not pregnant when she goes to visit Elizabeth. I would argue that we cannot *know* whether she is pregnant or not. See too the remarks of Evans (*St. Luke*, p. 170) and Laurentin (*Les Evangiles*, p. 37), where he notes that nothing is said in vv. 26-38 of Mary's conception, which is 'l'objet d'une ellipse'. He goes on, however, to make the more dubious claim that '[l]e fait est manifesté seulement par ses conséquences, dans l'épisode suivant'.

1.   F. Bovon, *Das Evangelium nach Lukas (Lk 1,1–9,50)* (Zürich: Benzinger/ Neukirchener Verlag, 1989), p. 80.

2.   As Spitta asks ('Die chronologische Notizen', p. 284), why would the narrator mention Mary's pregnancy in 2.5 if she were pregnant already in 1.39? Why would he not—as he does with Elizabeth in 1.57—simply report the birth in 2.6 with no prior reference to her pregnancy? J. Nolland, *Luke 1–9:20* (Dallas: Word Books, 1989), p. 67, avoids the question by pleading separate sources for 1.39-56 and 2.1-21. From a narrative critical point of view, the question remains.

3.   Gueuret is wrong therefore in her description of the greeting as a 'conjonction somatique' (*L'engendrement*, p. 72).

the narrator than what is seen. Though Gabriel gave the pregnant Elizabeth to Mary as sign, it is now Mary who becomes a sign for Elizabeth; but paradoxically she is a sign that is heard rather than seen.

The three references to Mary's greeting stress its importance. In v. 40 the narrator reports that Mary 'greeted Elizabeth' (ἠσπάσατο τὴν Ἐλισάβετ); in v. 41 that the child leaps when Elizabeth 'heard the greeting' (ἤκουσεν τὸν ἀσπασμόν); and in v. 44 Elizabeth reports the same thing, referring to 'the voice of your greeting' (ἡ φωνὴ τοῦ ἀσπασμοῦ). There is no doubt about its importance. What is strange, then, is that the narrator says nothing of its content. Marshall assures us that 'the oriental greeting was an extended affair',[1] and Ellis that it was 'a ceremonial act whose significance lay in the content of the message'.[2] Plummer feels constrained to remark that 'it is improbable that in her salutation Mary speaks to Elizabeth of the angelic visit'.[3] The narrative, however, gives no hint of any such thing, nor does it suggest that the greeting was at all extended. The impression is rather that as soon as Mary begins her greeting, John leaps in the womb and Elizabeth erupts into inspired speech: it seems neither 'an extended affair' nor 'a ceremonial act'. And if it is true that the significance of the ancient oriental greeting lay in its content, then this is an untypical instance, since the narrative significance of Mary's greeting lies not in its content, which is never reported, but in its effect, which is reported at length.

Its effect is to reinforce the sense of Mary as prime mover in the narrative. First of all, she has freely decided to make the journey into the Judaean hills:[4] in that sense she is the trigger. Once she arrives, it is her greeting that stirs John and Elizabeth: in a second sense, then, she appears as the trigger of the action. The decision not to report the greeting's content means that the narrator, having established the believing Mary as prime mover, can turn immediately to narrate the way in which John and Elizabeth interpret the sign of Mary's coming.

The first effect of Mary's greeting—and hence the first act of interpretation of the sign—is John's leap, reported by the narrator in v. 41 and interpreted later by Elizabeth in v. 44. Under the influence of the

---

1. Marshall, *Gospel*, p. 80.
2. E.E. Ellis, *The Gospel of Luke* (London: Nelson, 1966), p. 76.
3. Plummer, *Critical Commentary*, p. 28.
4. Though Marshall (*Gospel*, p. 77) speaks of Gabriel's 'implicit command' and later of Mary's 'obedience to the angelic message' (p. 80).

Holy Spirit, she is able to interpret both signs: the coming of Mary and the leap of John. The function of the leap is not immediately clear, since we are told when John leaps but not why.[1] It is true that Elizabeth interprets the leap as an expression of joy, but she does not say what has caused the joy. It is usually presumed that John leaps joyfully at the presence of the messiah whom Mary now carries in her womb.[2] Yet we have seen that the narrator has said nothing of the conception of Jesus. Mary may be pregnant, but we do not know. What we know with certainty is that Mary has put her faith in heaven's promise. The other possibility therefore is that it is not the presence of Jesus, but the presence of Mary the believer which stirs John in the womb; and there are reasons for thinking this is so.

First, Mary is the focus of the episode in a way Jesus is not: she is the one praised by Elizabeth and she is the one who in turn praises God. From a narrative point of view, then, it would be strange if the narrator were to have John leap before Jesus rather than before Mary at this point. It would diffuse the focus in a way he is careful to avoid. The narrative is careful also to associate the reactions of Elizabeth and John.[3] If therefore Elizabeth's reaction is a joyful acclamation of Mary as mother of the messiah and as woman of faith, then it would seem more likely that this is also the meaning of John's leap. If Elizabeth can interpret her child's leap, it is because his reaction is the same as hers; and she acclaims not Jesus but Mary. She may acclaim Mary in v. 43 as 'the mother of my lord', but this is subordinate to the climactic acclamation in v. 45 of Mary as 'she who believed' (ἡ

---

1. Some (for example H. Hendrickx, *The Infancy Narratives* [London: Geoffrey Chapman, 1984], p. 79) see in the leap the fulfilment of Gabriel's promise in v. 15 (πνεύματος ἁγίου πλησθήσεται ἔτι ἐκ κοιλίας μητρὸς αὐτοῦ). Yet on the basis of the textual evidence this is no more than possible. Even if it were so, it would only begin to answer the question of the leap's narrative function.

2. It is also presumed that this is a key point of the episode—that John and Jesus be brought together embryonically so that John may salute the messiah in a way that foreshadows his future ministry and asserts from the start the superiority of Jesus. Among many examples, see Schürmann, *Lukasevangelium*, p. 64, and Brown, *Birth of the Messiah*, p. 365.

3. To the point where Marshall (*Gospel*, p. 81) can claim of v. 44 that 'Elizabeth explains that she knew that Mary was to be the mother of the Messiah by the joyous movements of her unborn child', thus establishing a causal link between John's leap and Elizabeth's inspired knowledge.

πιστεύσασα).[1] John's leap, therefore, is primarily in praise of Mary as believer. He rightly interprets that it is faith which has brought her on the journey, and thus enabled the initiative to pass from heavenly to human character.

Furthermore, as Danker notes, in the Third Gospel 'the credentials of Jesus are validated not by John but by God'.[2] True, in 3.15-17 John does foretell the coming of Jesus, but in fairly general terms which are not quite confirmed in the unfolding of the Lukan narrative.[3] In the account of the baptism (3.21-22), John is not mentioned: it is God who validates Jesus' credentials. In 7.18-30, John sends to ask Jesus if he is 'the one to come' (ὁ ἐρχόμενος), and Jesus ends by validating John's credentials rather than vice versa.[4] Therefore, to have John leaping before Jesus in a way that acknowledges him as messiah at this early stage would also work against the consistent tendency of the Lukan narrative. It would seem, then, that John, like his mother, acclaims not Jesus but Mary.[5]

Verse 41 is the one point in the episode where the narrator abandons external narration to report the child's leap and the Holy Spirit's coming to Elizabeth. But it is not in order to offer psychological insight into the characters, since this is an episode where the narrator prefers to

1.   Verse 44 provides a transition from an accent upon Mary as mother (vv. 42-43) to an accent upon Mary as believer (v. 45). The narrator might have had Elizabeth say that it was the presence of the embryonic Jesus which stirred John to the joyful leap and which therefore enabled Elizabeth's recognition of Mary's true identity. But he chooses instead to have Elizabeth say that it was Mary's greeting. This shifts the focus from Mary's child to Mary herself, and from her conceiving to the greeting which has come at the end of a journey Mary has made as believer rather than mother.

2.   F.W. Danker, *Jesus and the New Age According to St. Luke: A Commentary on the Third Gospel* (St Louis: Clayton Publishing House, 1972), p. 45.

3.   John foretells the ministry of an unnamed eschatological judge, whom the later narrative will identify as Jesus. But the images John uses to describe this ministry are not a very accurate indication of the Third Gospel's understanding of how Jesus is eschatological judge, since at the heart of that understanding will lie the forgiveness of sin. John foretells the punishment of sin, and in vivid terms; but of sin's forgiveness he says nothing.

4.   It is not John, but the signs specified by Jesus in 7.22 which identify Jesus and validate his credentials.

5.   Interestingly, *Prot. Jas* 12.2 reads: 'when [Elizabeth] saw Mary she blessed her and said: Whence is this to me that the mother of my Lord should come unto me? for behold that which is in me leaped and blessed *thee* [emphasis mine]'.

have the characters offer what psychological insight there is rather than to offer it himself.[1] In v. 41, the narrator's inside view serves to report not the workings of the human psyche, but the workings of heaven in the human character.[2] The narrator habitually lets the characters speak for themselves, and only infringes his rule of external narration here in order to speak for heaven which cannot yet speak for itself.

The narrator introduces the Holy Spirit at a point where the action is set for the first time among human characters; and he does so for two reasons. First, the Holy Spirit is the conventional indication that what follows is to be prophetic speech,[3] and therefore in this context designates the character of what Elizabeth is about to say; and secondly, the mention of the Holy Spirit ensures that although the action is now between human beings it does not become wholly earthbound. The initiative has passed to human characters, but heaven still plays its part; and it does so quite differently than in the first two episodes. There it was heaven that moved first and the human being who responded. Now, however, the impulse of the Holy Spirit comes in the wake of Mary's greeting; and it comes at the point where Elizabeth offers her own interpretation of the sign of Mary's coming. For the first but not the last time in the infancy narrative, the Holy Spirit represents heaven's intervention in the process of human recognition to enable a character to interpret rightly signs which would otherwise be impenetrable.

Interpreting the Signs: Luke 1.42b-45

In the first two episodes, it was Gabriel who appeared as the prophetic figure, announcing the birth and interpreting its meaning. Now in the

---

1. The inspired Elizabeth gives no explicit description of her emotional state, though her ecstatic speech makes it clear enough. Elizabeth does, however, make explicit mention of the emotional state of John. And Mary, as she begins the hymn, describes her emotional state unambiguously—though the use of the two terms ψυχή and πνεῦμα suggests that her reaction is deeper than the emotional or psychological—on which see Plummer, *Critical Commentary*, p. 31.

2. This is different from the two inside views of vv. 5-38, both of which served to indicate the predictable reaction of the human being (fear, alarm) to the irruption of the numinous.

3. As in texts such as Num. 11.16-25; 24.2; 2 Sam. 23.2; 1 Chron. 12.18; Isa. 61.1; Mic. 3.8; Ezek. 2.2; 3.12, 14, 24; 8.3; 11.1, 5, 24; 37.1; 43.5; Neh. 9.30; Zech. 7.12.

third episode, it is no longer the heavenly messenger but Elizabeth and
the embryonic John who prophesy as they interpret and acclaim
Mary's arrival as the coming of 'she who believed' (ἡ πιστεύσασα).
For the first time in the Lukan narrative, then, human beings prophesy, albeit in unexpected ways.

In vv. 19-20, Gabriel had given heaven's forthright assessment of
Zechariah's doubt. But in vv. 26-38, the heavenly messenger says
nothing in response to Mary's word of faith. He departs wordlessly in
a way which leaves heaven silent in the face in Mary's faith. But the
assessment of her faith comes now as Elizabeth and John move to
centre stage. In vv. 42b-45, then, we have the narrative's dramatic
equivalent to vv. 19-20.[1] There Gabriel chided Zechariah for doubt;
now John and Elizabeth acclaim Mary's faith,[2] as again the narrator
leaves evaluation to his characters.[3]

Elizabeth effaces herself as soon as she begins speaking. Where
Mary had greeted her, she reverses the movement of the narrative and
acclaims Mary. She mentions herself twice in the speech (vv. 43 and
44), but in both cases it is to efface herself before the figure of Mary.
The one point at which she is not effaced is v. 44 when she interprets
the leap of John. One effect of this is to efface the narrator who may
report the leap in v. 41, but who leaves interpretation to his character.

Elizabeth opens with two forms of the passive participle 'blessed'
(εὐλογημένη and εὐλογημένος), which refer to the action of God
towards Mary and Jesus.[4] God lies concealed once more behind the
divine passive, but is implied as prime mover. He comes to the surface

---

1. This is one reason for considering vv. 26-56 as a unit, as does Meynet
(*Quelle est donc cette parole?*, pp. 153-55), though he gives other reasons.

2. See J. Dupont, 'Le Magnificat comme discours sur Dieu', *NRT* 102 (1980),
pp. 321-43, where he notes of Elizabeth's speech that '[c]es paroles se terminent par
une béatitude (v. 45) en évident contraste avec le reproche qui terminait l'annonce à
Zacharie (v. 20)' (p. 323).

3. This is a further reason for thinking that John leaps before Mary the believer
rather than before Jesus. The point of vv. 41-45 is to stage an inspired evaluation of
human faith. Therefore, to have John leaping before Jesus rather than Mary would
work against the thrust of the narrative in these verses.

4. On the participles as divine passives, see Bovon, *Evangelium*, p. 85. Brown
(*Birth of the Messiah*, p. 333) notes that 'in this participial sense 'blessed' is
properly addressed to God who is to be blessed by human beings. When it is
extended to men or women, it invokes on them the blessing of God'. In the NT,
however, God is referred to as εὐλογητός (as in 1.68) rather than εὐλογημένος.

of the narrative only in the last word of the speech where Elizabeth speaks of the 'fulfilment of what was spoken to her from the Lord' (τελείωσις τοῖς λελαλημένοις αὐτῇ παρὰ κυρίου). What was implicit at the start becomes explicit at the end. God may not be the overt focus of the speech, but he is its ground.

Mary, though the focus of the speech, is never named as Mary. She is 'blessed among women' (εὐλογημένη ἐν γυναιξίν) in v. 42, 'the mother of my lord' (ἡ μήτηρ τοῦ κυρίου μου) in v. 43, and 'she who believed' (ἡ πιστεύσασα) in v. 45. In each case, she is designated in a way that links her to the plan of God. It is not Mary in her own right who appears in the speech, but Mary in relation to God's plan. God may lurk beneath the surface of the narrative, but the way in which the narrator has Elizabeth address Mary looks to God.

The speech itself moves from a focus upon what God has done for Mary in v. 42 (εὐλογημένη) to a focus in v. 45 upon what Mary herself has done (πιστεύσασα). Yet it is precisely at the point where the accent falls upon what Mary has done that God is named explicitly in the narrative (παρὰ κυρίου). At the point where one might expect the focus to be triumphantly upon Mary, the narrator prefers to have Elizabeth focus upon God and his promise. It is also at that point that in referring to Mary the speech moves from the second person (σύ, σοῦ, σοῦ) to the third person (μακαρία ἡ πιστεύσασα, αὐτῇ). Elizabeth turns from addressing Mary directly to address a wider audience (including the readers) to whom she speaks about Mary and to whom she holds Mary up as a paragon of faith in the divine promise.[1]

Like Mary, Jesus is never named as Jesus as he was by Gabriel in v. 31. Instead he is 'blessed' (εὐλογημένος)[2] and 'the fruit of your womb' (ὁ καρπὸς τῆς κοιλίας σου) in v. 42 and 'my lord' (ὁ κύριος μου) in v. 43. In v. 42, he is named in a way that relates him

---

1.   M. Zerwick, *Biblical Greek* (trans. J. Smith; Rome: Biblical Institute Press, 1963) (p. 34) and BDF, pp. 81-82, point out that the third person can at times serve as a vocative. Even if that were so here, the question would be why the change in the form of the vocative.

2.   The participle εὐλογημένος is present tense, which might be judged a factor telling in favour of Mary being already pregnant. Yet the present could just as easily be read as having a future force, even if the force of εὐλογημένη is different (past, present and future). Alternatively, εὐλογημένος could be taken to mean that the one who is to be conceived and born is already blessed in the mind of God. Again it is not a matter of claiming that Mary is certainly not pregnant, but that we cannot yet be sure; and the present tense of εὐλογημένος cannot decide the issue.

to God (as the source of blessing) and to Mary (as his mother).[1] The case of v. 43 is more complex because for the first time the title 'lord' (κύριος) is used unmistakably of Jesus. Elsewhere it has been used of God,[2] and it will be used of God again in v. 45, though there in its anarthrous form which in the LXX is the form generally reserved for God.[3] Its application to Jesus here implies an unusual and radical relationship of Jesus to God, but the question is, what kind of relationship?[4] The messianic Ps. 110.1 (LXX) reads εἶπεν ὁ κύριος τῷ κυρίῳ μου ('The Lord said to my lord'), with 'lord' used to refer to both God and the Davidic messiah. Elizabeth's speech echoes the psalm with its reference to Jesus—already the Davidic messiah, according to Gabriel—as 'my lord' (ὁ κύριος μου), and to God in v. 45 as 'lord' (κύριος). In v. 43, therefore, Jesus is named in a way which relates him to God (as Davidic messiah) and to Elizabeth (as *her* lord).[5]

In the speech's presentation of the characters, the accent falls upon relationship. In the case of God, it is through the Holy Spirit that he relates, though differently here than in v. 35. The parallelism of v. 35 presented the Holy Spirit as a principle of power—power enough to enable a virginal conception: 'The Holy Spirit will come upon you, and the power of the Most High will overshadow you' (πνεῦμα ἅγιον ἐπελεύσεται ἐπὶ σὲ καὶ δύναμις ὑψίστου ἐπισκιάσει σοι). In vv. 41-45, however, the Holy Spirit appears not as a principle of power, but as a principle of knowledge. Under the influence of the Holy Spirit, Mary will embody the divine power in an extraordinary way. Under the influence of the Holy Spirit, John and Elizabeth embody the

---

1. Where the narrator in v. 41 has mentioned the reaction first of the son and then of the mother, now in v. 42 the narrator reverses the order, with Elizabeth mentioning first the mother and then the son. As soon as the speech begins Jesus is backgrounded.

2. See 1.6, 9, 11, 15, 16, 17, 25, 28, 32, 38.

3. On which see G. Quell, 'κύριος', *TDNT*, III, pp. 1058-59, where he notes that 'though there is a strong element of caprice in the tradition. . . the use of the article or not should enable us to see whether the singular nature of the name is implied' (p. 1059).

4. On Jesus as ὁ κύριος in the Third Gospel, see A. George, 'Jésus "Seigneur"', in *Etudes sur l'oeuvre de Luc* (Paris: Gabalda, 1978), pp. 236-55, especially pp. 245-51.

5. In this sense, the focus at this point is not so much upon Jesus himself as upon his relationship with both God and Elizabeth (μου).

divine knowledge in an extraordinary way;[1] and it is this inspired knowledge that enables the right interpretation of Mary's coming which John and Elizabeth offer. Where Zechariah sought an illicit knowledge which he was denied, his wife and and son are given a more marvellous knowledge by the gift of the Holy Spirit.

The narrator has divine power and divine knowledge converge in the Holy Spirit; and he has human characters drawn beyond powerlessness and ignorance by the Holy Spirit's impulse in order that the divine visitation may happen and be understood to happen. In that sense, the divine visitation is shown to mean that God shares with the human being his own power and knowledge;[2] and recognition of the visitation appears therefore as a perception of those moments when God shares his power and knowledge with the human being to overcome powerlessness and ignorance.

Completing Faith's Profile: Luke 1.46-56

As Elizabeth falls silent and the narrator turns to Mary in v. 46, nothing is said of the Holy Spirit. Mary's hymn is not inspired speech as was Elizabeth's prophecy, and its tone is therefore less ecstatic and more measured. Not that it is purely personal utterance: like Gabriel's speech in vv. 13-17, it is rich in biblical citation and echo. But still the narrator says nothing of the Holy Spirit's impulse, and this is in order to underscore the difference between prophecy and praise as modes of recognition of the divine visitation. In this episode, then, praise is added to prophecy as one of the twin fruits of faith, a second mode of the recognition that faith enables.

The narrator waits until now to insert the hymn when he might just as easily have decided to add it at the end of v. 38a. It would have been no problem for him to have Mary address Gabriel, or even to have her utter the hymn as a soliloquy once Gabriel had departed. Yet the narrator chooses to move differently, and the question is why. Between Mary's word of faith in v. 38 and her hymn of praise now, the narrator inserts Elizabeth's inspired evaluation of Mary's faith. Clearly he wants such an assessment as soon as possible after Mary's

---

1. Though, again, the reader is left uncertain as to whether John and Elizabeth know if Mary is pregnant or not.

2. On omnipotence and omniscience as the attributes of God in OT narrative, see Sternberg, *Poetics*, pp. 84-128.

word of faith, and he wants it to come not from an angel (as did the assessment of Zechariah's doubt in the first episode), but from a human character. The previous episode had Mary a notably solitary figure in her dialogue with Gabriel. At that point, the dramatization of faith was solely between the heavenly messenger and the human character. But once the narrator turns to the dramatization of faith's effects, as he does in this episode, the narration becomes less solitary and more social, with the circle expanding first to include Elizabeth and John. In the Magnificat, the circle will expand still further to include 'all generations' (πᾶσαι αἱ γενεαί) as the hymn expounds more fully the social implications of faith. The narrator, then, delays the Magnificat in order that it may take its climactic place in this pattern.

It is hard to specify any single character as the addressee of the Magnificat. It is true that in v. 44 Elizabeth strikes the note of joy which stirs Mary to voice her own joy;[1] yet the hymn meets Elizabeth's speech only obliquely and makes no mention of either Elizabeth or John. This is because it is not intended to be a response to what Elizabeth has said or even to what God has done for Elizabeth, but rather a response to the action of God understood more broadly. Mary therefore looks beyond Elizabeth to a wider audience, the extent of which is as large as 'all generations' (πᾶσαι αἱ γενεαί) she invokes in v. 48.

As one might expect in a hymn of praise such as this, the thrust is essentially theological, with the focus upon God.[2] Yet God himself is not addressed directly: he is spoken about, with the third person used throughout. The mode of address is horizontal rather than vertical. This is because the stress of the hymn is upon human recognition of God rather than upon God in himself. This is also the reason why the hymn says nothing of Jesus, which is all the more surprising after

---

1. In that sense, Elizabeth triggers the Magnificat. Yet there is a difference between the two expressions of joy, because Mary looks to God in a way not true of Elizabeth and John. Elizabeth expresses her own joy and the joy of her son at *Mary's* arrival, but Mary expresses her joy at *God's* visitation. Still, the link is made by the repetition of ἐν ἀγαλλιάσει in v. 44 and ἠγαλλίασεν in v 47.

2. See especially Dupont, 'Le Magnificat'. See also the comments of Laurentin, *Les Evangiles*, p. 199, where he writes that '[le théocentrisme] domine toute la scène, mais avec une discretion qui rayonne dans les signes mêmes de la Visitation'. He goes on to note of the Magnificat, that '[l]e théocentrisme triomphe' (p. 201).

Elizabeth's mention of him as 'my lord' (ὁ κύριος μοῦ) in v. 43. To have mentioned Jesus would inevitably have meant that the focus would have moved from Mary to him—in that sense from the human response to God's action to the action of God in Jesus; and that would not have served the narrator's purpose at a point where he wants to focus on the human recognition of God's action.

In a moment where the focus has moved decisively to Mary, the narrator effaces himself by introducing Mary's hymn with the briefest possible intrusion: 'And Mary said' (καὶ εἶπεν Μαριάμ), in contrast to vv. 41-42a which introduced Elizabeth's speech with a flourish.[1] The laconic style also ensures that the focus does not fall on Mary to the point where God himself might be obscured. Mary, like all the characters, must keep her place in the narrative world. The narration is therefore brief and external, with no indication of her reaction to John's leap or Elizabeth's speech; and, as in v. 38, the narrator has Mary ask not a single question when she might reasonably have asked many.

Power as Salvation

To see more of how the hymn functions in the narrative, there is a need to look back to v. 37. There Gabriel claimed omnipotence for God; and in v. 38 Mary accepted the claim, even though there was no precedent for the divine power bringing a child to birth by virginal conception. The key issue in her act of faith was God's power. But God's power in what sense? How does Mary understand the power that Gabriel has asserted? In what exactly does Mary put her faith? In v. 38, the narrator has given an answer only in broad outline, but a more nuanced answer comes now in the hymn, which defines the

---

1. Some have speculated that the original text contained the still briefer intrusion καὶ εἶπεν—hence leaving the scribes free to identify the unidentified subject as they felt inclined or driven, and hence prompting the text-critical question of who speaks the Magnificat: Mary or Elizabeth? The witnesses massively support the reading καὶ εἶπεν Μαριάμ, with the reading καὶ εἶπεν Ἐλισάβετ found only in three Latin MSS of late date (a, b, l*) and in one MS of Irenaeus (*Adv. Her.* 4.7.1), Jerome's translation of Origen's *In Lucam Homiliae* 7 and Nicetas of Remesiana (*De psalmodias bono* 9.11). Yet there have always been voices raised in support of the Elizabeth reading (for example A. Loisy, A. von Harnack, J. Creed, B. Easton, E. Klostermann, P. Winter, J. Drury, F. Danker and A. Gueuret). For a succinct and comprehensive discussion of the problem, see Brown, *Birth of the Messiah*, pp. 334-336. A narrative perspective strongly favours Mary as the speaker.

power of God in a way that looks back to v. 38 and forward into the
entire Lukan narrative.[1]

The first element of an answer comes in v. 47 where Mary extols
God as 'my saviour' (ὁ σωτήρ μου).[2] It is not immediately obvious
how God has shown himself Mary's saviour. She explains in v. 48 that
'he has looked upon the humility of his servant' (ἐπέβλεψεν ἐπὶ τὴν
ταπείνωσιν τῆς δούλης αὐτοῦ), but the explanation is so general
that one is left wondering how God has looked upon Mary's lowliness.
It seems an odd description of what has passed between Gabriel and
Mary in the previous episode. The description of God as 'my saviour'
would in fact sit more easily on the lips of Elizabeth, who has been
saved by God from the stigma of sterility. Yet the narrator places it
on the lips of Mary; and the reasons for his choice will emerge by the
end of the hymn.

In the hymn's first part (vv. 46b-49),[3] the accent falls upon God's
salvation as an act of power exercised in favour of a person. God is

---

1. R.P. Gordon describes the Song of Hannah as the clef sign of the entire
musical score of the Books of Samuel (*1 and 2 Samuel* [OTG; Sheffield: JSOT
Press, 1984], p. 26), and the same might be said of the Magnificat's function within
the Lukan narrative, looking as it does proleptically into the Gospel and Acts (on
which see Aletti, *L'art de raconter*, p. 74). But in a way not true of the Song of
Hannah, the Magnificat also serves as the Lukan clef sign for the score of the OT,
offering as it does a series of analepses which amount to a precise reading of the
Bible.

2. This is the first of the seven occurrences in the infancy narrative of words
falling within the semantic field of 'salvation'. Here we have God referred to as
σωτήρ; in 1.69, 71, 77, God's action is extolled as σωτηρία; and in 2.30, John is
described as σωτήριον. If the infancy narrative is concerned with the shape of the
divine visitation, then it is also concerned with the question of what salvation might
look like.

3. There are many different accounts of the hymn's structure, some of which are
more intricate than illuminating (on which see Brown, *Birth of the Messiah*,
pp. 355-57; Meynet, 'Dieu donne son nom', pp. 48-51; and Dupont, 'Le
Magnificat', pp. 329-30). The suggestion here is that it moves in two large
moments: vv. 46b-49 and vv. 50-55. In the first part, we have the praise of heaven
and the motive for praise; and in the second part, a series of images of the working of
divine power in history is framed by an inclusion with ἔλεος/ἐλέους the key lexical
item in the inclusion. Bovon (*Evangelium*, p. 91) and R.C. Tannehill ('The
Magnificat as Poem', *JBL* 93 [1974], pp. 263-75) also see the hymn as having two
large parts, but put the caesura after v. 50, with ἔλεος ending the first part and
ἐλέους the second part.

called not only 'my saviour' (v. 47), but also 'he who is mighty' (ὁ δυνατός) who has done 'great things for me' (μοι μεγάλα, v. 49). The naming of God as 'he who is mighty' looks back to vv. 37-38, and the praise of him as saviour implies that Mary has understood his power specifically as *saving* power. The hymn begins with Mary as subject of the two verbs of v. 46b-47; God is called not just 'saviour', but '*my* saviour'; Mary points to herself as 'his servant' (ἡ δούλη αὐτοῦ), looking back to v. 38; and she proclaims a future in which she will be named 'blessed' (μακαρία), because of what God has done for her. Throughout vv. 46b-49, the focus is on Mary as beneficiary of God's intervention. To this point, then, salvation is cast in terms of God's power in favour of a person.

In v. 49b however a new element appears, because there the accent falls upon the holiness of God: 'holy is his name' (ἅγιον τὸ ὄνομα αὐτοῦ).[1] At the turning point of the hymn, the focus shifts from God's power to God's holiness; and as Dupont notes, the new element that this introduces into the hymn is the element of transcendence.[2] Having mentioned God's holiness, the hymn immediately expands its horizon, looking beyond Mary to the mercy of God extending 'from generation to generation' (εἰς γενεὰς καὶ γενεάς). It is that unfailing mercy which will be the concrete manifestation of the divine holiness, that is, will reveal the holiness of God's name. Salvation, then, is understood not only as an isolated act of power in favour of a particular person, but as a manifestation of God's transcendent holiness which reaches beyond this act of power and this particular person to touch all generations with an enduring mercy.

Power as Mercy

In vv. 50-55, the hymn further defines its sense of the power of God, and this primarily through the inclusion spanning the verses. In v. 50, we read that 'his mercy [is] from generation to generation' (τὸ ἔλεος αὐτοῦ εἰς γενεὰς καὶ γενεάς); and this looks to vv. 54-55 where we

1. Meynet ('Dieu donne son nom', pp. 48-56) and D. Minguez ('Poetica generativa del Magnificat', *Bib* 61 [1980], pp. 57-77) both find the centre of the hymn in v. 49b. But set within the larger context of a narrative looking back to the Gabriel's climactic statement in v. 37, the hymn seems more concerned to define God's power in terms of God's holiness rather than vice versa. The key issue is power.

2. Dupont, 'Le Magnificat', p. 339.

find 'to remember [his] mercy...forever' (μνησθῆναι ἐλέους...εἰς τὸν αἰῶνα). In both cases, we have mention of God's mercy and of its endurance through time. Between the two elements of the inclusion, the hymn presents a series of images of God's power at work—a power, it appears, to save some (ταπεινούς, πεινῶντας, κενούς, 'Ισραήλ) and not to save others (ὑπερηφάνους, δυνάστας, πλουτοῦντας). The images of divine power offered in vv. 51-54a are images of a God who is prepared to immerse himself in the socio-economic world of the human being: the divine power which inscribes itself in human flesh also inscribes itself in the flesh of human society. The effect of the inclusion is to define God's power as a power governed by mercy. If, as Gabriel has put it in v. 37, 'nothing is impossible to God' (οὐκ ἀδυνατήσει παρὰ τοῦ θεοῦ πᾶν ῥῆμα), then so too does the divine mercy now appear limitless. Limitless power governed by unfailing mercy: this is how the hymn sees God as saviour.

If the accent in vv. 46b-49 was strongly personal, now in vv. 50-55 the accent is more public, with the figure of Mary less central.[1] She is not the uniquely privileged person to whom alone the saving power of God extends. If God is 'my saviour', then he is also saviour of 'those who fear him' (τοῖς φοβουμένοις αὐτόν [εἰς γενεὰς καὶ γενεάς]) and of 'Abraham and his descendants' ('Αβραὰμ καὶ τῷ σπέρματι αὐτοῦ [εἰς τὸν αἰῶνα]). The praise of the Magnificat is prompted by a particular moment in time, but it looks to the working of God's power which reaches beyond that moment to span all time—past, present and future. If the salvation of God reaches beyond the uniquely privileged person, then it also reaches beyond the uniquely privileged time. In that sense, the hymn begins with its focus on the figure of Mary, but then moves its focus elsewhere as it shapes a more inclusive vision of God's salvation, which is offered to all people at all times.

In v. 55, the figure of Abraham which has lurked in the background since the first episode is mentioned explicitly for the first time. The first episode raised the question of what the faith of Abraham might look like now and offered the figure of Zechariah as one who uses Abraham's words but does not share his faith. The second episode

1.   Mary is heard, but not seen, and this in order that her visualization of God's action may be the more effective. The less visible Mary, the more visible God's action.

continued to treat the question, offering the figure of Mary as one who does not use the words of Abraham but who does share his faith: in her, the faith of Abraham was shown without Abraham ever being mentioned. Now the narrator has Mary mention Abraham explicitly: the character rather than the narrator puts a name to her faith. It is Abrahamic: like Abraham, Mary puts her faith in the limitless power and unfailing mercy of God. His limitless power ensures that God will do the seemingly impossible thing he has promised; his unfailing mercy ensures that the divine action will reach beyond the privileged time and person. The return to Abraham at the hymn's end implies that all of God's saving interventions—including his intervention in Mary's life—open Israel's history to its beginning. Indeed, they make the beginning present in a way that subverts any sense of 'once upon a time'. The salvation of God which touched Abraham in the beginning is always available to those who, like Mary, come to share his faith and show themselves therefore to be truly 'his descendants' (τὸ σπέρμα αὐτοῦ).

The Birth of Human Memory
The hymn shapes its inclusive vision by having Mary set her exceptional experience of God's power within the context of Israel's experience of God's power.[1] Mary perceives the deeper implications of what has happened to her; and these are implications which could be drawn only from Scripture. Like Gabriel in the first two episodes (and unlike Zechariah), Mary appears as one who turns back to God's past action in order to understand what God is doing now and the future which this portends and which she proclaims. For the first time, the heavenly clue is taken up by a human character. Mary finds her way to faith because she reads the signs of the past aright.

The narrator has Mary trace a path through Scripture which accords with the hermeneutic offered by Gabriel in vv. 13-17.[2] There

---

1. As Dupont remarks: 'Marie ne peut s'exprimer qu'en se référant à l'expérience spirituelle d'Israël' ('Le Magnificat', p. 321). Given the dynamic images of God's action found throughout the hymn, the experience Mary evokes is not only spiritual in a restricted sense, but also social and historical. It is also worth noting that it is not a question of Mary's inability to express herself in any other way: it is a question of the narrator's decision. He could certainly have had her express herself differently.

2. It is because the narrator wants Mary to trace a path through Scripture that the

Scripture was understood as promise in its entirety. The same is true now, with the hymn composed like vv. 13-17 as a biblical tapestry drawing from all parts of Scripture.[1] Scripture is understood therefore as a unity. But the saving interventions of God to which Scripture bears witness are gathered up in a moment where Mary praises God 'because he who is mighty has done great things for me' (ὅτι ἐποίησέν μοι μεγάλα ὁ δυνατός); and this suggests that they all look to this final saving intervention. Scripture is understood as a promise in search of a fulfilment now imminent. The narrator, then, places on the lips of the woman of faith a hymn whose biblical hermeneutic matches the hermeneutic implied by the angel's first oracle; and it appears again that faith involves right reading of the Bible.

In his remarks on the last chapter of the Third Gospel, Aletti sees as central to the Emmaus story 'another resurrection: that of the memory'.[2] If in ch. 24 we have the resurrection of memory, then here in the first chapter we have the birth of memory.[3] In vv. 5-25, we saw how important right remembering was for a recognition of the divine visitation, and how Zechariah's failure was in part a failure of memory.[4] By contrast, the Magnificat is a triumph of right remem-

---

much discussed aorists occur. It has been suggested that they look to a Hebrew perfect which describes what God does habitually, the equivalent of a gnomic aorist (J. Ernst, *Das Evangelium nach Lukas* [Regensburg: Pustet, 1977], p. 87); that they translate the Hebrew prophetic perfect which describes future events as if they had already come to pass (F. Hauck, *Das Evangelium nach Lukas* [Leipzig: Deichert, 1934], p. 29); that they are inceptive aorists, which describe an action that has begun but is not yet complete (Schürmann, *Lukasevangelium*, p. 75); or that they reflect the church's later understanding of the effect of the death and resurrection of Jesus, now retrojected in the narrative (Brown, *Birth of the Messiah*, p. 363). Yet none of these answers the question of how the aorists function in the narrative. If the narrator wants Mary to define the present and future in terms of the past (and so define the past as promise in search of fulfilment), then the aorists make sense as both prolepsis and analepsis.

1.   For a comprehensive listing of the texts, see Plummer, *Critical Commentary*, pp. 30-31, and Brown, *Birth of the Messiah*, pp. 358-60 (Table XII).

2.   Aletti, *L'art de raconter*, p. 179.

3.   Aletti (*L'art de raconter*, p. 71) describes it as 'une mémoire à la puissance deux, puisque la mémoire divine ("il s'est souvenu") ravive, enclenche la mémoire humaine et la constitue comme récit'.

4.   The importance of remembering will emerge not only in the Emmaus episode, but also earlier in ch. 24 where the two men say to the women μνήσθητε ὡς ἐλάλησεν ὑμῖν (v. 6), and the narrator then reports of the women καὶ

bering, and of right remembering understood as right reading of Scripture. Because she remembers aright, Mary is able to understand the present moment in a way that secures the future. That understanding of the present and vision of the future are the ground of the praise voiced in the hymn. If memory does not come to birth, then the way to understanding and faith is blocked; and if that is so, then there will be no human recognition of God's visitation.

The Bible offers ample evidence that God has exercised his power to save some and to condemn others. That, according to Scripture, is the essence of his power—at least as the Magnificat sees it. If Mary is touched by the same power of the same God, then in ways not immediately obvious it will be for the same purpose. Read against the background of the biblical witness, Mary's extraordinary pregnancy emerges as the ultimate display of God's power—saving some, condemning others.

The Departure of Mary: Luke 1.56

At the end of the hymn, the narrator has Elizabeth make no reply, since she has by now performed her function in the episode,[1] and resumes the narration himself. Mary, we are told, stayed three months before returning home.[2] This prompts two questions. First, why does the narrator have Mary stay three months, when she might just as easily have stayed for a month or two? The effect of this is to highlight Mary as an independent agent—and incidentally to background

ἐμνήσθησαν τῶν ῥημάτων αὐτοῦ (v. 8). What Aletti calls the resurrection of memory presumes a death of memory after its birth. In that sense, Zechariah's failure of memory in the first episode anticipates the failure of memory—its death—later in the Gospel narrative.

1. To have had Elizabeth reply in some way (how is hard to imagine) would also have returned the focus to her in a way ill-suited to the thrust of the narration, which having focused on God with growing intensity in the Magnificat will return the focus to the figure of Mary.

2. The repetition of the name Mary in v. 56 has troubled some and been taken as an indication that it was Elizabeth rather than Mary who spoke the hymn originally. But it is simpler to see it as a way in which the narrator brings the narrative back from the lofty and generalizing heights of the late verses of Magnificat to the more mundane and individualized world of the concluding coda. To mention the name brings the focus back to the woman who has been elided as the hymn unfolded. But the focus will remain on her for only a moment.

Joseph—in a way that underscores the virginal conception of Jesus. In this episode, the narrator does this in three ways: (1) he has Mary leave for Judah without delay, with no mention of any reference to Joseph, (2) he has her stay three months, and (3) he has her return 'to her own house' (εἰς τὸν οἶκον αὐτῆς). What emerges therefore is a range of strategies to highlight Mary as independent agent and so confirm that the conception of Jesus has taken place or will take place as Gabriel has foretold, by the direct action of the Holy Spirit.

The second question is, why does the narrator have Mary return home before the birth?[1] At the level of narrative logistics, were Mary to have stayed for the birth, she would inevitably have had to yield centre stage to Elizabeth, Zechariah and the newborn John: it is hard to imagine how even the most adroit narrator might have managed it otherwise. Yet any backgrounding of Mary would undermine the epistemological thrust of the narrative to this point. Therefore the only way in which the narrator can avoid a backgrounding of Mary is to remove her from the scene before John is born. Alternatively, if

---

1.   This presumes that Mary does not stay for the birth, though there has been no shortage of commentators to claim that she stays; for example Plummer, *Critical Commentary*, pp. 34-35, Marshall, *Gospel*, p. 85 and as M.-J. Lagrange (*Evangile selon Saint Luc* [Paris: Gabalda, 1921], p. 51) points out, most of the Latin Fathers. This is hardly surprising, given how odd it seems that Mary would leave Elizabeth in her moment of both greatest need and greatest triumph. Yet however true it may be that Luke has a penchant for finishing one episode tidily before beginning another (on which see Plummer, *Critical Commentary*, p. 34; Ellis, *Commentary*, p. 74; Hendrickx, *Infancy Narratives*, p. 85), the most natural and obvious sense of the narrative as it stands is that Mary leaves for Nazareth before John is born, though it is doubtless the *lectio difficilior*. The question, then, is whether or not something so apparently odd may be understood in narrative terms. A.R.C. Leaney (*A Commentary on the Gospel according to St. Luke* [London: A. & C. Black, 1958], p. 88) resorts to guesswork at the level of sources and has Mary leave before the birth 'because it escaped [Luke] in his carrying out of the task of combining the narrative with the quite different source in chapter ii'. Brown (*Birth of the Messiah*, p. 338) and Fitzmyer (*Luke*, p. 369) both favour a pre-natal departure, but reject any attempt to plumb the psychology of such an odd departure and make no attempt to explain the manoeuvre in narrative terms. One further possibility is that Mary *did* stay for the birth, but that the narrator chooses not to mention it in the context of 1.39-80. From a narrative point of view, an answer to the question of why he would make such a choice would be the same as an answer to the question of why he has Mary leave before the birth. Either way, it is a question of why he wants to keep Mary and the ensuing episode apart.

the narrator were determined to leave Mary at centre stage, he would deny himself the possibility of bringing Zechariah from the far background to centre stage; and yet the dynamic of the narrative now demands not only the birth of John, but more especially the return of Zechariah, in order to show the fulfilment of Gabriel's promise and hence the complete reliability of heaven's word. Therefore, the need to foreground Zechariah and not to background Mary leads the narrator to have Mary return home before the birth.

At the same time, God and his action cannot be obscured; and the narrator removes Mary from the scene in a way which may seem odd, but which ensures that the focus in the narrative as a whole stays on God and his action. We saw earlier how any character who threatened to rival God as prime mover was removed from the scene; and this is what happens now to Mary. What matters is not that she stay, but that the promises of Gabriel be shown as fulfilled and the plan of God to be unfolding as predicted. Therefore, in order to ensure that God and his unfolding plan hold centre stage, the narrator removes Mary from the scene at a point where ordinarily she might be expected to stay. God may choose to collaborate with the human being, but that does not imply a dependence which might compromise his omnipotence.

Conclusion

This chapter set out to show that the narrative function of 1.39-56 is to stage the meeting of faith and interpretation, and to do so in a way that shows how faith in the promise and interpretation of the signs are intimately related—as intimately related as promise and fulfilment in the action of God. The narrator chooses to stage an encounter between the two women because Mary in the second episode has begun the process of faith in God's promise and Elizabeth in the first episode the process of right interpretation of the signs of fulfilment. Now the two modes of human recognition of God's visitation meet in a single narrative moment, and in a way that shows them to be two parts of a single process.

The episode has completed the profile of faith begun in the earlier episodes. Faith has appeared for the first time as the engine of the plot as Mary, after her word of faith in v. 38, takes the initiative and goes to visit Elizabeth, even though what Gabriel has said to her of Elizabeth cannot be construed as invitation or command. Once Mary arrives, it is her greeting that serves as the immediate trigger of the action that follows. The initiative therefore passes from God to Mary.

In the Magnificat understood as the birth of human memory, the narrator has had Mary reveal as the ground of her faith a right reading of past signs. Where Zechariah's doubt entailed a failure of memory, Mary comes to faith because she is able to look backwards and trace a path through Scripture in a way that accords with the understanding of Scripture as promise found first in Gabriel's speech in vv. 13-17. In that sense, the Magnificat looks back to her word of faith in v. 38 and reveals its hermeneutical ground. It also has Mary name her faith as Abrahamic, identifying her with the seed of Abraham and contrasting her with Zechariah who used the words of Abraham but did not share his faith. If the Magnificat lays bare the ground of faith, it also dramatizes praise of God as faith's first fruit.

In introducing the Holy Spirit, the narrator has also added a vital element to the profile of the process by which the signs of fulfilment are rightly interpreted. By the intervention of the Holy Spirit and the knowledge it brings, Elizabeth has taken a large step towards the full comprehension of God's action, which was beyond her in v. 25. Through the Holy Spirit, Elizabeth comes to the knowledge which allows right interpretation of both Mary's coming and John's leap—an act of interpretation that qualifies as the infancy narrative's first act of human prophecy. Just as Mary takes over from God as prime mover, Elizabeth takes over from Gabriel as prophetic interpreter.

It is again upon God and Mary rather than upon Jesus that the narrator chooses to focus in this episode. Both Elizabeth and John acclaim Mary as believer, and Mary in her hymn of praise looks resolutely to God, without ever mentioning Jesus.

This brings us to the point where we may assess Bovon's claim that 'the accent of the scene is on Jesus'.[1] Far from bearing the accent of the narration, it is impossible to know whether Jesus is there or not, given the narrator's reticence on the score of Mary's pregnancy. Moreover, Mary never mentions Jesus; Elizabeth mentions him as ὁ κύριος μου, but at a point where the focus is on Mary; and John leaps not before Jesus but before Mary. What is striking about the episode is how the focus does not fall on the figure of Jesus. This is because it is an episode concerned to narrate the human recognition of God's

---

1. Bovon, *Evangelium*, p. 80.

action rather than God's action itself.

An episode that has added such substance to the narration of the human response to God's action must be judged more than an intermezzo, supplement or epilogue. In the sweep of the infancy narrative, the episode has brought the readers to the threshold of the stories of fulfilment, knowing that God's visitation, insofar as it is promise, demands faith, and knowing too what faith involves—where it comes from and what it brings to birth. The readers also know that God's visitation, insofar as it is fulfilment, demands a right interpretation of ambiguous signs. As the shape of God's visitation shifts from promise to fulfilment, the question for the readers is what signs fulfilment of the promise might bring, and whether or not the characters will succeed in reading them aright.

Chapter 5

FROM INTERPRETATION TO PROCLAMATION IN LUKE 1.57-80

A Point of Transition

The episode of vv. 57-80 is both an end and a beginning. On the one hand, it brings the narrative to a point of rest, completing the story begun in vv. 5-25. Much of what was promised in the first episode is fulfilled: the promised son is born, his birth is greeted with joy, he is named John, Zechariah is released from his silence. Now more than ever Gabriel is shown to be as good as his word.[1] Moreover, there are points of similarity with the previous episode.[2] All of this suggests that this episode looks back to what has gone before and draws to a close the first phase of the infancy narrative.

At the same time, there are clear differences between this episode and both the opening scene[3] and the immediately preceding

1.   There are other similarities as well. After the seclusion of the previous two episodes, the scene is again set in the public arena. In the first episode, it was ὁ λαός at prayer; now it is the crowd of περίοικοι and συγγενεῖς. The public dimension returns to the narrative. Again we find a rite of Judaism mentioned but never narrated. In the first episode, it was the burning of incense in the sanctuary; now it is circumcision. In both cases the narrator chooses to focus the narrative elsewhere in a way which points beyond Judaism and its rites to the action of God conceived more broadly and less predictably. Moreover, there is a convergence at the point of biblical hermeneutic, with the reading of Scripture implied in Gabriel's speech in vv. 13-17 finding its match in the reading of Scripture implied in Zechariah's canticle in vv. 68-79.

2.   The narrator again chooses to have the action unfold between human characters, with heaven not wholly absent as the Holy Spirit appears once more. As in vv. 39-56, a human being sets the action in motion. In the previous episode, it was Mary with her decision to visit Elizabeth and her greeting upon arrival; now it is Elizabeth with the birth of John and her insistence upon the name.

3.   Verses 5-25 were situated for the most part in the Jerusalem Temple and then briefly in the house of Zechariah. Verses 57-80, however, are situated for the most

episode;[1] and the differences suggest that vv. 57-80 are as much a beginning as an end, that they not only look back to what has been, but also look ahead to what is coming. Indeed there are those who would see this episode as so tightly linked with the episodes of 2.1-40 that they would speak of a parallelism.[2] It would seem then that we are at a point of transition—a point where the narrator brings to a close the first phase of the infancy narrative in order to usher in the second.

As the narration of fulfilment gains momentum, the narrative's centre of gravity moves from faith in the promise to interpretation of the signs of fulfilment. In the first episode, the dumbstruck Zechariah and the pregnant Elizabeth were meagre first signs of fulfilment; but now in this last episode of the first phase, the signs of fulfilment are more substantial. The readers (like Elizabeth and Zechariah) know what the signs mean, but the crowd of 'neighbours' (περίοικοι), 'relatives' (συγγενεῖς) and 'all who heard' (πάντες οἱ ἀκούσαντες) do not; and central to the episode is the way in which the narrator draws the readers to follow the crowd as they grapple with puzzling signs.

In staging the move from promise to fulfilment, the episode also stages a move from faith to interpretation and from interpretation to proclamation. After the previous episode has staged the meeting of faith and interpretation in the meeting of two different characters (Mary and Elizabeth), this episode stages the convergence of faith and interpretation in a single character (Zechariah) in a way that brings the whole first phase of the infancy narrative to a point of convergence.

part in the house of Zechariah and then briefly in the Judaean hills and finally the desert. Zechariah and Elizabeth function differently in this episode. Zechariah comes to the point of faith, and gives voice to the prophecy and praise which are faith's fruit; and Elizabeth now serves as trigger of the action in a way she did not in the first episode.

1. In this episode, we have the presence of the crowd, the element of puzzlement, and the narration of fulfilment, all of which were absent from the previous episode.

2. So for instance Brown, *Birth of the Messiah*, pp. 374-75. It is true that both treat the birth, circumcision and naming of the child, that unusual or marvellous events accompany the child's appearance in a way that points to his future greatness, and in both cases a canticle follows the circumcision and naming. Yet, as Brown himself admits, the same elements are handled quite differently. In the case of John the marvellous events surround the circumcision and naming, where in the case of Jesus they surround the birth; and the two canticles are quite different in character.

The Sign of Fulfilment: Luke 1.57-58

The Brief Narration of the Birth: Luke 1.57

Mary has returned to Nazareth, but the narrator and the reader stay with Elizabeth, to whom the focus shifts and who for a brief moment becomes the fulcrum of the narrative. At the same time, the narrator opens with the dative 'And to Elizabeth' (τῇ δὲ Ἐλισάβετ), which suggests that she is more recipient than agent. If Elizabeth comes to the time of delivery, it is God's doing and not her own.[1] God may remain hidden behind the fixed rhythms of pregnancy and birth, but he remains prime mover, as again the divine power inscribes itself in human flesh, and now more explicitly in the shape of a newborn child.

In v. 57b, Elizabeth becomes the subject, with the verb ἐγέννησεν used to report the birth. Laurentin notes that γεννάω is usually applied to the father rather than the mother, since it refers normally to the initiative of generation.[2] The same verb appears earlier in v. 13 and with Elizabeth as subject, but there it is accompanied by the pronoun σοί ('to you'), which refers the initiative to Zechariah. Here however the use is absolute, with no mention of Zechariah, who for the moment is nowhere to be seen. At this point, the initiative passes wholly to Elizabeth, and it will remain with her until the end of v. 60. She who lurked in the shadows through most of vv. 5-25 and who deflected all attention from herself to Mary in vv. 39-56 now comes briefly to centre stage and, as believer, will trigger the action in this episode before she disappears from the narrative altogether.

More striking than the vocabulary of v. 57 is the brevity of the narration of the birth itself.[3] At the point which might be judged the

---

1. The verb πίμπλημι also catches the eye. Fitzmyer notes that ἐπλήσθη 'could simply denote the completion of the time of pregnancy; but in the Lukan narrative, which makes so much of fulfillment, the overtone is unmistakable' (*Luke*, p. 373). So too Schweizer (*Good News*, p. 38) and, more obliquely, D. Tiede (*Luke* [Minneapolis: Augsburg, 1988], pp. 57-58).

2. Laurentin, *Les Evangiles*, pp. 205-206. See for example Mt. 1.2-16. At the same time, the difference between γεννάω and τίκτω in first-century Koine should not be overstated, on which see BAGD, pp. 155, 816.

3. The majority of commentators pass over the extreme brevity of the narration in silence. Some, such as Brown (*Birth of the Messiah*, p. 375) and Tiede (*Luke*, p. 57), note the brevity, but make no attempt to explain why the narrator has it this way.

climax of the story reaching back to v. 5, we find only three words: καὶ ἐγέννησεν υἱόν ('and she gave birth to a son').[1] The brevity of the report suggests unmistakably that this is not where the narrative's centre of gravity lies: it is not primarily a story about John's birth. The factual fulfilment of Gabriel's promise is reported in the most laconic and matter-of-fact terms ('she gave birth to a son' [ἐγέννησεν υἱόν]), echoing Gabriel's words in v. 13 in a way which shows that what the angel said has happened just as the angel said ('she will give birth to a son' [γεννήσει υἱόν]). Yet what is narrated in much fuller terms is the human reaction to the birth. What interests the narrator, then, is not so much what has happened, but how the characters respond to it.

The Crowd's Recognition of God: Luke 1.58
The narrator does not focus on the figure of the newborn child, even though he is destined to play so decisive a role in the unfolding of the divine plan. It is odd too that the narrator delays the report of Elizabeth's reaction to the birth. In v. 25, he wasted no time in recounting her exultation at the pregnancy, but now in the climactic moment of birth, nothing is said of her reaction. In v. 58, we will be told that the neighbours and relatives rejoice with her, which implies that she was joyful at the birth. That is hardly surprising; but what is surprising is that the narrator delays the report and then reports Elizabeth's reaction through the reaction of the crowd. The effect of this is to shift the focus from Elizabeth in herself, even at the point where she has become the subject. The narrator also chooses to delay the report of Zechariah's reaction, of which nothing is said until v. 64. The delay serves to continue the total backgrounding of Zechariah, which began in v. 24. In these first two verses, then, John, Elizabeth and Zechariah are all elided in different ways; and this serves to focus on the crowd of 'neighbours' (περίοικοι) and 'relatives' (συγγενεῖς) who are very much to the fore in v. 58 and will remain so through much of the episode.

---

1. Again there is no visualization of the scene, which suggests that this episode too will be in an aural rather than visual mode. The one point at which the narration moves into a visual mode is vv. 62-63 where the crowd turns to Zechariah who asks for the writing-tablet and writes the name. But with Zechariah still dumb, the narrator has little choice. Where he has a choice in the episode, he opts for an aural mode of narration.

The crowd's reaction is reported without delay; and it confirms the truth of what Gabriel said in v. 14b. Their reaction is essentially theocentric, as they recognize God as subject and his action as a manifestation of his mercy, with ἔλεος echoing both v. 25 and the Magnificat and anticipating the Benedictus. At this point, the crowd read the signs well; and the accuracy of their interpretation stems from a knowledge of what God has done in the past: Scripture testifies that God can give children to old and sterile women. The problem of the crowd will come only once such patterns of continuity are disturbed and the signs turn strange. But for the moment there is no problem because the patterns of continuity are confirmed.

There was no visualisation of the birth scene; and we are told not that the neighbours and relatives see anything, but that they hear (ἤκουσαν).[1] As in the previous two episodes, the narrative is in an aural mode. Yet there is a difference here, because for the first time news of God's action moves beyond the small circle of the earlier episodes. In the first episode, neither Zechariah nor Elizabeth says anything to anyone; in the second episode, Mary speaks in the presence of Gabriel alone; and in the third episode, the revelation is kept within the tight circle of John, Elizabeth and Mary. True, in vv. 5-25 the People recognize something—that Zechariah has had an extraordinary experience of the numinous. But with Zechariah dumbstruck they hear nothing and therefore know nothing of the character of Zechariah's experience of the numinous; and the narrator has them say nothing to anyone. But now the crowd of neighbours and relatives hear a word which not only explains that God has acted, but which also describes how he has acted: Elizabeth has given birth. That still calls for interpretation, but at least the crowd in this episode know considerably more than the People in vv. 5-25; and later in the episode they will bear the word of God's action into the wider circle of the Judaean hill-country.

Although the focus shifts to the crowd and its reaction in v. 58, Elizabeth is not forgotten. Three times we have the third person singular pronoun (αὐτῆς, αὐτῆς, αὐτῇ), which ensures that she shares

---

1. This is no reason to suppose, as do Danker (*New Age*, p. 45), Gueuret (*L'engendrement*, p. 80), Brown (*Birth of the Messiah*, p. 368), Fitzmyer (*Luke*, p. 373) and Evans (*St. Luke*, p. 179) that Elizabeth was still in hiding when she gave birth. The information given in v. 24 was quite specific: Elizabeth hid herself for five months, not for the length of her pregnancy.

the spotlight, though as recipient of divine mercy rather than as agent in her own right. It also suggests that the crowd regard God's mercy as strictly personal, an effect reinforced by the text's silence about Zechariah and reminiscent of Elizabeth's self-regarding words in v. 25. Implied already is the crowd's inability to perceive the full scope of the divine mercy. As the narrative has it, God's favour is personal, but it is also much broader in scope.

Proclamation and Praise: Luke 1.59-64

The Importance of Naming: Luke 1.59-61
At v. 59 the narrator moves ahead in story time to the incident that bears the narrative weight of the episode. Although circumcision is mentioned first and naming as an addendum to circumcision, it is the naming which is the narrator's real concern, with the circumcision never mentioned again after v. 59. As in vv. 5-25, we have a Jewish rite mentioned, but never narrated; and the effect is the same as in the first episode. It stands in the narrative as an image of the way in which the divine action now unfolding surpasses (without rejecting) the world of Judaism, symbolized here as earlier by one of its rites. This is why the narrator chooses to associate the naming with the circumcision, even though the more usual Jewish practice seems to have been to name the child at birth.[1] It would have been easy enough to have Elizabeth insist immediately after the birth that the child was to be named John. Yet the narrator chooses to work differently in order to

---

1. The whole issue of naming in Jewish circles in NT times is somewhat confused—the link with circumcision, whether the child was named after the father or grandfather, who did the naming, and so on. Clear evidence of the association of naming with circumcision is not found among Palestinian Jews until several centuries later. At an earlier time, the practice seems to have been that the child was named at birth, as was also the practice in patriarchal times according to Gen. 4.1; 21.3; 25.25-26. Brown however notes that rabbinic tradition has Moses named at the time of circumcision (*Birth of the Messiah*, p. 369, citing *PRE* 48 [27c]). It has also been suggested (Ellis, *Gospel*, p. 75; Marshall, *Gospel*, p. 88; Ernst, *Lukasevangelium*, p. 91) that the association of naming and circumcision is the result of Hellenistic influence, since in ancient Greece a child was usually named seven or ten days after birth. From a narrative point of view, however, the key question is not the historical one, but the question of why the narrator chooses to associate circumcision and naming, whatever the historical facts may have been. He did not have to mention circumcision at all.

introduce the rite of circumcision, even though he will focus on the naming.

The eight-day gap also allows him to focus more upon the continuity of custom and the fact of human initiative. The use of the imperfect ἐκάλουν ('they were calling') suggests that the crowd had already begun to name the child after his father, on the assumption that custom would prevail and that there was no decision to be made in the matter.[1] God has shown mercy to Elizabeth in giving her a son in old age, but beyond that the initiative rests with the human being— or so at least it seems. In v. 59, the crowd is the subject of both verbs (ἦλθον and ἐκάλουν); and the sense is that in the name of human convention they have assumed the initiative. The narrator also delays Elizabeth's intervention until the time of circumcision. This too conveys a stronger sense of a convention followed unquestioningly, which makes Elizabeth's intervention when it comes all the more surprising and powerful—at least to the crowd if not to the reader.

In v. 59 Zechariah finally reappears in the narrative, though only as a name. No sooner does his name appear, however, than the focus shifts back to Elizabeth in v. 60, where she appears in the narrative for the last time. She is called 'his mother' (ἡ μήτηρ αὐτοῦ); and from now on this will be the pattern throughout the episode, where both Elizabeth and Zechariah are named not in their own right but in relation to John. This is the narrator's way of ensuring that the child, who is wholly passive throughout the episode, but who is central to the divine plan, remains lurking at centre stage. It is also a way of ensuring that Elizabeth and Zechariah appear in the narrative in relation to the divine plan now embodied in the newborn child, and therefore a way of insinuating the presence of God as prime mover. Neither John nor his parents are important in themselves.

Elizabeth's brusque rejoinder to the crowd[2] provokes the action which is the episode's real concern. But the future passive 'he will be called' (κληθήσεται) suggests both that the choice of name is not her decision and that she is not the one who will do the naming. It is God

---

1. Some read ἐκάλουν as a conative imperfect (Marshall, *Gospel*, p. 88; Lagrange, *Evangile*, p. 55), which is possible but forced. There is no great difficulty in reading the imperfect more naturally as referring to an action which continued throughout the eight days between birth and naming.

2. The strong formulation οὐχί ἀλλά implies more than a polite difference of opinion with the crowd.

who has chosen the name, and the task of implementing the divine choice belongs to Zechariah, as Gabriel has indicated in v. 13 ('you will call his name John', καλέσεις τὸ ὄνομα αὐτοῦ 'Ιωάννην). The form of Elizabeth's statement looks ahead to Zechariah's pronouncement in v. 63, where the future 'he will be called' (κληθήσεται) is replaced by the present 'is' (ἐστίν). Her statement is not itself proclamation, therefore, but looks ahead to Zechariah's proclamation. She predicts the fulfilment of Gabriel's prophecy in v. 13 (καλέσεις τὸ ὄμομα αὐτοῦ 'Ιωάννην) with its reference to Zechariah as the one who will do the naming, and thus reinforces the angelic prophecy in her last prophetic word.

Elizabeth's rejoinder prompts the question of how she has come to the knowledge that her words imply.[1] At times, the presumption is that the dumb Zechariah has somehow told Elizabeth the story of his encounter with Gabriel;[2] but the narrative has said nothing of any such exchange. Alternatively, it might be that Elizabeth here as in the previous episode is under the influence of the Holy Spirit—a suggestion which Plummer rightly regards as 'quite gratuitous'.[3] The narrator chooses not to tell the reader how Elizabeth knows; and the effect of this is to leave the 'how' of the divine action concealed. The will of heaven has been communicated to Elizabeth somehow; but the narrator

---

1.   In previous episodes there was no indication that Elizabeth knew of Gabriel's instruction concerning the child's name. She made no mention of John at all in v. 25 and referred to him simply as τὸ βρέφος in v. 44.

2.   Marshall (*Gospel*, p. 88), rejecting Creed's suggestion that Elizabeth had received a private revelation of the name (*St. Luke*, pp. 24-25), thinks it more likely that Zechariah had told Elizabeth of the angelic message. He cites Godet (*Commentary*, p. 108) who thinks that Zechariah must have told Elizabeth 'a hundred times over'. Plummer (*Critical Commentary*, p. 36) and Geldenhuys (*Commentary*, p. 91) suggest that Zechariah has communicated to Elizabeth in writing. Brown however thinks 'it would be banal to assume that Zechariah had informed [Elizabeth]', and prefers to see her outburst as 'a spontaneous and marvelous confirmation of God's plan' (*Birth of the Messiah*, p. 369). Fitzmyer puts the rhetorical question, 'would he not have communicated it to his wife in the interval before the child's birth?', but then goes on to claim that 'to ask that question is to fail to understand Luke's narrative, which was not meant to bear such scrutiny. Its simple account should be allowed to tell its own story' (*Luke*, p. 381). Luke's account may appear simple, but it is not simple; and the question of why the narrator does not tell us how Elizabeth knows is certainly pertinent, at least from a narrative-critical point of view.

3.   Plummer, *Critical Commentary*, 36.

leaves the details undisclosed in order to build into the episode for the first time the paradoxical combination of revelation and concealment which marks the presentation of God's action in vv. 57-80.

Neither at the end of v. 60 nor at the end of v. 61 does Elizabeth make any attempt to explain why the child should bear so unusual a name. Having foreshadowed the first public proclamation of the divine will, she falls silent and disappears from the narrative. Both God and the narrator are content to have Elizabeth declare the 'what' of the divine will, without ever declaring how she came to know it nor even that it is God's will rather than her own caprice which she voices. The readers at least know that she speaks for God, if not how she has come to know his will. But the characters know neither; and not surprisingly they reject what they take to be Elizabeth's decision, speak up in defence of convention and therefore turn to Zechariah.

The Birth of Human Proclamation: Luke 1.62-64

By having the crowd turn to Zechariah, the narrator strengthens the sense that for the neighbours and relatives the naming of the child is a matter for human decision, and for human decision along the lines prescribed by convention.[1] Clearly the crowd expects the dumbstruck patriarch to defend convention and reject the mysterious caprice of his wife. The sense is that Zechariah is the one in control. But then the narrator has Zechariah re-enter the narrative by making a gesture which signals his powerlessness in the face of the divine action: because he cannot speak, he requests 'a writing tablet' (πινακίδιον). His gesture of taking charge (as the crowd might see it) is in fact (as the readers know) a gesture signalling that heaven has the upper hand. At this point of the narrative, it is a question of who has control.

Somewhat puzzlingly, the narrator has the crowd make signs to Zechariah when they turn to him.[2] It is hard enough to imagine what

---

1.   The use of the optative θέλοι strengthens the sense that it is human decision which is the key. In the Koine Greek of the NT, the optative has all but disappeared, and is found only in Luke (in the present tense: Lk. 1.62; 9.46; 15.26; Acts 8.31; 10.17; 17.18; and in the aorist: Lk. 6.11; Acts 5.24; 26.29). The use here of ἄν with the optative adds what Lagrange (*Evangile*, p. 56) calls 'quelque chose de révérentiel', the note of deference reinforcing the mistaken sense that it is Zechariah who will decide the issue.

2.   Lagrange (*Evangile*, p. 56), Fitzmyer (*Luke*, p. 381), Brown (*Birth of the Messiah*, p. 369), Tiede (*Luke*, p. 59) and Marshall (*Gospel*, p. 88) all take it that

signs they might have made in order to put the question to Zechariah. If he really were deaf as well as dumb, then it would surely have been easier to write the question, but the writing comes later and from Zechariah. For the moment, the narrator has the crowd make signs to Zechariah, just as he himself has made signs to the People in v. 22. There has been no hint in the narrative that Zechariah was struck both deaf and dumb; and it would be crude tactics indeed on the narrator's part to make Zechariah deaf just for the moment so that he cannot hear Elizabeth's words and can therefore offer independent confirmation.[1] An answer to the question as to why the crowd makes signs to Zechariah must lie elsewhere.

It is first worth noting that 'they made signs' (ἐνένευον) in v. 62 is a different compound of the same verb used of Zechariah in v. 22, where we find διανεύων ('signing') in a periphrastic construction. The verbal link suggests that there is a link between the signing of Zechariah to the People earlier and the signing of the crowd to him now. But what kind of link? Gueuret claims that just as Zechariah was reduced to silence by unbelief, so now the crowd is reduced to silence not so much by unbelief as by incomprehension, with the difference suggested by the two different compounds used in the two different contexts.[2] But it is not clear that the problem is the crowd's silence, either literal or metaphorical.

Zechariah is deaf as well as dumb, though none of them suggests why or how this might be. Danker (*New Age*, p. 46) remarks that 'in the popular mind muteness and deafness would be inseparably connected', and Ellis (*Gospel*, p. 76) suggests the word may mean only a covert beckoning, intended to indicate not that Zechariah is deaf, but that Elizabeth should be kept in the dark. Leaney (*Commentary*, p. 88) and Fitzmyer (*Luke*, p. 381) point out however that the verb means 'to nod', which seems to disallow Ellis' sense of 'covert beckoning'. Underlying all of these proposals is a speculation which is not grounded in the narrative itself.

1.   This is the suggestion of Brown (*Birth of the Messiah*, p. 370) and Marshall (*Gospel*, p. 89).

2.   Gueuret, *L'engendrement*, pp. 88-89, in reply to which Laurentin (*Les Evangiles*, p. 208 n. 5) remarks that 'cette nuance peut jouer son rôle mais paraît subtile'. Judging Zechariah to be the real concern of the narrative at this point, she prefers to regard the seeming deafness as 'une expression outrancière de son châtiment'. But it is the crowd, not Zechariah, that is the narrative's real concern at this point, and it is therefore by attending to the crowd rather than to Zechariah that an answer may be found to the question of why the narrator has the crowd make signs to Zechariah.

What is clear is that they are seeking to overturn what they take to be Elizabeth's decision to call the child John. In this, they are unwittingly seeking to thwart the divine plan declared by Gabriel in v. 13; and in the attempt, they turn to Zechariah who in his own way has sought to thwart the divine plan in the first episode. As a result, Zechariah was struck silent in a way which forced him to use signs to communicate to the People (διανεύων). Now as they seek to enlist Zechariah's support in their unwitting attempt to thwart the divine plan, the narrator has the crowd use Zechariah's language of signs (ἐνένευον). They are like him because, though they seek to thwart the divine plan, they end up collaborating with it—again unwittingly. This is because in turning to Zechariah they draw him back into the narrative for the first time since v. 23, and not in a way which will thwart the divine plan but in a way which will accept and acclaim the divine plan as Zechariah breaks into praise. In this they resemble Zechariah in the first episode, where having been struck silent for his doubt he emerges from the sanctuary to become a sign to the People of God's action, and in this sense a collaborator of God despite himself. He who had threatened to thwart God's plan becomes God's collaborator. The same is true of the crowd in this episode: they who (unwittingly) threaten to thwart God's plan become (unwittingly) his collaborator.

From Zechariah's point of view, the signs of the crowd come at the end of a process of reading the signs of God's action—particularly the great signs of his own silence, his wife's pregnancy and his son's birth. He manages well enough to read the crowd's signs, and the question is how well he will have read the signs of God's action.

When his written answer comes in v. 63, it comes not as report of a decision he has made, but as a declaration of a state of affairs which transcends Zechariah's own power of choice: 'John is his name' ('Ιωάννης ἐστὶν ὄνομα αὐτοῦ). Gabriel's prophecy is fulfilled; and the declaration stands in the narrative as a symbol of Zechariah's acceptance of God's plan. It is also the birth of proclamation, as the future 'he will be called' (κληθήσεται) of v. 60 gives way to the present 'is' (ἐστίν): Zechariah publicly announces not that which will be, but that which already is. His announcement signals that he has read rightly the signs of God's action and that he reads the larger promise differently in the light of the fulfilment he has witnessed. Zechariah has come to the understanding and acceptance of the divine plan at which he baulked in the first episode; and this understanding and acceptance become the ground for public proclamation, however terse and cryptic it may be in its first moment. What Zechariah writes on the writing tablet is the small beginning of a process of proclamation which will gather momentum through the second phase of the infancy narrative and come to full flower in the public ministry of Jesus in the Gospel and the apostles in Acts.

Elizabeth and the readers know that this is a proclamation of the divine plan; but with no explanation of why the child is to be called John the crowd does not. The readers but not the crowd know that in seeming to confirm Elizabeth's decision Zechariah in fact confirms the decision of God, and that he does so freely, with no hint of heavenly manipulation or compulsion of any kind. Gabriel had said only that Zechariah would be silent until the child was born, leaving the decision to believe up to him. What emerges now is that Zechariah has made that decision. When his power of speech returns, he makes no effort to tell his story to the crowd, but instead blesses God in a moment of praise which the readers know is the fruit of faith.

Nor are the crowd given the chance to ask why the boy is to be called John. Their reaction is given in the terse two words which the narrator inserts into the sequence of Zechariah's response: ἐθαύμασαν πάντες ('all were amazed'). The effect of this is to shift the focus from Zechariah in his moment of triumph to the crowd; and this suggests that the narrator is more interested at this point in the crowd than in Zechariah. Unable to share the recognition to which Elizabeth and Zechariah have come, the best the crowd can manage is an amazement from which none is exempt, as πάντες ('all') makes clear.

The apparent certainties of v. 58 have been undermined, and the joy that the crowd then shared with Elizabeth has given way to bafflement. On the other hand, the crowd have also moved from a radical questioning of what Elizabeth has announced, a questioning which implies rejection, to an astonishment which implies incomprehension rather than rejection. The crowd are therefore open to the possibility of future clarification in a way they were not when first they turned to Zechariah for a decision.

From v. 58 to v. 66, it is the crowd that holds centre stage. With the exception of the infant John who is passive throughout, other characters come and go: Elizabeth disappears after v. 61 and Zechariah appears only once she has gone. The fact that Elizabeth and Zechariah are never allowed to appear together in the episode, but until v. 67 are presented only in relation to the crowd, underscores the crowd's importance.[1] It is also the crowd who make the first move at vital moments: it is they who presume to name the child after his father (to which Elizabeth reacts), and it is they who put the question to the child's father (to which Zechariah reacts). It is also true that the Benedictus is in some ways an answer to the question which they put in v. 66. Uncomprehending they may be, but their role in this episode is decisive: they are more than spectators or catalysts.

The narrator has Zechariah break into praise of God in v. 64, but makes no attempt to provide the text of his praise. This might seem odd at so climactic a point of the narrative, but it is a decision by the narrator which serves to show the focus of the episode. For the moment, it is the crowd rather than Zechariah who hold the narrator's interest. Therefore, rather than give the text of Zechariah's praise of God at this point, the narrator prefers to set the report of Zechariah's praise between two reports of the crowd's reaction (vv. 63b and 65).

The praise signals that Gabriel's promise in v. 20 has been fulfilled, and also that Zechariah, like Mary in the previous episode, is now open to the divine plan. Gabriel had predicted that Zechariah would give his newborn son the name of John; but the question was how Zechariah might fulfil the prediction. Reluctantly? Angrily? In compliance with his wife's will? Or in free obedience to God's will? The praise reported in v. 64 gives the answer. It is never said explicitly of Zechariah that he has come to faith, but the signs are there for the readers to interpret; and prime among these signs is praise of God, which the previous episode presented as the fruit of faith. After the brief report of his praise, however, the narrator turns away from Zechariah and back to the crowd of neighbours.

The Widening Circle: Luke 1.65-66

In vv. 65-66 the narrator interpolates a longer and more nuanced report of the crowd's reaction between the report of Zechariah's

---

1. This is also a way in which the narrator shifts the focus from the personal story of Zechariah and Elizabeth to God's action. The same technique appears in the narrator's decision never to have Zechariah and Mary meet. Were he interested in their personal stories, it would make sense to have them meet—in vv. 39-56 perhaps. But if he is interested in them only in relation to God's story, then there is no necessity to have them meet.

praise of God in v. 64b and the Benedictus. The interpolation amplifies the epistemological drama of the crowd, widening its circle in both place and time, and giving it a more complex modulation. Zechariah's insistence that the child's name is John was the birth of a proclamation which now moves beyond the circle of neighbours and relatives. The repetition of πάντας, πάντα and πάντες, as well as the use of ὅλη, suggests something that the readers know but which the crowd must come to recognize—that this birth is significant not just for Elizabeth and Zechariah, nor even just for the relatives, but has ramifications which touch everyone and everywhere. The question is whether or not they will come to that recognition and, if so, how.

From the amazement provoked by Zechariah's declaration in v. 63, the crowd now moves to fear in the wake of his praise of God in v. 64. Here as before fear is the standard human response to the irruption of the numinous. The crowd has come to a sense that God is stirring in unusual ways in the events they have witnessed. They recognized God's hand in enabling Elizabeth to give birth; and that recognition moved them to joy. Now they recognize God's hand in enabling Zechariah to speak; and that recognition moves them to fear. It is Zechariah's return to speech which suggests to the crowd that there may be more to this divine intervention than the undoing of the past in the life of a childless couple. Sterile women have given birth before by God's grace; but something new is afoot here. In v. 66, fear gives birth to a question which looks wonderingly to the future, understanding that God is shaping something but asking what this might be.

The fear, we are told, comes upon 'all the neighbours' (πάντας ... τοὺς περιοικοῦντας), which leaves the readers wondering what has happened to the relatives who in v. 58 were part of the crowd, and whose presence was insinuated again in v. 61 with the mention of 'your kindred' (συγγενεία). They are not mentioned here because in vv. 65-66 the perspective is spatial, where earlier in vv. 58-63 it was more familial, which is why the relatives were added to the neighbours. In v. 65, the light falls first on the neighbours and then broadens to include the entire hill-country of Judah. The narrator has the word of God's stirring spread beyond the narrow circles of the first three episodes. The purpose of the divine initiative remains unclear to many, but the word goes forth nonetheless. God is both concealed and revealed.

Those who hear the news in the Judaean hills store the memory of it 'in their heart' (ἐν τῇ καρδίᾳ αὐτῶν, v. 66). They hear of the signs but have no way of interpreting them rightly: for that they must wait. The news of God's stirring moves both outwards and inwards in what is another of the narrative's modulations of the interplay of horizontal and vertical.

This is the first of the infancy narrative's three references to a character or characters storing in their heart words and/or events which for the time being remain puzzling.[1] In v. 66 at least it implies three things: (1) words are heard which the crowd fail to understand; (2) the words have mysterious and portentous implications for the future of the one spoken about; (3) the act of storing in the heart implies not only incomprehension, but also an openness to clarification in the future, a preparedness to live with unclarity in the hope that there will come a time when the puzzling signs will disclose their true meaning. It remains to be seen whether it has the same meaning and effect in each of the infancy narrative's three instances.

In v. 66, the question, 'What then will this child be?' (τί ἄρα τὸ παιδίον τοῦτο ἔσται;) looks to the distant future when John will begin his public ministry. The news has spread in space from Zechariah's house to the entire hill-country; and now those who hear the news look from the present moment to a mysterious future. And just as joy gave way first to bafflement and then to amazement, so now amazement gives way to fear and finally to a less anguished sense that great things may be in store. Where the neighbours and relatives were geared to the past in their presumption that the child would be named after his father, so now 'all who heard' (πάντες οἱ ἀκούσαντες) are geared to the future, the shape of which will upset the patterns of human convention and the sense of unshakable continuities with the past.

The turn from the past (and the need to continue its ways without question) to the future (and the need to adjust to its disruptions in the belief that it is God who is doing the disrupting) is an important moment in the epistemological drama now unfolding; and it is the dramatization of this moment in the life of the neighbours, relatives and those who heard which has absorbed much of the narrative's

---

1.   It will be said of Mary in 2.19 and again in 2.51. A different verb is used in each case: ἔθεντο in v. 66, συνετήρει (with συμβάλλουσα) in 2.19, and διετήρει in 2.51.

energy through vv. 58-66. At the level of the rhetoric, the shift is signalled by the move from a statement of fact which seeks no reply (v. 61) to a question in search of an answer (v. 66). This turn to the future is also one of the ways in which this episode looks not only back to vv. 5-25, but also ahead to the stories which lie beyond.

To this point, the only inside views offered by the narrator have been the reports of the crowd's amazement at the end of v. 64 and of their fear in v. 65. In v. 66b, the narrator offers not an inside view, but a comment which moves ahead in time to note of John that 'the hand of the Lord was with him' (χεὶρ κυρίου ἦν μετ᾽ αὐτοῦ).[1] This is an unusually explicit intervention from a narrator who has been notably discreet.[2] But now with the birth and naming of John the action of God becomes more explicit; and as the action of God becomes more explicit, so too does the activity of the narrator. And yet he gives no hint as to how the hand of God was with John, as to what were the signs of God's presence and power in John's life. If the action of God now becomes more explicit, still its precise shape and purpose remain concealed if not from the readers then at least from the neighbours, relatives and those who heard. The narrator therefore embodies in his narration the same combination of revelation and concealment.

Private Interpretation: Luke 1.67-80

The narrator could well have decided to conclude the episode at v. 66, which is a natural point of rest, or alternatively to move straight to the report of John's growth and withdrawal to the desert which we now have as v. 80; but he decides instead to insert into the narrative a second lengthy canticle, the Benedictus.

1. It is not universally agreed that here we are dealing with a narratorial intervention. Schürmann (*Lukasevangelium*, p. 83 n. 21) and T. Zahn (*Das Evangelium des Lucas ausgelegt* [Leipzig: Deichert, 1930], p. 113), for example, prefer to see it as a continuation of the direct discourse of the crowd's question; and it is true that Codex Bezae shows an implicit present tense which would support or permit such a move. Yet the weight of both manuscript evidence and scholarly opinion strongly favours v. 66b as a narratorial intervention with a past tense verb.

2. Tiede (*Luke*, p. 59) describes it as 'an uncharacteristically direct comment by the narrator to supplement and confirm the readiness of the people to receive this child of divine promise'.

The Character of the Canticle

The Canticle as Soliloquy.[1] It is hard to know exactly when Zechariah speaks the canticle. It is assumed at times that it is at the end of the debate about the naming, with the neighbours and relatives still present. This is usually linked to the assumption that in the canticle the narrator provides the text of Zechariah's praise in v. 64.[2] Yet in v. 67 it is explicitly said that what follows is inspired utterance where nothing of the kind was said in v. 64. Furthermore, the ordering of the narrative suggests rather that the gathering of the neighbours and relatives disbands at some point during v. 65, with the news passing through them into the Judaean hills. Unless the gathering had disbanded there would have been no way in which 'all who heard' might have heard at all. Therefore, when Zechariah speaks the canticle seclusion has settled on the narrative once more, as Zechariah speaks in the presence of his son alone, with not even Elizabeth mentioned.

But it is not only in the presence of his son that Zechariah speaks the canticle. In vv. 76-79 he actually addresses the child, and the question is why the narrator has it this way, when he might as easily have continued the less specific mode of address of vv. 68-75 or have had Zechariah address God directly. Given John's inability to understand or respond, the communication is between the narrator and the reader rather than between Zechariah and his son; and within this context the effect of having Zechariah address John is to focus more strongly on the newborn child at the point where the canticle interprets his future ministry of preparation. In the verses leading to the Benedictus and in the early verses of the canticle itself, the focus has been upon Zechariah, upon the crowd of neighbours, relatives and 'all who heard', and upon God and his action. Now, however, as

---

1. On soliloquy in narrative, see Chatman, *Story and Discourse*, pp. 178-81, where he writes in terms applicable to the Benedictus:

> Soliloquy is perhaps best used as a term to refer to nonnaturalistic or 'expressionistic' narratives in which the only informational source is that of characters formally presenting, explaining and commenting on things. These are formal declamations—not speech or thought in the ordinary sense but a stylized merging of the two (p. 181).

2. The possibility is suggested by Plummer (*Critical Commentary*, p. 83) and asserted more confidently by Brown (*Birth of the Messiah*, p. 379) and Bovon (*Evangelium*, p. 103) who sees the first half as offering an example of the praise reported in v. 64.

Zechariah turns for the first time in the episode to the son who throughout has lurked in the background, the narrator makes the move all the more emphatic by having Zechariah actually address John.

This is one of the ways in which the Benedictus differs from the Magnificat: where Mary spoke of herself in vv. 46-49 and never mentioned the son she is to bear, Zechariah addresses his newborn son and never mentions himself. In the Benedictus, the focus is more on the son and less on the parent. This is because what is important is the unfolding plan of God in which Mary will continue to play a key role: hence the focus on her at the start of the Magnificat. Zechariah on the other hand is about to disappear from the narrative, and the key figure in the unfolding plan of God will be John rather than Zechariah: hence the mention of John and not Zechariah in the Benedictus.

That John can neither understand his father's words nor make any reply strengthens the sense of the hymn as soliloquy. If God's action is both revealed and concealed in the episode, then so too is the human response to it. The neighbours and relatives have seen the signs and 'those who heard' have heard about them; but the prophetic speech which interprets the signs is uttered in seclusion, heard by an uncomprehending John and the comprehending readers, but concealed from all the others. This is not yet the moment for the characters to hear and react to the kind of interpretation offered by Zechariah in the canticle: that will come in the infancy narrative's second phase once the messiah is born.

The Canticle as Convergence. In two ways, the Benedictus is a point of convergence in the first phase of the infancy narrative. First, Zechariah like Mary has received an angelic apparition; and now like Elizabeth he receives the inspiration of the Holy Spirit: 'he was filled with the Holy Spirit' (ἐπλήσθη πνεύματος ἁγίου). The two modes of heavenly revelation converge in him who speaks the canticle; and ironically they converge in him who initially baulked at God's initiative.

Secondly, the Benedictus is a point of convergence of praise and prophecy. In the previous episode, the narrator had Elizabeth prophesy and Mary praise God. Now in the canticle Zechariah does both together: he first praises God in vv. 68-75—in ways very like the

Magnificat[1]—and then prophesies in vv. 76-79, in ways which focus on John's role in the divine plan just as Elizabeth's prophecy focused on the role of Mary in the divine plan. In the previous episode, the narrator staged the meeting of praise and prophecy in the encounter of the two women; but now he stages the convergence of praise and prophecy in a single voice. In that sense, the Benedictus is a point of convergence not only in the way heaven comes to the human being, but also in the way the human being responds to the coming of heaven.

The Canticle as Cento. Like vv. 13-17 and the Magnificat, the Benedictus is composed as a biblical tapestry, 'a cento-like composition'[2] weaving together quotation, reference and echo from the Law, the Prophets and the Psalms.[3] The whole of Scripture converges in the canticle which begins as praise and ends as prophecy. Insofar as it gathers up all Scripture into a cry of praise and in doing so looks to the past, the Benedictus reveals the ground of Zechariah's faith as the Magnificat did of Mary's: faith requires the understanding of Scripture implied in vv. 13-17 and vv. 46-55, a right reading of the past. Insofar as it gathers up the whole of Scripture into a prophecy of John's ministry and in doing so looks to the future, the Benedictus declares how Scripture (understood as promise in its entirety) is coming to fulfilment in the events unfolding now and the future events they portend. Zechariah joins Mary as one who follows the biblical hermeneutic which in the first place came from heaven. Where he failed as a reader in the first episode, Zechariah is shown now to succeed.

The Movement of the Canticle
The Benedictus is, above all, prophetic interpretation—an interpretation of God's action now and in the future, an interpretation dependent upon a particular reading of Scripture, arising from faith and the extraordinary knowledge conferred by the Holy Spirit, and offered

1.   On the links between the Magnificat and Benedictus, see Laurentin, *Les Evangiles*, pp. 212-13.
2.   Fitzmyer, *Luke*, p. 376.
3.   For a concise presentation of the array of OT texts in the Benedictus, see Plummer, *Critical Commentary*, p. 39, and for a more detailed account, Brown, *Birth of the Messiah*, pp. 386-89 (Table XII).

not by Zechariah to the characters but by the narrator to the reader. To see more of how it functions as interpretation, we must now examine the movement of the canticle.

Proclaiming the Fact: Luke 1.68-69.[1] The opening verses of the Benedictus sound the note of praise and state the motive for praise: God has visited his people, with 'he has visited' (ἐπεσκέψατο) in v. 68 establishing and 'he will visit' (ἐπισκέψεται) in v. 78 reinforcing the presiding perspective.[2] The effect of the divine visitation is deliverance (ἐποίησεν λύτρωσιν), and the one through whom the deliverance comes is the Davidic messiah (κέρας σωτηρίας). We have, then, proclamation and praise of God's action.

After the first two verses, however, the thrust of the canticle will move from proclamation of God's visitation to an analeptic interpretation and proleptic reinterpretation of its mode.

Analeptic Interpretation: Luke 1.70-75. The prophetic interpretation of the divine visitation begins by looking backwards. This is as it was

---

1. The analysis that follows will suggest a simple three-part structuring of the canticle: vv. 68-69 (praise and the motive for praise), vv. 70-75 (analeptic interpretation of the divine visitation), and vv. 76-79 (proleptic reinterpretation of the divine visitation). Various more complex structures have been proposed, often at the level of the form of expression rather than at the level of the movement of the narrative. A. Vanhoye for instance ('Structure du "Benedictus"', *NTS* 12 [1965–66], pp. 382-89) and P. Auffret ('Note sur la structure littéraire de Lc 1,68-79', *NTS* 24 [1978], pp. 248-58) have argued for a chiastic structure with v. 72 the canticle's centre, but the suggestion has not won wide support (see Brown, *Birth of the Messiah*, p. 383 n. 28, and S. Farris, *The Hymns of Luke's Infancy Narratives: Their Origin, Meaning and Significance* [JSNTSup, 9; Sheffield: JSOT Press, 1985], p. 129, for arguments to the contrary).

2. ἐπισκέψεται in v. 78b provides the one real text-critical problem of the canticle. The future is attested by ℵ* B L W Θ 0177 *pc* sy^{s.p.} co, and the aorist ἐπεσκέψατο by ℵ2 A C D R Ξ Ψ 053.0130.0135 *f*^{1.13} 𝔐 latt sy^h; Ir^{lat}. W. Grundmann (*Das Evangelium nach Lukas* [Berlin: Evangelische Verlagsanstalt, 1961], p. 74), Lagrange (*Evangile*, p. 62), Fitzmyer (*Luke*, p. 388) and E. Klostermann (*Das Lukasevangelium* [Tübingen: Mohr, 1975], p. 28) prefer the future, while Benoit ('L'enfance', p. 185), Brown (*Birth of the Messiah*, p. 373) and Farris (*Hymns*, p. 128) favour the *lectio difficilior* of the aorist, even though the weight of manuscript evidence favours the future. Given the way the entire episode dramatizes a move from past to future, a move which the canticle itself embodies, the narrative context would suggest the future.

in the oracles of Gabriel and in vv. 51-55 of the Magnificat, so that by now the pattern is well established: look to the past in order to understand what God is doing now and what he will do in the future.[1] Right remembering is essential. Zechariah moves back through time from what God is doing now through the prophetic transmission of the Abrahamic promise to the Abrahamic promise itself, which here as in the Magnificat is understood as the seed of the divine visitation.

Where Gabriel in vv. 32-33 had spoken of the Davidic messiah in terms of royal power and government, Zechariah in vv. 68-75 speaks of the Davidic messiah in terms of military power and victory, with the image of 'a horn of salvation' (κέρας σωτηρίας) used to describe the mode of the divine visitation.[2] Zechariah also extols the mercy of God (ἔλεος in v. 72); but the concrete manifestation of mercy is understood here as military success guaranteeing Israel a peace which will allow undistracted and enduring service of God. The enemies are understood as those who act aggressively towards Israel, and so endanger the possibility of peaceful service of God. Both the need for salvation and the act of salvation itself, therefore, are understood in military terms; and fulfilment of the Abrahamic promise is understood in the same terms. In raising up a Davidic messiah capable of bringing victory of this kind and therefore lasting peace, God has shown his fidelity to the Abrahamic promise transmitted by the prophets.

Proleptic Reinterpretation: Luke 1.76-79. In the second half of the canticle, the aorist verbs give way to futures as the mode of interpretation becomes proleptic and Zechariah turns to the figure of John. What he offers in fact is a prophetic interpretation of John's prophetic interpretation of the role of the Davidic messiah. Zechariah has made it clear in v. 70 that it is the prophets who have transmitted and inter-

---

1. Here therefore as in the Magnificat we find aorist verbs.
2. Texts such as Ps. 18.3 and its parallel 2 Sam. 22.3 acclaim God as a horn of salvation. But in 1 Sam. 2.10 and Ezek. 29.21 the title is applied to a messianic figure; and in Ps. 132.17 it refers to a specifically Davidic messianic figure. Hence Fitzmyer's claim that ' "horn of salvation" must be understood here as a title for an agent of God's salvation in David's house, i.e. in a loose sense a messianic title' (*Luke*, p. 383). The military overtones of the title are echoed in v. 71 (σωτηρίαν ἐξ ἐχθρῶν ἡμῶν καὶ ἐκ χειρὸς πάντων τῶν μισούντων ἡμᾶς) and v. 74 (ἐκ χειρὸς ἐχθρῶν ῥυσθέντας).

preted the Abrahamic promise; and he himself has been placed among the prophets by the narrator in v. 67 ('he prophesied' [ἐπροφήτευσεν]).

Now Zechariah places John among the prophets ('you will be called a prophet of the Most High' [προφήτης ὑψίστου κληθήσῃ]), among those who will announce and interpret God's visitation of his people through the Davidic Messiah.

According to Zechariah, John will announce that the salvation of God will come through the Davidic Messiah in the form of forgiveness of sins: σωτηρία. . . ἐν ἀφέσει ἁμαρτιῶν (v. 77).[1] This will be the precursor's act of preparation, his interpretation of the Davidic messiah which is a substantial reinterpretation of what we saw in vv. 70-75. The precursor will prepare for the Davidic messiah by alerting the people to the signs of his coming; and the pre-eminent sign will be the forgiveness of sins. That 'the horn of salvation' will bring salvation through forgiveness implies that the real enemy is not the aggressive neighbour whose military pressure disallows peace, but the sin which disallows peace of another kind. This is the one piece of substantially new information given to the reader in the episode, and the significance of it for the direction and shape of the entire Lukan narrative is hard to overestimate.[2]

This forgiveness, we learn, will be the concrete manifestation of the mercy of God, no longer ἔλεος as it was in the Magnificat and in v. 72, but now the stronger and more dramatic σπλάγχνα ἐλέους of

1. The phrase γνῶσιν σωτηρίας is nowhere found in the OT, and seems to be a Lukan creation. As in the OT, γνῶσις here moves beyond a sense of factual knowledge to an experience of what is known (in this case, forgiveness). Similarly, the phrase ἄφεσις ἁμαρτιῶν is not found in the OT even if the idea of forgiveness is found frequently. The phrase does, however, occur in the Qumran texts, on which see H. Ringgren, *The Faith of Qumran* (Philadelphia: Fortress Press, 1963), pp. 120-25.
2. At the heart of the programmatic reading of Lk. 4.18-19, there is the announcement which the narrative applies to Jesus of a mission κηρύξαι αἰχμαλώτοις ἄφεσιν and ἀποστεῖλαι τεθραυσμένους ἐν ἀφέσει, where the literal meaning of ἄφεσις (release) and its figurative meaning (forgiveness) interplay in a way which foreshadows forgiveness as the great sign of Jesus as both prophet and king (see emblematic texts such as 5.17-26; 7.36-50; 15.1-32; 19.1-10; and the disputed 23.34b). In the climactic 24.47, the Risen Jesus is depicted as announcing the mission of the disciples to be the proclamation of μετάνοιαν εἰς ἄφεσιν ἁμαρτιῶν εἰς πάντα τὰ ἔθνη (see texts such as Acts 4.10-12; 5.31-32; 13.38).

v. 78a.[1] There is also the move from the image of the Davidic messiah as 'horn of salvation' to the image in v. 78b of the Davidic messiah as 'dawn from on high' (ἀνατολὴ ἐξ ὕψους).[2] The messiah appears as a presence (light) which drives out an absence (darkness) rather than a presence (power) which drives out another presence (enemies). A new depth of mercy is revealed as God's new and more spectacular display of power. It is this which will be the fulfilment of the promise made to Abraham; and it is this which will be the new and final visitation of God which demands recognition.

In v. 37, Gabriel claimed for God an unconditional power. In the Magnificat, this power was defined as salvation and mercy. Now in the Benedictus the power of God is defined not only in terms of salvation and mercy, but also—and more importantly from the point of view of the Lukan narrative—in terms of the forgiveness of sins. This is the point of convergence to which the narrative comes as it moves to the threshold of the Davidic messiah's birth.

In broad outline, the Benedictus moves from God to John to the messiah. Verses 68-75 begin by focusing on God and, though the messiah appears as 'a horn of salvation', the focus in the early verses remains upon God and his action, so that the first half of the canticle is theocentric, with the messiah a comparatively fleeting figure. But in vv. 76-79 the focus falls first upon John as prophetic interpreter of the messiah, with God now a subdued figure,[3] and then upon the messiah

---

1. σπλάγχνα refers literally to the vital organs (for example heart, liver, lungs), which were thought to be the seat of emotion. Metaphorically, it refers to 'the heart of mercy'; and the addition of it here to ἔλεους intensifies the reference. On the difference between the Greek and Hebrew understandings of σπλάγχνα, see Plummer, *Critical Commentary*, p. 43.

2.　The phrase ἀνατολὴ ἐξ ὕψους, found nowhere else, is tantalizing. Does it refer to John? Or God? Or the messiah? All three are possible, but the last seems most likely. ἀνατολή (literally 'rising', for example a heavenly body) occurs three times in the LXX for the Hebrew חמצ, 'sprout, shoot, scion', which is used to describe the Davidic heir. In v. 78b, it refers to the mode of the divine visitation, and the canticle has made it clear already that the mode is Davidic and messianic. Therefore it seems most likely that the figure of the messiah, described earlier as κέρας σωτηρίας, is described very differently here as ἀνατολὴ ἐξ ὕψους. For a full consideration of the possibilities and background, see Fitzmyer, *Luke*, p. 387, where he opts for a messianic interpretation.

3.　Especially if Fitzmyer (*Luke*, p. 385-86) is right that κύριος in v. 76b refers to the messiah. Marshall however is more guarded about authorial intention and

understood as 'dawn from on high' (ἀνατολὴ ἐξ ὕψους).

The movement of the canticle suggests that it will be John's task to prepare the way of God by enabling the people to move from a sense of messianic salvation as the fruit of military victory which leads to secure settlement in the land to a sense of messianic salvation as the fruit of forgiveness which leads to a journey into peace. In doing that, John will prepare the people to read the signs of the messiah when he comes. In moving from God through John to the messiah, and from past to present to future, the Benedictus reproduces on a small scale the movement of both the infancy narrative and the Third Gospel as a whole.

The Departure of John: Luke 1.80

As Zechariah falls silent, the voice of the narrator sounds once more in v. 80, amplifying and continuing the prolepsis of v. 66b. John is removed to the desert until the beginning of his public ministry, and Elizabeth and Zechariah disappear from the narrative forever. This ensures that, although the various characters come and go, the divine plan remains at centre stage.[1]

The withdrawal of John to the desert is another way in which the narrator builds into the narrative the paradox of revelation and concealment in the presentation of God's action. John is now a very concrete sign that God's plan is unfolding as promised; but, like Elizabeth in the first episode, he becomes a hidden sign. There was first the hiddenness of Zechariah's interpretation in the Benedictus, and now there is the hiddenness of the sign as the pattern of concealment continues. The paradox is that as the news of God's action spreads both sign and interpretation retire to concealment. The news moves into the

suggests that κύριος here would have been understood by Christian readers as referring to Jesus (*Gospel*, p. 93). It is more likely that in its anarthrous form as here it refers to God, who in v. 68 has been called κύριος. In v. 17 too κύριος referred clearly to God as did in the same verse ἐνώπιον αὐτοῦ in a phrase parallel to ἐνώπιον κυρίου in v. 76. Although Jesus was referred to by Elizabeth—echoing Psalm 110—as ὁ κύριος μου in v. 43, the weight of evidence suggests that in v. 76 κύριος refers to God.

1. From the point of view of narrative logistics too it serves the narrator's purpose to move John to the desert, since it is there that he will appear when the account of his public ministry begins at the start of ch. 3.

hills, but Zechariah and Elizabeth disappear from the narrative and John withdraws to the desert. Heaven is left wholly in command.

Conclusion

This has been an episode in which the narrator has decisively demonstrated the reliability of heaven's word. The divine promise may seem strange, even impossible, but it is to be trusted. The first glimmer of fulfilment of Gabriel's prophecies came in the first episode, with Zechariah struck dumb as predicted and Elizabeth conceiving as predicted; but in this episode the narration of fulfilment has gained new momentum as John is born, the crowd rejoices and Zechariah is freed from his silence. Fulfilment appears as a process which reveals both the reliability of the heavenly promise in all its detail, and the reliability of the heavenly messenger.

The analysis in this chapter has shown how the episode also underscores the profile of faith offered in the first three episodes. Faith has again stirred the action as Elizabeth intervenes to insist upon the name given by heaven; and again the action has been set between human characters, though now among a larger cast as the crowd expands the circle. The narrator again introduces the Holy Spirit at the point of interpretation of the signs of God's action.

The narrator has prophecy and praise converge in the Benedictus, and so brings to a climax the narration of the characters' recognition of the divine visitation in the first phase of the infancy narrative. The prophecy voiced by Elizabeth and the praise voiced by Mary in the previous episode now find a single voice in Zechariah; and the irony is that he who baulked at faith in the first episode now voices a climactic recognition of God's action in this fourth episode. In the first part of the Benedictus (vv. 68-75), the narrator shows that where memory failed in the first episode it now triumphs as it did in the Magnificat; and in the second part of the Benedictus (vv. 76-79) it emerges that Zechariah has come to look beyond the birth as something for him personally to its wider ramifications as part of God's plan.

The analysis has also shown how the episode adds to the narrative the element of proclamation, which looks to the following episodes, as the news of God's action moves beyond the private arena into a wider milieu. In his insistence that 'John is his name' ('Ιωάννης ἐστὶν ὄνομα αὐτοῦ), Zechariah shows that he has rightly interpreted the signs of fulfilment and makes the narrative's first public proclamation. This and his cry of praise in v. 64 stir the less assured but more public proclamation that the neighbours and relatives take into the hill-country. In the first two episodes, the narrative was set in the context of solitary encounters between Gabriel and a human character;[1] and in the third episode, it was set in the context of the encounter between two blood relatives. Now, however, the news of God's action spreads—albeit very vaguely and tentatively—beyond such arenas and their privacies into a wider circle which includes not only blood relatives but also neighbours and 'all who heard' in the Judaean hills.

The narrator has the crowd of neighbours, relatives and 'all who heard' play a surprisingly important role in the episode. They move from protest at the infringement of convention to a vague recognition that God is astir in unusual ways and an openness to the future that this promises. They do not come to the point of faith, and yet despite themselves they become collaborators with God. First, it is they who draw Zechariah back into the action in a way which ensures the fulfilment of Gabriel's prophecy in v. 20; and secondly, it is they who take the news of God's action beyond the narrow circle of the earlier episodes into the hills of Judah.

In the narrator's presentation of God's action, there has been a paradoxical combination of revelation and concealment. Heaven is shown to be as good as its word as Gabriel's prophecy of v. 20 is fulfilled; and yet the divine action remains hidden in different ways. Neither Elizabeth nor Zechariah explains why the child is to be named John, even though the name is odd enough to draw consternation from the crowd; nothing is said of how Elizabeth is brought to a knowledge of the divine will; we are not told what the signs were that the hand of the Lord was with John; and Jesus is never mentioned explicitly.

The same is true of the narration of the human response to God's action. Elizabeth comes to a knowledge of God's plan, but we are not told how; Zechariah speaks the canticle as a virtual soliloquy; and nothing is said of what John did in the desert. In the first four episodes of the infancy narrative, the process of revelation and response has only begun. Gabriel has announced the 'what' of God's action, but the

---

1. In 1.5-25, ὁ λαός are mentioned before and after Zechariah's encounter in the sanctuary. But the solitariness of the encounter is stressed, with not even the accompanying clergy mentioned, and nothing is said of ὁ λαός spreading the news (such as they perceive it) beyond the Temple precincts.

narrative has only begun to show the 'how' of its unfolding. The narrator has shown more of what is required to recognize the moment of God's visitation; and yet there are points of unclarity which demand that more of the story be told.

The episode has been full of transitions. John has made the transition of birth and then gone to the desert; Zechariah has come from silence to praise of God and proclamation of his action; the crowd has moved from joy to protest to amazement to fear and finally to a questioning which looks to the future; the narrative's sense of God's power has moved from salvation through mercy to forgiveness; the news of God's action has moved from private to public world; and the transition from promise to fulfilment and therefore from faith to interpretation has marked the episode. Having in this first phase of the infancy narrative deployed the elements of both God's visitation and the human recognition of it, the narrator is now poised to make the great transition from John to Jesus.

Part II

THE GESTATION OF THE NARRATIVE

Chapter 6

INTERPRETING ANGELS IN LUKE 2.1-21

Continuity and Discontinuity

The connection between 2.1-21[1] and the episodes of the first phase of
the infancy narrative is complex. There are discontinuities enough to
have Bultmann claim that '[c]hap. 2 is not only fully intelligible on its
own without chap. 1, but every section of it is opposed to any combination with an introductory story'.[2] It is true that the narrative

---

1. Commentators are divided as to where to place v. 21. Some (for example
Lagrange, George, Schürmann, Brown, Muñoz Iglesias and Bovon) see it as the
conclusion of the birth narrative. Others however (for example Plummer, Creed,
Ernst, Laurentin, Ellis, Marshall, Gueuret and Fitzmyer) prefer to see it as the
opening verse of the following episode; and there are solid enough reasons to
support their choice (for which see Laurentin, *Les Evangiles*, p. 238). The decision
here to include v. 21 with vv. 1-20 is not guided by any unshakable conviction that it
must be associated with these verses rather than with vv. 22-40. My reasons for
reading v. 21 as the conclusion of the birth narrative will appear in the analysis that
follows; but in the end a decision about segmentation here can never reach a point of
certainty. Like v. 40, v. 21 serves as a hinge; and therefore any hard and fast
decision about segmentation is artificial and unfaithful to the nature of the reading
process.

2. Bultmann, *History of the Synoptic Tradition*, p. 294. He goes on to note in
support of his claim that '[t]he Baptist and his parents have no further part to play in
Lk. 2. Even more important is: (1) The motif of the angel's promise in 1:30-33 has
no sequel in Lk. 2, but is rather in contradiction to the angelic message in 2:11-14;
(2) The marriage of Joseph and Mary contemplated in 1:27 is simply presupposed in
chap. 2, whereas it has to be reported in the previous chapter'. Bultmann has
identified the problem, but proposed an answer which may make sense from his own
source-oriented point of view, where the finished text is seen largely as a collage of
traditional elements arranged by a redactor, but which makes less sense from a
narrative point of view, since it takes no account of the essentially sequential
character of the narrative transaction. For the reader, there is, indeed there must be, a
connection of some kind between what has been recounted in a narrative and what

changes key with its setting now in the world of the Roman Empire rather than the world of Judaism, and that v. 1 reads as the beginning rather than the continuation of a narrative. It is also true that the accent falls more upon what has happened than upon what will happen, and that the one character to survive from earlier episodes is Mary, though even she appears differently.[1]

Yet for all the shifts there are clear links with what has gone before.[2] The fulfilment of Gabriel's prophecies in 1.30-35 gains momentum; again the action which triggers the narrative—here the census—is never narrated; the narrator again has God communicate through an angel; the news of the shepherds prompts amazement in all who hear it and, in the case of Mary, a storing in the heart similar to v. 66. As a whole too the episode is shaped in ways similar to the previous episode. A birth is followed by an announcement concerning the child's identity; those to whom the announcement is made spread the news; and this in turn prompts amazement in those who hear. Here again we have the Lukan technique of reprise.

The divine visitation becomes more explicit with the messiah's birth; yet paradoxically—as this chapter will show—the ways of human

follows immediately: if not, then the whole narrative transaction dissolves into chaos, with the narrator showing himself or herself either incompetent or untrustworthy, and the readers left in the lurch. Presuming that Luke is both competent and trustworthy, and presuming too that he is more than a compiler of ill-fitting traditional elements, the challenge to the readers (and the critics) is to decide not whether there is any connection between chs. 1 and 2, but what exactly its character might be.

1.   Joseph was mentioned in 1.27 and in this episode appears actively. But he was so shadowy a presence in the earlier episode that he could hardly be judged a character. Compare this to the apocryphal accounts, in all of which Joseph becomes a key character.

2.   The continuation of the John–Jesus parallelism is often noted, though with less conviction than in earlier episodes. Brown remarks that '[t]here is a parallelism between the birth stories of JBap. . . and of Jesus. . . even if it is not so perfect as the parallelism of the two annunciations' (*Birth of the Messiah*, p. 408). Earlier he points out defects of the parallelism (*Birth of the Messiah*, pp. 374-75). A. George ('Le parallèle entre Jean-Baptiste et Jésus en Lc 1–2', in *Etudes*, pp. 47-48), Fitzmyer (*Luke*, p. 392), Bovon (*Evangelium*, p. 117), Laurentin (*Les Evangiles*, pp. 37-38) and Ernst (*Evangelium*, p. 99) are among those who note that, although the parallelism continues, there are important differences. While attention to the continuing parallelism focuses on the superficial similarities between the two episodes, it does not throw light upon their different narrative functions.

recognition become more arduous, since God visits his people in ways more surprising than ever. The fulfilment of Gabriel's prophecies in 1.30-35 begins, just as in the previous episode the fulfilment of his prophecies in 1.13-20 began; but the shape of fulfilment now is considerably less predictable than it was in the story of John's birth.

In vv. 1-21 the narrator presents signs of fulfilment which seem at odds with the meaning of the event, and right interpretation of them is therefore cast as a challenge. This is again an episode in which the narrator is less concerned with what has happened and more concerned with what it means and how human beings respond to it.

The Sway of Caesar: Luke 2.1-5

It may seem arbitrary to read vv. 1-5 rather than vv. 1-7 as the first section of the episode;[1] yet there are narrative reasons for doing so. In the first five verses, the narrator sets the context for the episode by reporting the imperial decree and the obedience of Joseph and Mary in response to it. In v. 6 as elsewhere in the Lukan narrative, the initial ἐγένετο signals a shift[2]—a shift from the realm of Caesar's sway to the very different realm of God's sway. The authority of Caesar brings Joseph and Mary to Bethlehem, but the readers know that it is the authority of God which brings the child to birth. What begins in v. 1 is the narration of the implementation of Caesar's plan, but what resumes in v. 6 is the narration of the implementation of God's plan; and this brings with it a change of subject as the initiative passes from Caesar (and Joseph) to Mary. The two narrative programmes are related, but quite distinct: hence the decision to make the break after v. 5.

To the question of why the narrator begins with the imperial decree of a universal census, different answers are possible.[3] From the point

1. See, for example, the remark of Ernst (*Evangelium*, p. 99): 'Der Abschnitt gibt folgende natürliche Gliederung zu erkennen: 2,1-7...2,8-14...2,15-20'. Similarly Brown, *Birth of the Messiah*, p. 410.

2. On the Lukan use of the formula ἐγένετο δέ ἐν τῷ + infinitive, see Aletti, *L'art de raconter*, p. 137 n. 11, where he points out that it occurs either at the beginning or a turning point of an episode.

3. The most straightforward and unsatisfactory answer is the claim of Muñoz Iglesias that it is simply because the census was a historical fact (S. Muñoz Iglesias, *Los Evangelios de la Infancia*, III [Madrid: Biblioteca de autores cristianos, 1987], p. 74). Despite his attempt to prove the historical reliability of the Lukan account, the

of view of narrative logistics, the imperial decree serves to bring Joseph and Mary from Nazareth to Bethlehem for the birth—that the one born may match Jewish expectation that the Davidic messiah be born at Bethlehem. Moreover, as with the introduction of 1.5-7, the report of the census serves to embed the narration of God's visitation: God appears from within the human world.[1] Where in 1.5-7 it was the world of Jewish politics and religion, now it is the larger and more secular world of the Roman Empire; and this might be read as the narrator's way of pointing to the wider significance of Jesus.[2]

Yet there is more to be said. The narrator chooses to begin the second phase of the infancy narrative with the story of a human initiative which sets the action in motion. The initiative is an act of human authority from the centre of the world and including the whole world. In both 1.5 and 3.1 the reference to royal authority functions primarily as a chronological marker, but the reference to Augustus in 2.1 does not. Neither Herod in 1.5 nor Tiberius and his minions in 3.1 do anything: they are simply named. But in 2.1 Augustus, without appearing on the stage of the narrative, acts: it is from him that the decree goes forth. The narrator presents him therefore as one who takes the initiative and exercises authority. In v. 2, we see that the imperial power is mediated from Caesar through the governor Quirinius. Not only a source, but also a line of authority is evoked.[3]

The imperial decree implies two things: first a possession (and

lack of evidence makes the claim impossible to prove (on which see Brown, *Birth of the Messiah*, pp. 547-56). As always in these situations, the prime question for a narrative approach is, why did the narrator choose to include the element, whether historically factual or not?—though if we know that it is not historically factual, the question becomes, why did the narrator choose to include a fictional element into his narrative? In this case, however, we cannot be sure whether or not the census was historically factual or not.

1. The more precise suggestion of Schweizer (*Good News*, p. 48) is that the purpose is 'to show how God speaks in an earthly historical event. . . rather than in a philosophical system explaining the world or in a myth embodying a universal truth which would be true apart from its mythic presentation'.

2. See, for example, Marshall, *Gospel*, p. 98 and Brown, *Birth of the Messiah*, pp. 414-15.

3. Both source and line are suggested by the repetition of ἀπογράφεσθαι (v. 1), referring to the imperial decree, ἀπογραφή (v. 2), locating the census during the governorship of Quirinius, ἀπογράφεσθαι (v. 3) and ἀπογράψασθαι (v. 5), referring to compliance with the imperial decree.

therefore control) of those who are counted, 'the whole world' (πᾶσαν τὴν οἰκουμένην),[1] and secondly a compulsion, with the narrator describing the decree as δόγμα,[2] and reporting that it was met by prompt and universal obedience. It is not an act which in any way requires interpretation on the part of the characters. What it requires from them is compliance.

As the narrator recounts the obedience of Joseph and Mary to the decree (v. 4), Joseph appears in an active role for the first and only time in the infancy narrative. Until now the narrator has had Mary take the initiative in the narrative, with Joseph appearing as no more than a name.[3] But now he has Joseph take the initiative, with Mary not mentioned at all in v. 4. When she is mentioned in v. 5, it is as an appendix to the action, in the midst of which, initially at least, Mary remains passive. She is named, and her condition is described, but she does nothing.

The imperial decree is shown to have two contrasting effects. On the one hand, it ensures that Joseph and Mary are brought to Bethlehem for the birth, with Caesar appearing as one who unwittingly collaborates with God's plan in ensuring that the circumstances

---

1.   Gueuret, *L'engendrement*, p. 108, captures well the symbolic force of the census: 'Recenser un peuple recouvre une opération de comptabilité. Il s'agit de dresser les listes de ceux qui, par ordre du gouvernement, viennent se faire inscrire. L'empereur romain pose là un acte de prise de possession de ses sujets, eux en état de soumission'.

2.   In classical Greek, the first meaning of δόγμα (opinion, philosophical position, deriving from δοκεῖν) is usually replaced by the secondary meaning (public decree, ordinance), on which see G. Kittel, 'δόγμα', *TWNT*, II, pp. 233-34; and in NT Greek this is always the case (again see Kittel), whether it refers to the emperor as here (also Acts 17.7), or the apostles (Acts 16.4), or the Mosaic law (Col. 2.14; Eph. 2.15). In technical Roman usage, δόγμα implies an imperial consultation of the Senate leading to a senatorial decree. Here in the narrative what matters is not the detail of its technical usage, but that it represents an exercise of authority which leaves no room for personal decision.

3.   The narrator has had Mary take the initiative in asking her question in 1.34, in speaking her word of faith in 1.38, in visiting Elizabeth in 1.39, in speaking her praise in 1.46-55, and in returning home in 1.56. In none of these cases is it said that Mary is impelled by the Holy Spirit or driven in any way by the power of heaven. It is hardly accidental that Luke has women as the prime human protagonists in his early episodes, and that his one egregious failure is a man. This has built into the narrative the vision of the overturning of the status quo which finds voice in the Magnificat.

of the Davidic messiah's birth are right; but on the other hand, it upsets what might seem to be God's plan, since it ensures that the circumstances of the birth are in other ways decidedly strange. In that sense, Caesar appears as one who (again unwittingly) works against the divine plan. This suggests that the relationship between the realm of Caesar and the realm of God is complex. The narrator implies that it is neither collaboration nor opposition; but more detailed judgments are left to the readers to formulate as the episode unfolds.

The Sway of God: Luke 2.6-14

To this point, the narrator has evoked the source and line of a human authority which is universal in scope, which implies possession and demands obedience, and which has contrasting effects as regards the plan of God. At v. 6, however, the narrator moves to resume the narration of the exercise of divine authority, which will show itself to be quite different.

The Brief Narration of the Birth: Luke 2.6-7

Given how crucial the birth is from many points of view, it is remarkable that it is recounted in so terse a style.[1] While in the apocryphal versions it is reported in detail and is accompanied by an array of marvellous signs,[2] here it is narrated in a single verse focusing on

---

1. As with the narration of John's birth in the preceding episode, many remark the brevity without tackling the question of why the narrator might have it this way (for example Brown, *Birth of the Messiah*, p. 418, Schürmann, *Lukasevangelium*, p. 98, Lagrange, *Evangile*, pp. 70-71, Muñoz Iglesias, *Evangelios*, III, p. 75, Ernst, *Evangelium*, p. 105, Laurentin, *Les Evangiles*, p. 223, and Nolland, *Luke*, p. 105). From a narrative-critical viewpoint, the question is *why* the narration is so brief.

2. In the *Prot. Jas* 18.1–20.3, Joseph, having left Mary in a cave while he goes seeking a midwife, suddenly sees the whole creation frozen into stillness for a moment. Having found the midwife, he returns to the cave to find it covered by a cloud, which is followed by an unbearably bright light issuing from the cave. They enter the cave, and the midwife verifies Mary's virginal condition; her hand is burnt away as a result; but she is then healed by touching the newborn child. The *Armenian Infancy Gospel* (8.7) has the earth raised and the heavens lowered, and even has Joseph meet Eve, whom he brings to meet Mary and Jesus (8.9-10). The *Latin Infancy Gospel* (Arundel MS, 73-74) has the midwife describe how Mary worships the newborn child, how the cave is filled with both bright light and sweet perfume,

the 'what' but not the 'how'. We are not told when the child is born, though v. 8 will hint that it was during the night.[1] Verse 6 implies that Joseph and Mary have been in Bethlehem for some time, but does not specify how long.[2] We are told where the birth does not happen ('in the inn' [ἐν τῷ καταλύματι]), but not exactly where it does happen. The mention of the manger in v. 7 suggests that it was in a space reserved for animals, but more than that we are not told.[3] Joseph disappears from the narrative at the critical moment; and although v. 18 will suggest that there were others present, if not at the birth then at least shortly afterwards, there is no hint of this in v. 7. Nothing is said of the inner response of either Joseph or Mary to the birth, the narrator preferring a wholly external mode of narration: Joseph vanishes and Mary is presented solely in terms of what she does. Then above and beyond all of this, the narrator says nothing of why God may want things this way. If he is as all-powerful as Gabriel claimed in 1.37, then God might have managed better the birth of the messiah. We are given the strange fact by the narrator, but no interpretation.

Having made his first appearance in the narrative in v. 4, Joseph disappears from the scene once Mary returns to centre stage for the first time since 1.56. In describing the exercise and effect of imperial authority, the narrator had Joseph take the initiative (with Mary little

---

and how a chorus of invisible beings chants Amen. She then fearfully bends to touch the child, and notices that he is weightless and noiseless, without defilement of any kind, his body radiant. She concludes: 'While I held him, and looked at his face, he smiled at me with the most sweet smile, and opened his eyes and looked sharply on me. And suddenly there came forth from his eyes a great light like a brilliant flash of lightning'. The Lukan account could hardly be more different. Compare too the extraordinary portents that Suetonius associates with the birth of Augustus, cited in F. Martin (ed.), *Narrative Parallels to the New Testament* (Atlanta: Scholars Press, 1988), pp. 160-61.

1.   Compare the *Armenian Infancy Gospel* (8.5) which tells us that the birth took place at midday on Thursday 6 January, and even that the weather was exceptionally cold.

2.   Given that they have been in Bethlehem for some time, it is surprising that the narrator waits until v. 7b to reveal that there was no space ἐν τῷ καταλύματι, which would perhaps have come more naturally at the end of v. 6. But to have mentioned the fact then would have committed the narrator to a description of the place where eventually the child was born, and also of the process by which they found it. The delay serves terse narration.

3.   Again the apocryphal accounts are very detailed in their description of the place, with the majority favouring a cave.

more than an addendum); but now as the narrator turns to describe the exercise and effect of divine authority, he has Mary regain the initiative (with Joseph hardly even an addendum). The focus is on her alone;[1] and she is the subject of the three verbs in v. 7 (ἔτεκεν, ἐσπαργάνωσεν, ἀνέκλινεν). This suggests that she who has been so privileged in the first phase and to whom the initiative now passes may prove to be the one to offer the interpretation which the narrator has left to the characters. She seems uniquely qualified for the task. Yet it remains to be seen whether that will determine the narrator's choice.

The report of Mary's actions after the birth presents a puzzling combination. As a pair they seem banal given what the reader knows to be the significance of the event.[2] The swaddling is an ordinary human initiative, so ordinary in fact that interpreters through the ages have pondered it, convinced that there must be more to it than meets

1.   One of the effects of the narrator's addition of the qualifiers αὐτῆς τὸν πρωτότοκον to the bare τὸν υἱόν (cf. 1.57) is to strengthen the focus on Mary by underscoring the child's relationship to her. It is also true that the description of the newborn as πρωτότοκος looks forward to 2.23. But to read its prime effect in this episode as strengthening the focus on Mary removes the need for elaborate speculation as to the meaning of πρωτότοκος here—much of which has focused on the question of whether or not Mary had further children. If the narrator had intended to assert that Jesus was Mary's only child, then he had at his disposal the word μονογενής which he himself uses in 7.12. As Marshall (*Gospel*, p. 106) notes, the word πρωτότοκος 'allows that Mary had later children, but need not *demand* this' (on which see J.-B. Frey, 'La signification du terme πρωτότοκος d'après une inscription juive', *Bib* 11 [1930], pp. 373-90). Schürmann (*Lukasevangelium*, 104) and Danker (*New Age*, p. 25) claim that Jesus as the first-born is the one who will inherit the kingdom and so be the messiah. Bovon (*Evangelium*, p. 121) asks whether it is a christological title, 'der den Herrn in seiner Inkarnation wie in seiner Auferstehung als die führende Gestalt der neuen Menschheit bezeichnen will' (see Rom. 8.29; Col. 1.15, 18; Heb. 1.6; Rev. 1.5). He insists (with Schneider, *Evangelium*, p. 66) that it refers to a special relationship to God rather than to other brothers and sisters. Suggestions of this kind presume that Jesus is the focus of the narrative at this point, and that πρωτότοκος must therefore tell us most about him. But if Mary is the focus, then it may be that πρωτότοκος tells us more about her than about Jesus. The apocryphal gospels find Mary's being alone at the time of birth unacceptable, and as a result supply the figure of a midwife, who in the *Protoevangelium of James* becomes a key character (19.1–20.3), and in the *Latin Infancy Gospel* (Arundel MS) even becomes the narrator (pp. 73-74).

2.   Compare again the apocryphal accounts, which might be judged more fitting with their abundance of marvellous phenomena following the birth, on which see my earlier note.

the eye.[1] From a narrative point of view what matters is that at the point where the narrator moves from the narration of Caesar's sway to the narration of God's sway, we again have a story of human initiative, and of the most ordinary kind: a woman gives birth and then swaddles the newborn. The readers might have expected God to take the initiative immediately and in more dramatic fashion.

It is even more surprising that Mary's second action is to place the child in a manger. If the first action seems banal, this second action seems absurd—again given what the readers know to be the identity of the newborn.[2] Born into the human circle, the messiah is nonetheless born outside the human circle.[3] To the question 'why the manger?', the narrator offers one immediate answer: 'because there was no place for them in the inn' (διότι οὐκ ἦν αὐτοῖς τόπος ἐν τῷ καταλύματι). This is not interpretation, but simple reportage of fact at one level: the newborn messiah is put in so extraordinary a place as an indirect result of Caesar's decree, since the census has ensured that no other or better accommodation for the birth can be found in Bethlehem. After the grandeur of Gabriel's promise to Mary in 1.30-35, the poverty of such circumstances is strange.

---

1. Some have suggested with reason that a text like Wis. 7.4-6 may throw some light on the swaddling, since there Solomon announces—in the midst of a long reflection on what makes for good kingship—that ἐν σπαργάνοις ἀνετράφην καὶ ἐν φροντίσιν, οὐδεὶς γὰρ βασιλέων ἑτέραν ἔσχεν γενέσεως ἀρχήν, μία δὲ πάντων εἴσοδος εἰς τὸν βίον ἔξοδός τε ἴση. For a full report of the many patristic understandings of the swaddling, see A. Serra, *E C'Era La Madre di Gesù* (Milan: Edizioni Cens Marianum, 1989), pp. 232-84.

2. This is an example of what the Russian formalists (especially Viktor Shklovsky) call 'defamiliarization', where there is a disorientating association which leads to a revision of the elements associated. Here it is the association of messiah and manger which is disorientating, and which demands a revision of messianic expectation. On the various forms of defamiliarization in the Gospels, see J.L. Resseguie, 'Defamiliarization and the Gospels', *BTB* 20 (1990), pp. 147-53.

3. This is to differ with C.H. Giblin, 'Reflections on the Sign of the Manger', *CBQ* 29 (1967), pp. 87-101 and Brown, *Birth of the Messiah*, pp. 419-20, who claim that 'Jesus is born in the city of David, not in lodgings like an alien, but in a manger where God sustains His people' (Brown, *Birth of the Messiah*, p. 420). The placing of the child in the manger would seem to make him considerably more alien than a birth in lodgings; and that the manger looks symbolically to God's sustenance of his people cannot be assumed. The reference to Isa. 1.3 mentioned by both Giblin and Brown is possible, though as always, given Luke's consistently allusive use of Scripture, it is hard to be sure.

The Switch to the Shepherds: Luke 2.8-9

At v. 8, the narrator switches unexpectedly from the newborn child to the shepherds who will play a decisive role from now until the end of the episode.[1] Heaven seizes the initiative, with the characters again found in a space reserved for animals. Not only that, but it is also night, so that both the time and place of the next phase of the divine visitation are odd; and the narrator says nothing of why God should choose to send angels at night to shepherds in the fields.

From a narrative point of view, however, the prime question is not why God might choose the shepherds to receive the revelation, but why the narrator makes the sudden switch away from the birth scene when he might easily and more naturally have turned to the reaction of Mary and Joseph. He prefers instead to background both parents and child, and to turn to the fields outside Bethlehem. Verses 1-5 have told of human initiative; and vv. 6-7, if they have begun the narration of God's sway, have still focused on human initiative, as if God, having set things in motion in earlier episodes, has now departed the scene. But in v. 8 the divine initiative is reasserted in unexpected ways.

As in the first two episodes, heaven triggers the real action of the episode. It may have seemed as the episode began that it was Caesar who, with the census, was prime mover of the plot. But in v. 9 it is again an angel who stirs the real action as the heavens open once more. Like Gabriel in 1.11, the angel is introduced anonymously, but unlike Gabriel he remains nameless throughout. Gabriel named himself in the first episode in order to establish his authority after Zechariah had questioned it, and in the first two episodes to show how his promises were fulfilments of old promises, promises made in a biblical past of which Gabriel himself was symbol and representative. There was, therefore, good reason to identify the messenger in the first two episodes. But, given that the shepherds at no stage question his authority, the angel here has no need to assert his authority or reliability, and his function is different: he will announce the birth and interpret its strange circumstances. Therefore there is not the same need to identify the messenger: it is enough to identify him as God's messenger.

That the news is made to come from heaven through the angel suggests that as with the promises made through Gabriel so now with

---

1. To the point where Bovon's claim (*Evangelium*, p. 129) that '[d]er Leser empfindet die VV 15-20 als eine Antiklimax' must be judged mistaken.

the birth: the initiative at every turn rests directly with heaven. It is God who has intervened directly to bring the child to birth (1.35), and it is God who now intervenes directly to announce and interpret the fact of fulfilment. In the case of John, his conception was the result of natural process *aided* by God (1.24), and interpretation of his birth the work of the human being aided by the Holy Spirit (1.68-79). At the point of both fact and interpretation, the workings of heaven were less direct. In the case of Jesus, heaven does not so much aid as replace the human being at the point of both fact and interpretation.

In v. 9, the narrator has 'the glory of the Lord' (δόξα κυρίου) shine around the shepherds, with the image of light in darkness strengthening the sense that the fulfilment of the prophecy of 1.78b-79a has begun. It also underscores the fact that, with the birth of Jesus, the presence of God becomes more overt.[1] As Laurentin notes: 'At Christmas, the presence of God is no longer engulfed in Mary's womb, but becomes engulfing: the divine presence engulfs the shepherds'.[2] Surprisingly perhaps, the glory of the Lord surrounds not the newborn child, as in the *Protoevangelium of James*,[3] but the shepherds. This is because it is not so much the bare fact of the birth which absorbs the narrator's interest as the interpretation of the birth and its circumstances which heaven now offers, and the reaction of the shepherds to the angel's interpretation.

The Interpretation of Heaven: Luke 2.10-12
As he begins to speak, the angel makes no attempt to introduce himself, nor does he mention God as the one who has sent him to make the proclamation: the angel himself is the subject of εὐαγγελίζομαι ('I announce good news'). Again the prime mover lies hidden, with the focus on what has happened and what it means rather than upon

---

1.   In neither of the appearances of Gabriel was he accompanied by the δόξα κυρίου. He was accompanied by the memory of his OT appearances in a way which focused more on him. But now the anonymous angel is accompanied by the δόξα κυρίου in a way which focuses more upon God.

2.   Laurentin, *Les Evangiles*, p. 228.

3.   The same is true of the *Armenian Infancy Gospel* (9.3) and the *Arabic Infancy Gospel* (3.1). The *Latin Infancy Gospel* (Arundel MS) goes further and has Jesus *as* light. In para. 73, we read: 'And when the light had come forth, Mary worshipped him...And the light itself which was born increased and darkened the light of the sun with the brightness of its shining...This light was born just as dew descends on the earth from heaven'.

either the one who has made it happen or the messenger he now sends. In the messenger's words, there is a complementarity between 'to you' (ὑμῖν) and 'to all the People' (παντὶ τῷ λαῷ).[1] On the one hand, the proclamation is made in a secluded place and to the shepherds personally, but on the other they are entrusted with news that concerns all of the People.[2] Again, public and private dimensions converge in the narrative, and here, as Bovon notes, in a way that points to the mediating function of the shepherds.[3]

Verse 11 gives the content of the proclamation and the reason for joy. The shepherds are told a number of things known already to the readers:

1. what has happened (ἐτέχθη)
2. when it has happened (σήμερον)[4]

1. ἥτις in v. 10 is usually taken as equivalent of ἥ, yielding versions such as the RSV: 'I bring you news of a great joy *which* will come to all the people'—suggesting that the angel announces the *future* joy which will come to all. A more strictly correct translation of ἥτις as 'such as' would produce the different version: 'I bring you news of great joy *such as* will come to all the people'—which suggests rather that the angel announces a *present* joy to the shepherds which will be followed by the *future* joy of all the people. The second is preferable in the narrative context.

2. It has been argued that λαός here includes the Gentiles, since it clearly does in texts such as Acts 15.14 and 18.10 (K. Rengstorf, *Das Evangelium nach Lukas* [Göttingen: Vandenhoeck & Ruprecht, 1962], p. 41; Geldenhuys, *Commentary*, p. 119; H.H. Oliver, 'The Lukan Birth Stories and the Purpose of Luke–Acts', *NTS* 10 [1963–64], pp. 202-26, here 221). But in every other instance of the singular λαός in the Lukan narrative it refers to Israel, especially when found in the phrase πᾶς ὁ λαός (Lk. 3.21; 7.29; 8.47; 18.43; 19.48; 21.38; 24.19). Where a clear universalist connotation enters the narrative in 2.31, the plural παντῶν τῶν λαῶν is found. It seems best then to conclude with S.G. Wilson that 'while admitting that a reference to the new people of God, both Jews and Gentiles, is possible in 2:10... it is unlikely' (*The Gentile and the Gentile Mission in Luke-Acts* [Cambridge: Cambridge University Press, 1973], p. 35).

3. Bovon, *Evangelium*, p. 125.

4. σήμερον is a characteristic Lukan expression, which is found 20 times in the Lukan narrative and which captures the Lukan sense of realized eschatology, the sense that the prophecies are *now* fulfilled. Other more arcane suggestions are that σήμερον here is a cultic usage looking to a pastoral feast which coincided with the birth of Jesus (P. Winter, 'On the Margin of Luke I–II', *ST* 12 [1958], pp. 103-107, here p. 105), or to the Christian celebration of Jesus' birth (G. Erdmann, *Die Vorgeschichten des Lukas- und Matthäusevangeliums und Vergils vierte Ekloge* [Göttingen: Vandenhoeck & Ruprecht, 1932], pp. 18-19), that it is an echo of Ps.

3. who has been born (σωτήρ, χριστὸς, κύριος), with the unnamed child identified in terms of the role he will play
4. where it has happened (ἐν πόλει Δαυίδ).

For the first time in the Lukan narrative Jesus is called saviour (σωτήρ), since in the title's one earlier appearance it referred to God.[1] The Benedictus spoke obliquely of 'a horn of salvation' (κέρας σωτηρίας), the one as yet unknown who would bring God's salvation. But now the identity of the shadowy figure is known—the saviour himself, he who brings the salvation of God which the narrator has been careful to define from 1.47 until now. The Benedictus' image of the horn of salvation gives way to the newborn child whom the image seems hardly to fit. If the redefinition of salvation as forgiveness seemed strange, then the proclamation of a newborn child as saviour seems even stranger.[2]

The title 'saviour' (σωτήρ) combines elements both sacral and secular. The Magnificat and Benedictus have made it clear how the title relates Jesus to God and how it therefore has a sacral edge. But in another way the title 'saviour' resumes the contrast between the sway of Caesar and the sway of God, since this was a title used of rulers in the Hellenistic world, and applied specifically to Caesar Augustus, chiefly as the architect of the *pax augusta*.[3] If Augustus was hailed

2.7—ἐγὼ σήμερον γεγέννηκά σε (Brown, *Birth of the Messiah*, p. 425), or a polemic against the expectation that the messiah would be born an adult (Muñoz Iglesias, *Evangelios*, III, p. 128). Of these, only the echo of Psalm 2 holds any interest for a narrative-critical study, but as always in such cases there is the problem of the allusive use of Scripture found throughout the Lukan narrative.

1. That was in the Magnificat where Mary proclaimed that ἠγαλλίασεν τὸ πνεῦμά μου ἐπὶ τῷ θεῷ τῷ σωτῆρί μου.

2. All the more so since the angelic proclamation uses the present tense ἐστιν rather than a future. The newborn child is already σωτήρ and χριστὸς κύριος.

3. The reign of Augustus as sole ruler of the empire began in 30 BC; and in a short time he put an end to the continual conflict that had followed the assassination of Julius Caesar in 44 BC—so much so that in 29 BC the doors of the shrine of Janus in the Roman Forum were finally closed. The widely shared sense of Augustus as the architect of peace is celebrated by Virgil in the Fourth Eclogue, which hails the reign of Augustus as 'a glorious age of pastoral rule over a world made peaceful by virtue' (Brown, *Birth of the Messiah*, p. 415). Later in his reign, the Greek cities of Asia Minor adopted Augustus' birthday (23 September) as the beginning of the new year and acclaimed him as σωτήρ (see the citation of the Priene inscription in Danker, *New Age*, p. 24); and an inscription at Lycia refers to Augustus in these

throughout the empire as the source of salvation and peace, so too were God and his messiah in the Benedictus. The real question therefore concerns how we are to understand salvation and peace and how they come about. The *pax augusta* and the *pax christi* are not necessarily identical, especially if what the Benedictus says of God's peace is right—that it comes as the fruit of forgiveness.

In the third of the titles, 'lord' (κύριος), there is the same mingling of sacral and secular. To this point of the infancy narrative it has been used of God and Jesus, which makes its sacral character clear. But it was also a title widely used in the Hellenistic world of both gods and rulers, as recognition of a source of power.[1]

The second of the three titles, messiah (χριστός), is wholly Jewish and wholly sacral in character. What is unusual is the way it is linked with κύριος.[2] It is one thing to claim that Jesus is the Davidic messiah, as is done in the title χριστός, used here for the first time of Jesus; but it is another thing to associate the messiah with God in the way that is done by the juxtaposition of χριστός and the anarthrous κύριος, which until now has been reserved for God.[3] On the one hand, the effect of the juxtaposition is to associate the Davidic messiah and God in an unusual way. On the other hand, the effect of titles such as 'saviour' and 'lord', which if not exclusively Hellenistic were at least used widely to refer to the imperial power, contrasts the Davidic

---

terms: θεὸν Σεβαστὸν, θεοῦ υἱὸ[ν], Καίσαρα αὐτοκράτορα γῆς καὶ θαλάσσης, τὸν εὐεργέτ[ην] καὶ σωτῆρα τοῦ σύνπαντο[ς] κόσμου (cited in R. Cagnat [ed.], *Inscriptiones Graecae Ad Res Romanas Pertinentes*, III [Paris: Leroux, 1906], p. 719).

1.   On this, see the detailed discussion of W. Foerster, 'κύριος', *TDNT*, III, pp. 1046-58.

2.   W. Grundmann ('χρίω', *TDNT*, IX, p. 533 n. 276) argues that the phrase should be translated 'Christ (and) Lord'; and another possibility is to treat χριστός as an adjective, reading 'an anointed lord'. Some ancient versions read χριστὸς κυρίου (β r¹ sy^hpal Tat Ephr); and this is favoured by P. Winter ('Lukanische Miszellen', *ZNW* 49 [1958], pp. 65-77). Yet the manuscript evidence is so weak that the suggestion, however attractive, must be judged doubtful. Others have claimed that the addition of κύριος is intended to clarify the Jewish term χριστός for Hellenistic readers (Schürmann, *Lukasevangelium*, pp. 111-12; Laurentin, *Structure*, pp. 127-130). For a thorough canvassing of opinion, see Muñoz Iglesias, *Evangelios*, III, pp. 129-45.

3.   The one instance where it refers unequivocally to Jesus is 1.43, and there it has the article.

messiah with the Roman emperor in a way that continues and specifies the contrast between Caesar and God established in the early verses of the episode.[1] The combination of the sacral and the secular in the titles reinforces the process of defamiliarization already at work in the episode in phenomena such as the newborn messiah in a manger and an angel appearing to shepherds. Worlds converge unexpectedly in a way that defamiliarizes and in that sense redefines both.

A more startling juxtaposition comes in v. 12 where the angel offers the shepherds a sign they have not sought. The angel reports to the shepherds the surprising details that the narrator gave the readers in v. 7b: 'she wrapped him in swaddling cloths and laid him in a manger' (βρέφος ἐσπαργανωμένον καὶ κείμενον ἐν φάτνῃ). After the grandeur of the angelic proclamation, this seems banal, even absurd.[2] As far as the shepherds are concerned, one wonders what the function of the sign might be. There is not the bare minimum of detail to guide them on their way: they are not told where to look, who the child's parents are or what the child's name is; and far from serving as a sign which might confirm the angel's proclamation, it seems more a sign designed to overturn any expectation they may have had of the Davidic messiah and so test the shepherds' powers of credulity.

As far as the readers are concerned, the function of the sign is easier to determine. Where in v. 7 the narrator made it seem that the placing of the child in the manger was the result of misfortune coming in the wake of the imperial decree, the angel in v. 12 makes it clear that this is the way God wants it. Hence he offers not a word of explanation of the strange sign he announces. The reason given by the narrator for placing the child in the manger ('because there was no place for them in the inn' [διότι οὐκ ἦν αὐτοῖς τόπος ἐν τῷ καταλύματι]) is shown not to be the real reason. It is not as if God wanted the Davidic messiah born in a royal palace, but that events

---

1.   Given the cluster of titles, it is perhaps surprising that we do not find among them υἱὸς ὑψίστου or υἱὸς θεοῦ, which were so striking a part of Gabriel's proclamation in 1.31-33, 35. Those titles were placed on Gabriel's lips at that point because the narrator was keen to stress the initiative of God in the conception of Jesus, and the exceptional relationship with God that that initiative entailed. But now his interests are different: he is keen instead to stress the role of the one born, to focus more upon the meaning of the birth than upon the initiative of God.

2.   Compare again the startling signs accompanying the birth in the apocryphal accounts, and even the star in the Matthean infancy narrative.

intervened to thwart the divine plan. As the spokesman of heaven, the angel makes it clear that not only the birth, but also its peculiar circumstances, are as God wanted it. An answer to the question, 'who is in control?', comes from heaven itself, and an answer which shows that the 'how' of divine control is paradoxical. The angel's speech, then, has a double function: it announces and interprets the birth for the shepherds, and interprets the circumstances of the birth for the readers.

The Supporting Chorus: Luke 2.13-14

Before the shepherds have time to reply in any way, they are met by a second surprise as the angel is joined by the host of heaven. The angels are introduced by the narrator as 'a multitude of the heavenly host' (πλῆθος στρατιᾶς οὐρανίου), which with its military overtone strikes an ironic note after the Benedictus's redefinition of salvation as the fruit not of military might but of forgiveness. The function of the heavenly host is again interpretative, as the angels proclaim the meaning and effect of the divine action as glory in heaven to God and peace on earth (δόξα ἐν ὑψίστοις θεῷ καὶ ἐπὶ γῆς εἰρήνη ἐν ἀνθρώποις).[1]

In the act of praise, the glory that touched earth in v. 9 returns to God. Like the Magnificat and the Benedictus, the chorus of the heavenly host is essentially theocentric, with the newborn messiah nowhere mentioned. The angels acclaim God and the effect of his action, without ever naming the one in whom his action takes shape. But in twelve verses God has barely been mentioned, and now the narrator has the interpreting chorus intervene to ensure that the prime mover is duly recognized in an act of praise.

The chorus may look to God, but it also focuses on the earthly effect of God's action, an effect which is described as 'peace' (εἰρήνη). This is not the first time the word has appeared in the infancy narrative. It appeared in 1.79 as the last word of the Benedictus, where it described the effect of the enlightened human being's recognition that God has fulfilled his promise—climactically in the forgiveness of sins. In 2.29, 'peace' (εἰρήνη) will appear again to

---

1.   Some versions read the nominative εὐδοκία (ℵ² B² L Θ Ξ Ψ 053 f¹·¹³ 𝔐 sy bo; Or^pt Eus Epiph). Yet there is stronger manuscript support for the genitive εὐδοκίας (ℵ* A B* D W *pc* vg^pt sa; Or^lat); and, as Metzger points out (*Textual Commentary*, p. 133), it is the *lectio difficilior*.

describe the effect of God's fulfilment of his promise to Simeon, though it will not be linked there to the forgiveness of sins. Later in the Gospel, it will appear in 19.38 in a context very like that of 2.14. As Jesus enters Jerusalem, the crowd of disciples[1] will proclaim 'in heaven peace and glory in the highest' (ἐν οὐρανῷ εἰρήνη καὶ δόξα ἐν ὑψίστοις), with both 'glory' (δόξα) and 'peace' (εἰρήνη) referred to heaven, and heaven therefore acknowledged as the source of the peace which comes with the recognition that God has fulfilled his promise. Then in 19.42 the narrator will have Jesus say of Jerusalem: 'If only you knew even today the things that make for peace' (εἰ ἔγνως τῇ ἡμέρᾳ ταύτῃ καὶ σὺ τὰ πρὸς εἰρήνην)—and this just before 19.44 where Jesus foresees the destruction of Jerusalem 'because you did not know the moment of your visitation' (ἀνθ' ὧν οὐκ ἔγνως τὸν καιρὸν τῆς ἐπισκοπῆς σου). The effect of this is to link 'the moment of the visitation' (τὸν καιρὸν τῆς ἐπισκοπῆς) and 'the things that make for peace' (τὰ πρὸς εἰρήνην) in the same way as in 2.14, and again to tie 'peace' (εἰρήνη) to the recognition that God has fulfilled his promise.

Peace is proclaimed for ἀνθρώποις εὐδοκίας, which moves the scope of God's action and the possibility of human recognition of it beyond the bounds of Israel.[2] Through vv. 11-14 the focus has expanded in three steps: from the shepherds (ὑμῖν) to Israel (πᾶς λαός) and now beyond Israel to ἀνθρώποις εὐδοκίας. But what is the force of εὐδοκίας?[3] If, as the weight of opinion now suggests, it

---

1.　Who are described as τὸ πλῆθος τῶν μαθητῶν χαίροντες αἰνεῖν τὸν θεόν, which is reminiscent of the description of the angels in 2.13.

2.　With its implied universalism, ἀνθρώποις εὐδοκίας represents a step forward from the angelic proclamation of a joy which is ὑμῖν and παντὶ τῷ λαῷ. The focus expands from the shepherds to Israel and finally to all ἀνθρώποις εὐδοκίας.

3.　The readings of εὐδοκία (nominative) and εὐδοκίας (genitive) have given rise to two different renderings. First, εὐδοκία has been understood to have the same status as δόξα and εἰρήνη; and this produces the translation found in the KJV and elsewhere: 'Glory to God in the highest, and on earth peace, good will toward [or among] men'. This gives the chorus a triple structure. Secondly, εὐδοκίας has been understood as referring either to the good will that belongs to human beings or as the good will that God displays towards earth. This gives the chorus a double or parallel structure, and produces either the translation found in the Vulgate (and many later Roman Catholic versions): 'Gloria in altissimis Deo et in terra pax hominibus bonae voluntatis', or a translation such as the RSV: 'Glory to God in the highest, and on earth peace among men with whom he is pleased'. Accepting the reading of

refers to divine favour rather than human good will, the question arises as to why the narrator does not have εὐδοκίας αὐτοῦ in order to remove the ambiguity to which the history of interpretation well testifies.[1] But other questions suggest themselves. Might the narrator have decided to omit the αὐτοῦ? And if he did, then why? Certainly the omission creates an ambiguity; and yet if this is an ambiguity which serves the narrator's purpose, and therefore an ambiguity he has a vested interest in creating, it may not after all be so necessary to choose between divine favour and human good will.

The bare εὐδοκίας serves the narrator's purpose because it captures both a sense of God's favour moving from heaven to earth and of human good will moving from earth to heaven. In that sense, it expresses in a single word the two-way vertical movement which marks the chorus of the angels. If the divine visitation and human recognition of it are parts of a single process, then so too are the coming of God's favour to earth and the good will which opens the human being to receive God's favour. This single process with its double movement is captured nicely by the ambiguous εὐδοκίας in a way that confirms the narrative's sense of the necessary link between theology and epistemology, between divine visitation and human recognition.

Narrating Human Response: Luke 2.15-21

The Shepherds' Decision: Luke 2.15
The interpreting chorus has shown that the angels know the truth of the puzzling sign; and the question is whether the human characters will show themselves equally perceptive. The angels have led the way, and the human characters are called to follow.

With the return of the angels to heaven, the narrative shifts from

---

εὐδοκίας, it is a question of whether it applies to God or to human beings. Fitzmyer (*Luke*, pp. 411-12) offers an array of arguments (including parallels from Qumran texts) in favour of εὐδοκίας as applying to God rather than to human beings, and in doing so he is voicing a wide consensus of recent opinion, which is reflected in the recent versions, all of which adopt a translation which refers εὐδοκίας to God rather than to human beings.

1. For a similar objection (accepted by Brown, *Birth of the Messiah*, p. 404), see A. Feuillet, 'Les hommes de bonne volonté ou les hommes que Dieu aime: Note sur la traduction de Luc 2,14b', *Bulletin de l'Association Guillaume Budé* 4 (1974), pp. 91-92.

the vertical to the horizontal, as the narrator has the shepherds speak
not to the angels but to each other. The implication of what they say is
that they freely decide to go to Bethlehem—their decision contrasting
with the obedience demanded by the imperial decree,[1] and the imperfect 'they were saying' (ἐλάλουν) implying that their decision was
more a process than a flash of inspiration. They recognize that it is
God himself who stands behind the revelation. It is no illusion or
human concoction: 'the Lord has made known to us' (ὁ κύριος
ἐγνώρισεν ἡμῖν). That they decide to go shows that they in their way
have come to faith. Undaunted by the peculiar sign they have been
given, they are prepared to accept the reliability of the messenger.

By the end of v. 15, it is clear that the shepherds know where to go,
who is behind the revelation, and what to look for. What is not so
clear is why the narrator has them go. They themselves say: 'let us see
the thing that has happened' (ἴδωμεν τὸ ῥῆμα τοῦτο τὸ γεγονός).[2]
Seeing is the point; but why do they want or need to see? There is no
hint that they need to see in order to verify what the angel has said;
and their words in v. 15 give no hint of puzzlement or questioning.
The indications are that like Mary in 1.39-56 they go not in order to
believe, but because they believe; and they will see because they
believe. The narrator has the shepherds go in order to secure the point
made in earlier episodes that it is faith that stirs the action and to make
the new point that it is faith that confers sight.

With the use of the verb 'let us see' (ἴδωμεν) the mode of narration
becomes more strongly visual; and it becomes more apparent that,
once the messiah is born (that is, once the sign of fulfilment appears),
the aural and the visual begin to interact in a way that is new in the
infancy narrative. The shepherds who have heard the word of the
angel do not go to hear another word (as did Mary to Elizabeth), since
they do the speaking once they arrive and there is no report of anyone
else saying anything. They go to see the sign and to pass on the inter-

---

1. On which see Gueuret, *L'engendrement*, p. 116. Where the imperial decree
demands of the characters the kind of compliance reported in v. 3, the divine
visitation demands of them a free response arising from interpretation of what has
been seen and heard. The point has emerged in all the human characters of the first
phase and is reinforced now as the second phase begins.

2. Here there seems to be a play on the ambiguity of ῥῆμα, with the shepherds
going to see both what heaven has uttered ('the word') and what heaven has enacted
('the thing').

pretative word they have heard to those who may have witnessed the facts, but who need to hear a word of interpretation so that the facts may become a sign that leads to understanding; and when eventually the shepherds depart the scene in v. 20, they will be shown praising God 'for all they had heard and seen' (ἐπὶ πᾶσιν οἷς ἤκουσαν καὶ εἶδον). It is hearing and seeing that produce praise.

Shepherds as Angels: Luke 2.16-17
The impression in v. 16 is that the shepherds find the child immediately,[1] though what they find when they arrive is not quite what the angel promised. We are told first that they find the parents, of whom the angel has said nothing; and then we are told that they find the child laid in the manger, with nothing said of the swaddling cloths mentioned by both the narrator in v. 7 and the angel in v. 12. The way in which what they find is reported suggests that the narration is focalized through the eyes of the shepherds themselves. The readers see with the shepherds—another way in which the visual enters the narration more decisively.

First, they notice Mary and Joseph, about whom the angel has said nothing, though the shepherds can hardly have failed to wonder who the parents of such a child might be; and the mention of both Mary and Joseph suggests that the shepherds judge them to be the parents. They next see the baby, noticing not the commonplace detail of the swaddling cloths of which nothing is said, but the most unusual place where the child lies, which the angel has announced with no word of explanation. Verse 17 begins with the word 'seeing' (ἰδόντες); but it is v. 16 that recounts the process of the shepherds' seeing, and so has the readers see with them.

Once the shepherds come to the birth scene, the narrative moves to a point of convergence which is more than merely physical. There is first the convergence of the two realms juxtaposed until now—the realm of Caesar, who has ensured a birth in Bethlehem, and the realm of God, who has revealed the birth's meaning to the shepherds. This implies a second convergence of fact and interpretation. The shepherds

1. Lagrange (*Evangile*, p. 79) and Plummer (*Critical Commentary*, p. 60) claim that the compound form ἀνευρίσκω implies finding after a search. Yet there is nothing in the narrative which suggests this. If anything, the participle σπεύσαντες suggests the opposite. In Acts 21.4, the same verb appears without any obvious sense of search or struggle.

come to the birth scene not having seen the fact, but knowing the interpretation; those at the birth scene have seen the fact, but do not know the interpretation. Once the shepherds see and those at the birth scene hear, the convergence is achieved.

In v. 17, the narrator uses the verb 'they made known' (ἐγνώρισαν), another form of which he used in the shepherds' speech in v.15 (ἐγνώρισεν). The effect of the verbal link is to associate the shepherds with the angels. There is a second verbal link with λαληθέντος ('saying') in v. 17 and λαληθέντων ('saying') in v. 18; and then the narrator has the shepherds return praising God, using 'glorifying and praising God' (δοξάζοντες καὶ αἰνοῦντες τὸν θεόν, v. 20), just as earlier he had described the angelic host as 'praising God and saying glory in the highest to God' (αἰνούντων τὸν θεὸν καὶ λεγόντων δόξα ἐν ὑψίστοις θεῷ, vv. 13b-14a). The paradox, as the narrator has it, is that shepherds become interpreting angels; and like the angels, they do not worship the child in the way of the Matthean magi (Mt. 2.11).[1] This is another of the narrative's ways of ensuring that the focus remains on the human response to the birth and the revelation of its meaning.

From Puzzlement to Pondering: Luke 2.18-19

In narrating the reaction to the shepherds' story, the narrator unexpectedly introduces a group that he calls 'all who heard' (πάντες οἱ ἀκούσαντες), about whom nothing was said in vv. 6-7 and about whom no detail is given now. Who they are, where they came from, or how they came to be there we are not told, since their presence in the narrative is strictly functional: the narrator has no interest in them for their own sake. They are important rather for what they do; having seen the newborn child, they now hear the shepherds' story and marvel at what they hear. Having seen the fact (a child born in such poor circumstances), they are astonished by the shepherds' interpretation of it.

Their astonishment implies incomprehension; and the way in which the narrator frames their reaction suggests that they are puzzled for three reasons. First, the news itself is astonishing enough—that such a child should be the saviour; secondly, the messengers themselves are

---

1. See Danker, *New Age*, p. 29. Compare too the *Arabic Infancy Gospel* (4.1) and the *Armenian Infancy Gospel* (10.2) which both have the shepherds worship Jesus.

almost as astonishing, which is why the narrator includes the redundant 'by the shepherds' (ὑπὸ τῶν ποιμένων), focusing on the extraordinary fact of such a message brought by such messengers who themselves have been visited by angels; and thirdly, the equally redundant 'to them' (πρὸς αὐτούς) suggests that the crowd is also astonished that they should be the recipients of such news.

In turning first to 'all who heard' in v. 18, the narrator points to the essentially public character of the announcement which, as the angel has declared in v. 10, is 'a great joy for all the People' (χαρὰν μεγάλην. . . παντὶ τῷ λαῷ). Mary and Joseph are never addressed personally by the shepherds, as they will be later by Simeon. At this stage, they take their place among 'all who heard', and are made therefore to share the astonishment of the crowd. Yet in recounting Mary's personal reaction in v. 19, the narrator implies that here, as in v. 10 where the joy was both 'to you' (ὑμῖν) and 'to all the People' (παντὶ τῷ λαῷ), the public dimension stands in tension with the private.

It seems strange at first that Mary should be in any way astonished after what she has heard from Gabriel.[1] Some prefer to resolve the difficulty by claiming that she does not share the amazement or incomprehension of the crowd.[2] Yet that presumes that Mary is not included among 'all who heard' in v. 18; and it would seem strange that the narrator would report her response in terms so similar to those in which he has reported the reaction of 'all who heard' in 1.66

---

1. This appears to be one of those points where chs. 1 and 2 of the infancy narrative are at odds. Yet seen through the lens of narrative criticism rather than source criticism this is not necessarily the case.

2. See for example Plummer, *Critical Commentary*, p. 60, where he claims that Mary 'could have no such astonishment', because of the revelations made to her and Joseph, and judges the δέ at the start of v. 19 to imply that Mary did not share the common amazement. Laurentin (*Les Evangiles*, p. 236 n. 23) disputes the claim of Gueuret (*L'engendrement*, p. 124) regarding Mary in 2.19 that '[c]'est plutôt son non-savoir qui est souligné'. He prefers to see the evangelist stressing Mary's contemplative response and her role as source of the infancy narrative. Gueuret goes too far in claiming that Mary's 'non-savoir' is stressed at this point, since what is stressed more is the way she deals with her 'non-savoir'. But Laurentin deals too lightly with the element of 'non-savoir' in his determination to read the verse as Luke's oblique reference to Mary as source of the Lukan narrative—an ultimately unprovable claim which, even if it were provable, would throw little light on how the narrative works.

if he intended her response to be so different. The language is not identical,[1] which suggests that there is something different about Mary's response, as one might expect given the revelation she has received. But the difference is not a difference between puzzled incomprehension on the one hand and knowing appreciation on the other. Mary is astonished and uncomprehending, though for different reasons than the others who heard.

For Mary what is puzzling is that her child should be born in this way.[2] Gabriel promised the birth and revealed to her the child's role and identity, but he said nothing of a birth in such circumstances. Therefore it is not just one strange detail which she must ponder, but the whole configuration of promise and fulfilment to this point, as is suggested by the phrase 'all these things' (πάντα...τὰ ῥήματα ταῦτα).[3] For Mary, as for the reader, the circumstances of the birth must have seemed the result of misadventure; and what astonishes her now is that the 'how' of the birth should also prove to be part of God's plan. For the others who have heard, however, the reason for astonishment is different, because unlike Mary and the readers they know nothing of the child's role and identity. They are therefore astonished that a child born in such circumstances should be saviour, messiah and lord.

What emerges in v. 19 is that because of what she knows Mary handles her astonishment and incomprehension creatively. The question, then, is not whether faith includes incomprehension, but what faith does with incomprehension.[4] For faith and incomprehension to cohabit creatively there is a need to do what Mary is reported as doing in v. 19: 'she kept all these things, pondering them in her heart' (πάντα συνετήρει τὰ ῥήματα ταῦτα συμβάλλουσα ἐν τῇ καρδίᾳ

1.   1.66 reads ἔθεντο πάντες οἱ ἀκούσαντες ἐν τῇ καρδίᾳ αὐτῶν, and 2.19 reads ἡ δὲ Μαριὰμ πάντα συνετήρει τὰ ῥήματα ταῦτα συμβάλλουσα ἐν τῇ καρδίᾳ αὐτῆς. The main difference is that the verbs in 2.19 are more active than ἔθεντο in 1.66. Apart from the wording, a further important difference is that Mary's puzzlement is within the context of faith and the crowd's was not.

2.   This may also be true of Joseph, but the readers know nothing of how much Joseph knows.

3.   This is to understand τὰ ῥήματα not simply as 'words' (as in 1.66), but also as 'things' in the sense of 'events'.

4.   Another reason for the introduction of οἱ ἀκούσαντες is to provide a background against which the narrator might narrate Mary's reaction. In this sense again, they are strictly functional.

αὐτῆς).[1] That her pondering was more than a momentary questioning is suggested by the use of the imperfect 'she kept' (συνετήρει), which is at times translated 'treasure, cherish' to avoid the hint of incomprehension, but which here has the more neutral sense of 'keep, preserve'. The less neutral and more important word is the participle συμβάλλουσα ('pondering'), which specifies how Mary kept all these things in her heart. W.C. van Unnik has done most to clarify the meaning of the word and concludes that it means to interpret obscure events, hitting upon the right meaning, often with divine help.[2] In the case of Mary, there is no suggestion of divine help, but she is certainly alert to the obscurity of the shepherds' visit and revelation.

The process implied by συνετήρει is a process of interpretation, an attempt, as συμβάλλουσα further indicates, to put the pieces together in order to see the pattern, a grappling with strange signs of fulfilment. After the shepherds' visit and revelation, Mary has more pieces than she had before, and she will have still more after each of the remaining episodes of the infancy narrative. What she begins in v. 19 is the process of putting the pieces together in an act of interpretation which will enable a recognition of the pattern. What we see therefore is that not only does faith not exclude such a process, but positively demands it. In that sense, Mary's word of faith in 1.38 is shown to be the beginning, not the end, of a journey that is growing more complex.

A Chorus of Praise: Luke 2.20
In v. 20, the focus returns to the shepherds, who like the angels praise and glorify God—δοξάζοντες καὶ αἰνοῦντες τὸν θεόν, as the narrator has it in language similar to vv. 13-14. The glory that touched earth in the appearance of the angel to the shepherds now returns to heaven in their praise of God to whom alone glory belongs. Hidden he may be—and behind deeply puzzling signs—but this does not mean that God lies beyond the powers of human recognition. In

---

1. G. Schneider, *Das Evangelium nach Lukas*, I (2 vols; Gütersloh: Gütersloher Verlagshaus, 1977), p. 68, is right in noting of v. 19 that it has a paranetic force: 'Wie Maria soll der Leser die Geschehnisse gläubig meditieren und so die richtige Bedeutung treffen'.

2. W. C. van Unnik, 'Die rechte Bedeutung des Wortes 'treffen', Lukas II,19', in *Sparsa Collecta: The Collected Essays of W.C. van Unnik I* (Leiden: Brill, 1973), pp. 72-91 (pp. 79-86 on συμβάλλουσα).

v. 20, the narrator dramatizes both right recognition of the divine visitation and praise as its fruit.

The shepherds recognize the coherence between what they have heard and what they have seen. The narrator has them put fact and interpretation together in a way that reveals a coherence in the midst of all that tells against it; and it is that vision of coherence which stirs them to praise. They have believed what they have heard and, because of the revelation, have understood what they have seen; and it is that combination of faith and understanding which opens the way to both praise of God and proclamation to human beings. Their praise is prompted not only by the coherence between what they have heard and what they have seen, but also by the fact that God chooses to visit his people in the midst of poverty and powerlessness, in a manger and among shepherds.

At this point, we turn to the question, why the shepherds as the recipients of the revelation?[1]—to which corresponds the question, why background the parents by making them the recipients of the shepherds' revelation rather than the agents as Elizabeth and Zechariah were in the previous episode? The shepherds suit the narrator's purpose for a number of reasons:

---

1. Various suggestions have been made as to the symbolic significance of the shepherds: that they appear in the narrative because of their lowliness (Fitzmyer, *Luke*, p. 408), or their ritual uncleanness (see *b. Sanh.* 25b)—a suggestion made by R. Murphy, 'On Shepherds', *BT* 1 (1964), pp. 986-91, and G. Lohfink, 'Weinachten und die Armut', *GL* 35 (1962), pp. 401-405, but rejected by Dibelius, *Jungfrauensohn und Krippenkind*, p. 66—or because pagan gods tend to reveal themselves to rustics who are symbolic of paradisal innocence (Bultmann, *History of the Synoptic Tradition*, pp. 298-99), or even of the early Christian missionaries and preachers (L. Legrand, 'L'Evangile aux bergers: Essai sur le genre littéraire de Luc II, 8-20', *RB* 75 [1968], pp. 161-87). Muñoz Iglesias claims that the shepherds appear because there was an historical recollection of them at the birth scene (*Evangelios*, III, p. 121) and Jeremias because they owned the stall where the birth took place ('ποιμήν', *TDNT*, VI, p. 491), which also explains how the shepherds knew where to look. None of these suggestions is based upon narrative criteria, attention to which stirs less interest in the symbolic force of the shepherds and more in their narrative function.

1. They match the image of 1.79: 'to those sitting in darkness and the shadow of death' (τοῖς ἐν σκότει καὶ σκιᾷ θανάτου καθημένοις), with its reminiscence of Isa. 9.1.[1]

2. They show that the marginal have less trouble than others in believing the angelic message. The pious priest Zechariah should have believed more easily, but did not. Now in untroubled style the shepherds discover the coherence between fact and interpretation, and so find their way to proclamation and to praise of God for showing himself in so unexpected a way (that is, in the midst of poverty).

3. They have not witnessed the birth and must therefore believe what they are told by the angel and then decide to go to Bethlehem.

4. Their physical isolation means that only they will hear the angelic revelation and that 'all who heard' will therefore have to believe them, however unlikely they may seem as messengers.

5. They show that for them as for 'all who heard' interpretation of the sign comes from outside, that right interpretation and the understanding it enables are not simply a human concoction.

Another Obedience: Luke 2.21

For the other characters, it has been more a matter of puzzlement than praise that God has shown himself in so unexpected a way (that is, through the shepherds). Yet puzzlement at God's new intervention does not preclude obedience to the old command, as now they name the child in obedience to Gabriel's command.

The child, who has not appeared since v. 16, now reappears, though he remains wholly passive. The parents are there implicitly, but they are not mentioned explicitly in a verse in which all but one of the verbs is passive.[2] In v. 31b, Gabriel had said to Mary: 'you will call

---

1. In the LXX, Isa. 9.1 reads: ὁ λαός ὁ πορευόμενος ἐν σκότει ἴδετε φῶς μέγα· οἱ κατοικοῦντες ἐν χώρᾳ καὶ σκιᾷ θανάτου φῶς λάμψει ἐφ' ὑμᾶς. Just as the Benedictus, in service of its vision of salvation-through-forgiveness, abandons the military imagery of Isa. 9.1-6, so now we find not soldiers, but shepherds—and shepherds who will rejoice not because of the spoils of battle, but ἐπὶ πᾶσιν οἷς ἤκουσαν καὶ εἶδον.

2. Only περιτεμεῖν is active, though even then it is not said who performs the

his name Jesus' (καλέσεις τὸ ὄνομα αὐτοῦ 'Ιησοῦν); but now she is elided by the passive 'he was called' (ἐκλήθη). In contrast to 1.57-80, we are not told who names the child.[1] What matters for the narrator is not who does the naming, but that the child be named in accordance with the divine will communicated by Gabriel, who appears as the anonymous 'angel' in a way which elides him too and looks to the unfolding of the divine plan which remains at centre stage. The refusal to specify the parents in v. 21 works in the same direction as the decision to make not them but the shepherds the first human characters to proclaim and interpret the birth: it ensures that the initiative is seen to belong to God rather than to the parents.

Circumcision is mentioned, but as in 1.57-80 it is not narrated: again it is the naming that is stressed. The characters are shown to be doubly obedient—now to both the demands of the law and the will of God communicated through Gabriel, just as at the start of the episode they were shown as under the sway of both Caesar and God. Yet the emphasis earlier was on the birth as fulfilment of the divine decree rather than on the census as fulfilment of the imperial decree; and now the emphasis is on the naming as fulfilment of the divine decree rather than on the circumcision as fulfilment of the Mosaic decree. What is ultimately decisive is not the command of Caesar or Moses, but the command of God.

Conclusion

The first episode of the second phase of the infancy narrative has dealt with a fact and its interpretation. The fact has been the birth of the Davidic messiah promised by Gabriel in 1.30-35; and it has been narrated in unexpected style. After the grandeur of Gabriel's prophecy, the circumstances of the birth seem wrong. The initial impression is that such circumstances could only be the regrettable result of the census and its displacement. Yet the angelic revelation, which interprets both the birth and its circumstances, makes it clear that the oddness of fulfilment is itself part of God's plan. God has decreed the strange sign of the messiah in the manger, and shows himself therefore to be in control, but in puzzling ways.

circumcision. On the elision of the parents here, see Gueuret, *L'engendrement*, pp. 126-27, followed by Laurentin, *Les Evangiles*, pp. 239-41.

1.   Compare also Mt. 1.25, which makes it clear that Joseph named the child.

Throughout the episode, the stress has been less on the fact than on its interpretation. The narrator does not focus on the birth nor on the figure of the newborn messiah, but upon the reactions to the birth. The birth itself is reported in brief and laconic terms, and is accompanied by none of the extraordinary signs found in the apocryphal gospels. No sooner is the child born than the focus shifts elsewhere;[1] the glory of the Lord shines neither from nor around him but from heaven and around the shepherds; and neither the angels nor the shepherds worship the newborn child. Again the narrator shows himself less interested in the fact of fulfilment than in the mode of fulfilment and the mode of human response to the 'what' and 'how' of fulfilment.

What needs to be discovered—and not without difficulty—is the meaning of the birth; and for that to happen, heaven must intervene. Right interpretation of the birth is not the result of human invention or exertion: it is the revelation of heaven. This is made clear by the angelic revelation, just as the angelic revelations in the first two episodes insisted upon the divine initiative. Left to their own devices, the human characters have no way of discovering the meaning of the birth and its circumstances.

Yet even heaven's intervention to interpret the birth is odd, since it is made not to a priest in the sanctuary but to shepherds in the fields. The readers may have expected the parents—or at least Mary—to be the chief agent of proclamation and interpretation of the birth. This is as it was in the previous episode, where Elizabeth and especially Zechariah played a role denied to Mary (and Joseph) in this episode. Here the parents are backgrounded and the direction in which the news moves is reversed. In the previous episode, the news moved from the birth scene into the countryside. Now it moves from the countryside to the birth scene; and it does so in a way which stresses that the interpretation offered is the gift of heaven rather than some human concoction.

The shepherds are told of the messiah's birth, but are given a sign which seems absurd. Those at the birth scene are doubly perplexed— that a child born in such circumstances should be the messiah and that

---

1.   Which is why Ernst's claim that '[m]it der Geburt Jesu. . . kommt die lk Kindheitserzählung zu ihrem eigentlichen Höhepunkt' is unconvincing (*Evangelium*, p. 99). If the birth were the 'Höhepunkt'—as one might expect it should be—the narrator would surely dwell at greater length upon it.

the interpretation of the birth should have been delivered to shepherds. Whatever of Joseph, about whom we know virtually nothing, Mary is in a unique situation. She knows that her child is the messiah, but Gabriel had said nothing of a birth in such circumstances, which cannot have failed to puzzle her; and then, after Gabriel's silence on the point, to have shepherds arrive with the key of interpretation can only have added to the puzzlement. Even when heaven intervenes, there is still a task that remains for the human being. If heaven's promise and the mode of its fulfilment are strange, then so too is the way heaven intervenes to interpret fulfilment.

Chapter 7

INSPIRED INTERPRETATION IN LUKE 2.22-40

A Return to Religion

From the secular world of the last four episodes, the narrative in vv. 22-40 returns to the specifically religious world of Judaism and to the sacral space of the Temple, with the characters who announce extraordinary things about the newborn child not improbable figures like the shepherds, but pious Jews like Zechariah and Elizabeth in the first episode.

Laurentin discerns in this episode 'converging trajectories' which make it 'a point of arrival', since in this episode, as he reads it, the Lord comes finally and triumphantly to his Temple in fulfilment of the prophecy of Mal. 3.1.[1] If that is so, then it is strange that the patterns of elision work in such a way that only v. 34 in the whole episode refers specifically to Jesus. If the narrator were concerned to recount the climactic coming of the Lord to his Temple, then surely the figure of Jesus would be accentuated in a way he is not in fact. It is again a question of deciding where the narrative finds its focus and of identifying the data that justify the decision about narrative focus.

The claim in this chapter is that the episode focuses less on Jesus in himself and more on the way the characters interpret God's action in Jesus. In this episode, very different characters in a very different setting are faced with the task of interpreting rightly the great sign of fulfilment—the sign of Jesus himself. Under the influence of the Holy Spirit, they succeed in their task, and their interpretation becomes proclamation—a proclamation of God's action no longer shrouded in

---

1.   Laurentin, *Les Evangiles*, p. 82. See too his statement in *Structure*, p. 63: 'On est. . . conduit à formuler ainsi l'idée directrice de *Luc 1–2*: L'entrée de Jésus au temple inaugure l'habitation eschatologique de la 'Gloire', c'est-à-dire de Yahweh, promise par les prophètes'.

seclusion or set on the rim of the human circle, but located in the Temple itself.

The Sway of the Law: Luke 2.22-24

In v. 21, the demands of the law were implied, but in vv. 22-24, they are made explicit. In a way that seems strange in so compressed a narrative, the narrator mentions the law three times: in v. 22, we have 'according to the law of Moses' (κατὰ τὸν νόμον Μωϋσέως), in v. 23 'in the law of the Lord' (ἐν νόμῳ κυρίου), and in v. 24 'in the law of the Lord' (ἐν τῷ νόμῳ κυρίου). Not only that, but the law is also cited twice.[1] In the previous episode, the narration of the birth was set against the background of imperial authority. Now the narration of the coming of Jesus to the Temple is set against the background of Mosaic authority; and we find human beings as obedient to the demand of the law as they were in 2.1-5 to the demand of Caesar.[2]

Yet the situation is more complex than this, given that the narrator in v. 22 refers to the law as 'the law of Moses' (ὁ νόμος Μωϋσέως), but then in vv. 23 and 24 refers to the law as 'the law of the Lord' (ὁ νόμος κυρίου). The shift from 'Moses' to 'the Lord' is dictated by the referent in the statement in v. 22 that the parents bring Jesus to Jerusalem 'to present [him] to the Lord' (παραστῆσαι τῷ κυρίῳ); and it serves two narrative purposes. First, it declares a difference between the authority of Caesar and the authority of Moses. Caesar may unwittingly collaborate with the divine plan, but it is nowhere said that the emperor exercises the authority of God. But now with the

---

1. The citations are free-wheeling. Verse 23 blends LXX Exod. 13.2 (ἁγίασόν μοι πᾶν πρωτότοκον πρωτογενὲς διανοῖγον πᾶσαν μήτραν), 13.12 (ἀφελεῖς πᾶν διανοῖγον μήτραν, τὰ ἀρσενικά, τῷ κυρίῳ) and 13.15 (διὰ τοῦτο ἐγὼ θύω τῷ κυρίῳ πᾶν διανοῖγον μήτραν, τὰ ἀρσενικά, καὶ πᾶν πρωτότοκον τῶν υἱῶν μου λυτρώσομαι) and perhaps Num. 8.15-16 which refers to the consecration of the Levites. The citation in v. 24 is a form of LXX Lev. 12.8 (ἐὰν δὲ μὴ εὑρίσκη ἡ χεὶρ αὐτῆς τὸ ἱκανὸν εἰς ἀμνόν, καὶ λήμψεται δύο τρυγόνας ἢ δύο νεοσσοὺς περιστερῶν, μίαν εἰς ὁλοκαύτωμα καὶ μίαν περὶ ἁμαρτίας, καὶ ἐξιλάσεται περὶ αὐτῆς ὁ ἱερεύς, καὶ καθαρισθήσεται).

2. In fact they are shown to be more than obedient, since there was no demand by the law that a newborn son be brought to the sanctuary in person in order to be redeemed. Neh. 10.37 mentions the act of bringing the first-born to the sanctuary as a mark of special devotion, but there was nothing either in the law or even custom which made this obligatory.

twofold reference to the law as 'the law of the Lord', the narrator leaves no doubt that the law of Moses is of God. It bears an authority which exceeds any human authority.

Secondly, the move from 'Moses' to 'the Lord' shifts the accent from Moses to God. Moses has been absent from the narrative until this point, with the accent falling instead upon the figures of Abraham and David. Yet no sooner is Moses mentioned for the first time in the infancy narrative than he vanishes; and this is in order that God rather than Moses appear as prime mover. Both the name of Moses and the rites specified by the Mosaic law are elided. Again the purpose of the visit to Jerusalem will never be narrated. We are told in vv. 22-24 that Mary and Joseph take the child to the Temple to perform the rites of purification and presentation, and in v. 39 that they leave having performed the rites; but of the actual performance of the rites nothing is said.[1] This is as we have seen in 1.5-25, where the incense-burning was not narrated, and in both 1.57-80 and 2.21 where the circumcision was never narrated. The decision not to narrate these rites casts the focus elsewhere.

One of the oddities of these first verses is the apparent confusion of the two Mosaic stipulations—the purification of the mother after the birth of a male child, and the presentation of the first-born male to God.[2] The narrator mentions first the purification, though the mention

1. Marshall (*Gospel*, p. 117) claims that the fact that there is no mention of the redemption price being paid means that Jesus is not being redeemed but consecrated to the Lord. Yet we cannot be sure that the price was not paid. If anything, v. 39 suggests that it was. The same might be said in reply to J. McHugh (*The Mother of Jesus in the New Testament* [London: Darton, Longman & Todd, 1975], p. 101) who argues that there is no mention of the redemption price because '[i]t is impossible to think of him as being (in the Mosaic sense) "redeemed"'.

2. Creed (*St. Luke*, p. 39) notes an 'imperfect understanding of the legal requirement', and Brown (*Birth of the Messiah*, p. 447) notes that 'Luke seems to have confused [purification and presentation]'. Bultmann (*History of the Synoptic Tradition*, p. 299) explains the confusion as a result of the secondary insertion of vv. 22b-23, which concern the presentation, into vv. 22a and 24, which concern the purification. Schürmann (*Lukasevangelium*, p. 122) sees the confusion as the result of the reworking of a Palestinian source by a Hellenistic Christian writer. Fitzmyer (*Luke*, p. 421) sees the narration at this point as shaped by a general desire on Luke's part to explain something of the birth customs of Palestinian Judaism to his predominantly Gentile readers; and Ernst (*Evangelium*, p. 115) claims that the uncertainty shows 'dass der Autor an einer zuverlässigen Überlieferung von historischen Details nicht interessiert ist', but does not say why this

is complicated by the use of αὐτῶν ('their') rather than αὐτῆς ('her') which might be expected, since it was only the mother who had to undergo the rite of purification.[1] But if the narrator is more concerned with focus in the narrative than with an exact report of the Mosaic legislation, then αὐτῶν makes sense. It ensures that the focus does not fall exclusively on any of the key human characters—Mary, Joseph or Jesus. What matters at this point is that the law rather than any of the characters appear as prime mover in the narrative, just as at the start of the previous episode the narrator made Caesar seem prime mover. In the same way now he sets a context for the narration of God's intervention.[2]

Having mentioned the purification, the narrator turns to the presentation of the child,[3] and for the first time God is mentioned explicitly:

might be so. A narrative approach must seek to do so.

1. The MSS vary on the point. Only one cursive (76) supports the reading αὐτῆς, which spread from the Complutensian Polyglott Bible (1514) into various editions. The Vulgate has the ambiguous *eius*, from which may derive the masculine form αὐτοῦ found in D 2174* *pc* lat sy[s] sa[ms], though Metzger reads αὐτοῦ as a transcriptional error (*Textual Commentary*, p. 134). Other witnesses omit the pronoun altogether (435 *pc* bo[pt] Ir[lat]). Some judge αὐτῆς to be the original text, altered to αὐτοῦ in the belief that Mary could not be impure. But it seems unlikely that the scribes would have transferred the need for purification from Mary to Jesus. It seems even less likely that they would opt for the conflation αὐτῶν, as Hauck (*Evangelium*, p. 41) and Easton (*Gospel*, p. 26) suggest. In the end, the weight of external evidence favours αὐτῶν, and points to the alternatives as attempts to ease the difficulty.

Various suggestions have been made as to why the narrator prefers αὐτῶν. Some take it to mean the purification of Jesus and his parents (Zahn, Grundmann, Schürmann); others the purification of Mary and Joseph (Plummer, Klostermann, Gächter, Ellis); and others see it as referring to Jesus and Mary (Origen, Lagrange, Creed). Another suggestion (Laurentin, *Les Evangiles*, p. 97) is that αὐτῶν refers to the Jews, making an inclusion with λύτρωσιν Ἰερουσαλήμ in v. 38.

2. It might be objected that it would have suited the narrator's purpose just as well (and have avoided any hint of sloppy grammar) if he had used no pronoun at all and have spoken simply of αἱ ἡμέραι τοῦ καθαρισμοῦ. But what the addition of αὐτῶν adds is a stronger sense of *human initiative*, and this prepares for the contrast with the divine initiative which the episode will narrate.

3. Many commentators see 1 Samuel 1–2 as the inspiration of the narrative at this point (Creed, *St. Luke*, p. 39, A. George, 'La présentation de Jésus au Temple', *AsSeign* 2.11 [1970], p. 31, Ernst, *Evangelium*, p. 115, Schürmann, *Lukasevangelium*, p. 122, Brown, *Birth of the Messiah*, pp. 450-51, Fitzmyer, *Luke*, p. 421, Bovon, *Evangelium*, p. 140). However, both Laurentin (*Les*

'they brought him to Jerusalem to present [him] to the Lord' (ἀνήγαγον αὐτὸν εἰς Ἰεροσόλυμα παραστῆσαι τῷ κυρίῳ).[1] From now on, the law will no longer be referred to as 'the law of Moses' as in v. 22, but three times as 'the law of the Lord' (vv. 23, 24, 39). The shift of focus from Moses to God begins the more general shift from the narration of obedience to the Mosaic law, in which the law itself appears as prime mover, to the narration of the divine intervention, in which God will appear as prime mover. It is again a question of who or what has the initiative.

The odd character of the messiah's coming is underscored in v. 24 with the presentation of the parents as people of modest means, unable to afford the lamb and bird prescribed for the purification, and offering instead the two birds prescribed as a concession to those of modest means.[2] This serves the same purpose as the report in the

---

Evangiles, p. 95) and Muñoz Iglesias (*Evangelios*, III, p. 169) note the differences between the story of Samuel and the narration of the presentation of Jesus here. This raises again the complex question of the Lukan use of Scripture.

1.   Some (for example Brown, *Birth of the Messiah*, p. 445, Ernst, *Evangelium*, p. 113, Laurentin, *Les Evangiles*, pp. 83-89, McHugh, *Mother of Jesus*, p. 102; but against see Muñoz Iglesias, *Evangelios*, III, pp. 166-67, and Bovon, *Evangelium*, p. 140) argue that the prophecies of Malachi underlie the account of the presentation of Jesus in the Temple. The claim is that where Mal. 3.1a refers to the ministry of John (LXX: ἰδοὺ ἐγὼ ἐξαποστέλλω τὸν ἄγγελόν μου καὶ ἐπιβλέψεται ὁδὸν πρὸ προσώπου μου), Mal. 3.1b refers to the coming of Jesus to the Temple (LXX: καὶ ἐξαίφνης ἥξει εἰς τὸν ναὸν ἑαυτοῦ κύριος). It is true that in 7.27 Luke has Jesus adapt Mal. 3.1a (changing Malachi's μου to σου) to describe John's ministry; but this does not mean that vv. 22-40 must be read in the light of Mal. 3.1b—all the more so since John has exercised no ministry of preparation before vv. 22-40. It is possible to read Lk. 19.45–21.38 as the paradoxical fulfilment of Mal. 3.1b; but it is hard to read Lk. 2.22-40 as foreshadowing Lk. 19.45–21.38. Moreover, as Bovon notes, to see the presentation of Jesus as the coming of the Lord to the Temple as foretold in Mal. 3.1 presumes that the Lord is absent from the Temple; and yet there is nothing in the infancy narrative to suggest that God is absent from the Temple.

2.   See Lev. 5.11; 12.8. Ernst (*Evangelium*, p. 114) is right in noting that this reveals the actual socioeconomic background of Joseph and Mary in no great detail. See too the comment of Plummer (*Critical Commentary*, p. 65) that '[o]nly well-to-do people offered a lamb and a pigeon. Neither here nor elsewhere in NT have we any evidence that our Lord or His parents were among the abjectly poor'. While this is true, there remains a gap between the grandeur of Gabriel's promise in 1.32-33 and the circumstances of its fulfilment.

previous episode that the messiah was born outside the inn and laid in the manger: it emphasizes the strangeness of the circumstances into which he has been born. The notice comes as no surprise to the well-informed readers; but it ensures that for the less well-informed characters the task of recognizing and rightly interpreting the messiah's coming will prove challenging.

For the first time in the infancy narrative, Jerusalem is named;[1] and it occurs in the form Ἱεροσόλυμα . In v. 25, the city is again named, but this time as Ἱερουσαλήμ; and the combination raises the question of whether any special significance may be attached to the different forms of the city's name.[2] Accepting that the LXX form Ἱερουσαλήμ has a sacral resonance where the secular form Ἱεροσόλυμα does not, the juxtaposition of the two forms means that the sacral and secular mingle here as they did in the previous episode in the titles 'saviour' and 'lord'. This enhances a more general effect in the infancy narrative. Not only titles applied to Jesus and now different forms of the name Jerusalem, but also the alternation of sacral space (the Temple) and secular space (the home of Zechariah, Nazareth, the birth-place in Bethlehem, the fields near Bethlehem) ensure that the narrative moves between worlds in a way which underscores the fact that no person, no time, no place is unaffected by the messiah's coming.

The Sway of the Spirit: Luke 2.25-38

The Switch to Simeon: Luke 2.25-27

In a switch not unlike the move to the shepherds in 2:8, the narrator turns unexpectedly to the figure of Simeon in v. 25; and as he does he begins the narration of the interpretation of the signs of fulfilment in

---

1.   For a somewhat convoluted account of the reasons for the narrator's decision not to name Jerusalem until now, see Gueuret, *L'engendrement*, pp. 232-40.

2.   It has been widely proposed that the difference between the two forms of the name in the Third Gospel is more than casual—in particular that Ἱεροσόλυμα is a geographical term, where Ἱερουσαλήμ is a sacral term, since in extra-Christian literature Ἱερουσαλήμ is found only in Greek versions of the OT and in the apocrypha, and it is the sole term used in the LXX. Moreover, both non-Jewish and Jewish authors use Ἱεροσόλυμα in secular works. This leads Jeremias to claim that the form Ἱερουσαλήμ acquired 'Dignität und sakralen Klang' ('ΙΕΡΟΥΣΑΛΗΜ/ ΙΕΡΟΥΣΟΛΥΜΑ', *ZNW* 65 [1974], p. 275). For a full canvassing of opinion and a fresh sifting of the evidence, see D.D. Sylva, 'Ierousalêm and Hierosoluma in Luke–Acts', *ZNW* 74 (1983), pp. 207-21.

this episode. At first, the focus is upon the man Simeon and his piety, which is described in terms of his devotion to the law and cult (δίκαιος καὶ εὐλαβής[1]) and his faith in God's promise (προσδεχόμενος παράκλησιν τοῦ Ἰσραήλ).[2] At this point, he is like Zechariah and Elizabeth in the first episode.

The presentation of Simeon becomes less conventional and more detailed at the end of v. 25 where the narrator reveals that 'the Holy Spirit was upon him' (πνεῦμα ἦν ἅγιον ἐπ' αὐτόν).[3] In its report of how the Holy Spirit was upon Simeon, the narrative moves from the conventional 'righteous and devout' (δίκαιος καὶ εὐλαβής) to the precise and personal 'looking for the consolation of Israel' (προσδεχόμενος παράκλησιν τοῦ Ἰσραήλ), and then to the still more precise and personal 'the Holy Spirit was upon him' (πνεῦμα ἦν ἅγιον ἐπ' αὐτόν). In v. 26 the narrator abandons his external mode of narration and makes the key revelation that Simeon has received a

---

1.   εὐλαβής is found only in Luke–Acts in the NT (Acts 2.5; 8.2; 22.12 as well as here). It has the literal sense of 'taking hold well', which leads to the extended sense of 'cautious', which the Vulgate translates as *timoratus*. Though Plutarch uses the noun εὐλάβεια to mean caution specifically with regard to religious duty or hesitancy before the gods (*Cam.* 21.2; *Num.* 22.7; *Aem.* 3.2; *Moralia* 549e, 568c), this sense is not found in classical Greek. See the remarks of Plummer (*Critical Commentary*, p. 66) on Plato's use of both δίκαιος and εὐλαβής in his description of the ideal statesman. But with reference to Simeon, its sense is exclusively religious and is best rendered 'God-fearing'.

2.   παράκλησις introduces for the first time in the episode an echo of Second Isaiah, who will become a more recognizable voice as the narrative unfolds. It evokes texts such as Isa. 40.1; 49.13; 51.3, as well as Isa. 61.2 and 66.13 from Third Isaiah.

3.   Plummer (*Critical Commentary*, p. 66) argues that the meaning here is not 'the Holy Spirit' but 'an influence which was holy' on the basis of the anarthrous form and the unusual word order (πνεῦμα ἦν ἅγιον), which is different from what is found in the following verse (τοῦ πνεύματος τοῦ ἁγίου). Yet, as Brown (*Birth of the Messiah*, p. 438) points out, the anarthrous form has occurred before in the infancy narrative where the reference was to the Holy Spirit (1.15, 35, 41, 67); and the word order is not enough in itself to decide the issue, especially given that the next verse clearly does refer to the Holy Spirit. Plummer also claims that the accusative ἐπ' αὐτόν 'indicates the coming, rather than the resting, of the holy influence; the prophetic impulse'. Yet the imperfect verb suggests a state rather than an impulse, with the logic of the narrative being that vv. 25-26 report a charismatic state and v. 27 a charismatic impulse.

private revelation by the Holy Spirit.[1] At that point, we have moved a long way from the first notice that Simeon was 'righteous and devout'; and we have moved a long way inwards.

This does not mean that we are given any profound psychological insight into Simeon: that is not the narrator's purpose. He is not interested in Simeon in himself,[2] but in Simeon as one who (like Zechariah and Mary) had received a divine promise. Therefore, the way in which Simeon is presented throws light not upon the workings of his psyche, but upon him as one who has received (and believed) a double divine promise—the communal promise of the consolation of Israel and the personal promise that he would not see death until he had seen the one through whom the consolation of Israel would come.

Like Zechariah in the first episode, the shepherds received a heavenly revelation through an angel. But now like Elizabeth in the third episode and Zechariah in the fourth, Simeon receives a heavenly revelation through the Holy Spirit. The second phase of the infancy narrative therefore reproduces the pattern of the first. A further difference between Simeon and the shepherds is that with the shepherds the narrator described the angel's revelation in vv. 8-14, whereas with Simeon the revelation mentioned by the narrator in v. 26 is left outside the frame of the narrative. This is because in vv. 8-14 the revelation was a proclamation of something that had happened, where in v. 26 it is a promise of something that will happen. What matters therefore is not so much the promise as its fulfilment; and it is that upon which the narrator concentrates.

---

1.   The action described by the noun χρῆμα has a range of meanings (on which see B. Reicke, 'χρηματίζω', *TWNT*, IX, pp. 469-71). It can mean in general a business transaction, or, in the religious context, the divine response given to one who consults an oracle, or less specifically a divine admonition or a teaching given from heaven (see Jer. 25.30; 33.2; Job 40.8). The passive form as here can refer either to the divine communication, or to the person who receives the communication (as in Mt. 2.12, 22; Acts 10.22; Heb. 8.5; 9.7).

2.   This is why, for all that we are told, there is much that we are not told about Simeon. It is almost always assumed, for instance, that he is old, with the *Gospel of Pseudo-Matthew* 15.2 even putting his age at 112. Yet the narrator says nothing to allow the assumption of old age: Simeon may be an old man, but we do not know. Some have him a priest (for example Nolland, *Luke*, pp. 119, 120-21, 124-25), and *Acts Pil.* 2.2.1 makes him High Priest, with *Prot. Jas* 24.4 making him the successor to Zechariah in the high priestly office. But again the narrator gives no indication that he was a priest, with the blessing of v. 34 not necessarily priestly.

After the introduction of Simeon in vv. 25-26, the narration of the promise's fulfilment begins in v. 27. In the previous episode, the narrator had the shepherds come freely and in faith to the birth scene, but now by contrast he has Simeon come to the Temple under the impulse of the Holy Spirit. Simeon's act of faith in the divine promise lies outside the frame of the narrative; and he comes to the Temple with the same qualified freedom we have seen already in inspired characters such as Elizabeth in the third episode and Zechariah in the fourth. The impulse of the Holy Spirit may not abolish human freedom, but it does qualify it. The difference between Simeon here and the inspired characters of earlier episodes is that the Holy Spirit—initially at least—inspires Simeon to act rather than speak. This is the infancy narrative's first and only instance of action under the influence of the Holy Spirit, and as such it adds an important element to the narrative's understanding of the influence of the Holy Spirit. In the previous episode, the shepherds heard the angelic revelation and then of their own free will decided to act. Now, however, the Holy Spirit intervenes at the point of both revelation and action. The action of the Holy Spirit is both more inward and more comprehensive than the action of the angel.

For all that the narrator is detailed in his description of the action of the Holy Spirit on Simeon in both past and present, the mind and heart of Simeon remain closed to the readers, with no indication of what he knows or how he feels. The sense is that he comes to the Temple under the impulse of the Holy Spirit (ἐν τῷ πνεύματι), but without knowing what awaits him when he arrives. He has been promised that he will see the messiah, but for the readers the question is whether he will recognize the messiah, given the odd circumstances of the messiah's appearance.

In v. 27b, the narrator refers to Mary and Joseph as 'the parents' (οἱ γονεῖς), which some have taken to indicate an ignorance on the narrator's part of the virginal conception of Jesus and so to serve as proof that the second phase of the infancy narrative is compiled from a different source.[1] Yet there are good narrative reasons for a narrator who is well aware of the virginal conception to refer to Mary and Joseph as 'the parents' nonetheless. For one thing, the emphasis here is on their religious and social role rather than on them personally; and

---

1. On which see Plummer, *Critical Commentary*, p. 67.

the description of them as 'the parents' captures that well. Secondly, to name them in relation to Jesus (as 'the parents' does) allows the narrator to shift the focus from them as the ones who bring Jesus to the Temple to Jesus himself as the one about whom Simeon will prophesy. At the point where the narrative will focus on Jesus for the first time, the description of them as 'the parents' looks away from Mary and Joseph to the figure of Jesus.

In v. 21, the narrator named Jesus for the first time, waiting for the characters to name the child before he himself made the move. Until that moment, the parents had been named as 'Mary' (Μαριάμ) and 'Joseph' (Ἰωσήφ) throughout 2.1-21.[1] But once Jesus is named, their names disappear from the infancy narrative, with the sole exception of v. 34 where Mary is referred to by the narrator as 'Mary his mother' (Μαριάμ ἡ μήτηρ αὐτοῦ) at a point where Simeon focuses on her specifically. Through this and the following episode the focus moves slowly but surely from the parents to Jesus; and the shift is reflected in the way the characters are named by the narrator.

Inspired Interpretation: Luke 2.28-33
The answer to the question of whether Simeon will recognize the messiah comes in both action (v. 28a) and word (vv. 28b-32): under the influence of the Holy Spirit he both recognizes and interprets 'the messiah of the Lord' (ὁ χριστὸς κυρίου). The narrator has Simeon take the initiative as he takes the child in his arms in a gesture symbolizing the new concreteness and immediacy of God's action.[2] Zechariah had no physical contact with the newborn John during the Benedictus; and the sole report of physical contact with the newborn Jesus in 2.6-21 was Mary swaddling him and placing him in the manger. But now, with the action of God growing steadily more overt, a human character is shown for the first time holding the newborn child. For the first but not the last time the fulfilment exceeds the promise made to Simeon. Yet there is a paradox, because although he holds Jesus in his arms, Simeon blesses not the child but God.[3]

---

1. Joseph was named as Ἰωσήφ in vv. 4 and 16, and Mary as Μαριάμ in vv. 5, 16 and 19.

2. On the connection between holding the child ('conjonction somatique') and recognizing the meaning of the child ('performance cognitive'), see Gueuret, *L'engendrement*, pp. 130-31.

3. Compare the *Gospel of Pseudo-Matthew* 15.2, which even has Simeon

The effacement of Jesus before God continues once Simeon begins to speak, since the Nunc Dimittis looks not to Jesus, who here as in 2.14 is never mentioned explicitly,[1] but is described obliquely as 'your salvation, a light for the revelation of the Gentiles and the glory of your People, Israel' (τὸ σωτήριόν σου, φῶς εἰς ἀποκάλυψιν ἐθνῶν καὶ δόξαν λαοῦ σου 'Ισραήλ).[2] In the first and third cases, the reference to God is explicit, with the second person singular pronoun; and in the second case, 'light' (φῶς) recalls 1.78-79 where the coming of light into darkness was the key image of what God would do through the Davidic messiah. The Nunc Dimittis therefore speaks not so much about Jesus in himself as about what God is doing through Jesus.

The hymn is also the first time in the infancy narrative that a character addresses God directly. Gabriel in his oracles, Elizabeth in her prophetic cry, Mary in the Magnificat, Zechariah in the Benedictus and the angels in the Gloria have all spoken of God in the third person, but now Simeon speaks to God in the second person. The effect of this is both to accentuate God in a way that makes the Nunc Dimittis more radically theocentric than either the Magnificat or the Benedictus.

Verse 28 has Simeon blessing God, but the text of his praise is not given. What is given in the Nunc Dimittis is the motive for praise: God has fulfilled his promise. But the hymn not only states the motive for praise; like the earlier hymns it also interprets God's action.[3] Once again the narrator leaves interpretation to one of his characters, with the hymn interpreting the moment of encounter in the Temple in a way that looks beyond the encounter itself to the larger meaning of

prostrate himself before the child.

1. Compare the *Arabic Infancy Gospel* 6.1, which has Simeon address Jesus in the Nunc Dimittis.

2. A connection is at times made between the description of Jesus as δόξα here and the supposed link with Mal. 3.1-2 (on which see my earlier note). OT texts such as 1 Kgs 8.10-11 and Ezek. 44.4 make it clear that the δόξα was the sign of the divine indwelling in the Temple. But there is a need to distinguish between the sign of the presence and the presence itself. Jesus as the Davidic messiah enters the Temple as a unique sign of the divine presence, but that does not mean that he enters as the presence itself in the way implied by Mal. 3.1-2.

3. This means that a cry such as μεγαλύνει or εὐλογητός is omitted and that before v. 29 there is an unwritten but implied ὅτι. The effect of this is to focus more intensely upon the interpretative moment which comes in vv. 29-32.

God's action in Jesus. The promise made by the Holy Spirit to Simeon was that he would see the messiah; yet now by the Holy Spirit's impulse he not only sees but he interprets what he sees. Again the fulfilment of the promise draws him beyond the bare terms of the promise itself.

What we have in the Nunc Dimittis as interpretation of God's action is more comprehensive than anything found in the earlier hymns. In the Magnificat, the focus was strongly upon God's action towards Mary, with wider perspectives serving to interpret her experience; in the Benedictus, it was more upon God's action towards Israel, with the presiding perspective nationalistic. Now in the Nunc Dimittis, the focus is upon God's action towards all peoples. In the progression from the Magnificat to the Benedictus to the Nunc Dimittis, we see how as God's action grows more overt so too does the human interpretation of it grow more comprehensive; and this is a progression which anticipates the movement of the Lukan narrative itself.

The universalism which first glimmered in v. 50 of the Magnificat is heard now in full voice; and God's action is seen to move beyond the nationalistic bounds set by the Benedictus. Indeed, in its interpretation of the divine action the Nunc Dimittis mentions first the Gentiles and then Israel;[1] and the Gentiles are referred to twice, with 'of all the peoples' (πάντων τῶν λαῶν) in v. 31, and 'a light for the revelation of the Gentiles' (φῶς εἰς ἀποκάλυψιν ἐθνῶν) in v. 32.[2]

---

1. Brown (*Birth of the Messiah*, p. 459) speaks of 'a subordinated universalism', which is true in the sense that, although the Gentiles are mentioned first and twice in the hymn, its climax is the δόξα which the messiah's coming means for Israel. Though the hymns move from Mary to Israel to all people, the Nunc Dimittis returns the focus finally to Israel since it is with Israel that the Gospel narrative will begin its account of the ministry of John and Jesus.

2. G.D. Kilpatrick, 'ΛΑΟΙ at Luke II. 31 and Acts IV. 25, 27', *JTS* 16 (1965), p. 127, has argued that if in Acts 4.25-27 λαῶν refers to the tribes of Israel in contrast to the Gentiles, then the meaning in 2.31 is the same. He goes on to claim that v. 32a refers to a light for the Gentiles to see, which would mean that the entire hymn would refer to Israel. Yet it would seem odd if the plural λαῶν in v. 31 and the singular λαός in v. 32b (which clearly refers to Israel) had the same meaning. In 3.6 the narrator will cite Isaiah (LXX 40.5) to the effect that ὄψεται πᾶσα σὰρξ τὸ σωτήριον τοῦ θεοῦ, and here in v. 31—which also refers to the scope of salvation—it would seem that λαῶν refers to the two groups mentioned in v. 32, ἐθνῶν and Ἰσραήλ—on which see Plummer, *Critical Commentary*, p. 69, and Brown, *Birth of the Messiah*, p. 440. Such a reading of λαῶν also fits better with the

The pattern is the same as in the Magnificat. Simeon first mentions the peace which comes to him personally (vv. 29-30), just as Mary first mentioned the joy which was hers (1.46b-47); then the focus expands to include all peoples (vv. 31-32a), just as in the Magnificat it expanded to include 'the God-fearers' (οἱ φοβούμενοι θεόν, 1.50); and finally the accent falls on the glory which comes to Israel (v. 32a), just as the Magnificat ended with a proclamation of God's enduring fidelity to Israel (1.54-55).

The language of the Nunc Dimittis is different from anything in the Magnificat or Benedictus. There is not the same scriptural tapestry, since the biblical hermeneutic has been well enough established in the first phase of the infancy narrative. Although the use of Scripture is as allusive as ever, the voice of Second Isaiah sounds recognizably;[1] and this is in service of the different christology which the Nunc Dimittis articulates—the vision of a messiah who is for all peoples.

Yet there is a paradox at work in the hymn. On the one hand, the strongly visual language gives the impression that the divine action is already so overt that the signs of it are there for all to see. But on the other hand, it is not at all obvious that the child newly born to such parents is 'your salvation, which you have prepared before all peoples, a light for the revelation of the Gentiles and the glory of your People, Israel' (τὸ σωτήριόν σου ὃ ἡτοίμασας κατὰ πρόσωπον πάντων τῶν λαῶν, φῶς εἰς ἀποκάλυψιν ἐθνῶν καὶ δόξαν λαοῦ σου Ἰσραήλ). There is a marked discrepancy between the grandeur of the proclamation and the poverty of the signs, just as there was in 2.10-12. Simeon, however, recognizes the messiah despite the oddness of the circumstances of the messiah's appearance.

His speech makes it clear that it is not by misadventure that the Davidic messiah should appear as simply another newborn child of parents of modest means: this is the way God wants it. In this sense, Simeon's interpretative speech serves the same function as the angel's interpretative speech in v. 12. It declares that the signs of God's action may be strange, but that this is part of the divine plan. His speech also

infancy narrative's expanding focus from the individual to the nation to the world.

1. Texts from Second Isaiah which echo in the Nunc Dimittis are Isa. 40.5; 42.6; 46.13; 49.6; 52.9-10. For more detailed attention to the echoes, see Brown, *Birth of the Messiah*, pp. 458-59, and in particular M. Miyoshi, 'Jesu Darstellung oder Reinigung im Tempel unter Berücksichtigung von "Nunc Dimittis"', *AJBI* 4 (1978), pp. 85-115, especially pp. 95-98.

makes it clear that right interpretation of the strange signs of fulfilment is not beyond the human being; and the fact that his own interpretation is made under the Holy Spirit's influence shows that it is not some human fabrication, but is heaven's revelation.[1]

Simeon interprets the meaning of the messiah's coming as εἰρήνη (peace for himself) and φῶς (salvation and light for all),[2] with 'light' specified further as ἀποκάλυψις ('revelation' for the Gentiles) and δόξα (glory for Israel).[3] The εἰρήνη he experiences now, but the σωτήριον (the φῶς and δόξα) are present embryonically, and only the future will reveal how the child is 'salvation' (σωτήριον), how he is 'light' (φῶς) ' for the Gentiles and 'glory' (δόξα) for Israel. In that sense, Simeon both recognizes a present fulfilment and looks to a future which he himself will not see. He sees the messiah, but he will not see the full effects of the messiah's coming; and yet in these he puts his faith as he looks to the future. He knows that the comforting of Israel is now certain, that the time of his waiting has come to an end.

In believing without seeing fully, Simeon is like Mary in 1.38, as

---

1.   It is not said explicitly of Simeon (nor will it be of Anna) that he speaks under the influence of the Holy Spirit, as it was of Elizabeth in 1.41 and Zechariah in 1.67. But it is implied by ἐν τῷ πνεύματι in v. 27, understood as referring not only to his coming to the Temple but also to what he does and says once he arrives. In the case of Anna, the term προφῆτις in v. 36 looks forward to her utterance in v. 38 and implies the influence of the Holy Spirit without stating it explicitly. In the second phase of the infancy narrative, the influence of the Holy Spirit is more enduring and implicit than in the first phase, where it was more momentary and explicit.

2.   The syntax of φῶς is ambiguous. Is it linked with δόξαν, with both in apposition to σωτήριον? Or is it, like ἀποκάλυψιν, governed by the preposition εἰς? Some (for example Creed, *St. Luke*, p. 41) favour the former, while others (for example Fitzmyer, *Luke*, p. 428) prefer the latter. In Isa. 60.1, φῶς and δόξα are coordinated, but there both are referred to Israel rather than to Israel and the Gentiles as in the Nunc Dimittis. The Benedictus linked salvation for Israel (v. 77) with the image of light (vv. 78b-79a); and for all its growing universalism, the infancy narrative has carefully distinguished between Israel and the Gentiles. This suggests that δόξαν is governed by εἰς and is coordinated with ἀποκάλυψιν rather than with φῶς.

3.   For the Gentiles, the light will mean ἀποκάλυψις because it will mean the unveiling of both promise and fulfilment, and the unveiling therefore of the truth of Israel's identity as mediator of the promise and its fulfilment. For Israel it will mean δόξα because it will mean the fulfilment of a promise they have long known, and a recognition of the truth of Israel's identity as mediator of a universal promise.

his description of himself as 'your servant' (τὸν δοῦλόν σου) and the verbatim repetition of 'according to your word' (κατὰ τὸ ῥῆμά σου) suggest. He is also like Mary in the Magnificat as she proclaims the future effects of the divine intervention 'forever' (εἰς τὸν αἰῶνα), and like Zechariah in the Benedictus as he looks to the less distant future of his son's ministry as precursor. Like them, Simeon discerns the shape of a future he will not see. But like Mary and unlike Zechariah initially, Simeon has not asked to see. In that respect, he is like Abraham; and insofar as that is true, the narrator modulates further his answer to the question first implied in 1.5-25: what might the faith of Abraham look like now?[1]

Once Simeon falls silent, the narrator has Mary and Joseph[2] astonished (θαυμάζοντες), as he did the neighbours and relatives in 1.63 and 'all who heard' in 2.18. In both previous instances, it signalled incomprehension, and there is no reason to think that it does not carry the same nuance here. As with the visit and announcement of the shepherds, Mary and Joseph are puzzled—which is not surprising, given that Simeon offers no explanation of how he comes to recognize the child as messiah, and that he speaks of the child's universal significance in a way neither Gabriel or the shepherds did.[3] From a narrative point of view, their astonishment serves to underline the mysterious character of a divine visitation which has Simeon suddenly appear

1.   Marshall (*Gospel*, p. 120) notes how unusual δέσποτα is as a term for God in the NT (Acts 4.24; Rev. 6.10; and perhaps Jude 4, though there it more likely refers to Christ as in 2 Pet. 2.1). He also claims that 'it is the appropriate correlative to δοῦλος, signifying a master of slaves'; but in 1.38 it was the far more common term κύριος which was used with δούλη. It is possible that the use of the unusual δέσποτα points to the figure of Abraham, since that is (part of) how Abraham addresses God in Gen. 15.8. A further link with Abraham is that in Gen. 15.15 Abraham receives a promise from God that he will die in peace.

2.   Joseph and Mary are styled respectively ὁ πατὴρ αὐτοῦ and ἡ μήτηρ. They are again named not in their own right, but in a way that relates them to Jesus; and the effect of this is to underscore again that they are important not in themselves, but only in relation to Jesus. A number of witnesses read Ιωσήφ ([A] Θ [Ψ] 053 *f*[13] 𝔐 it vg^mss sy^p.h.bo^Pt), with ὁ πατὴρ αὐτοῦ read by ℵ B D L W 1. 700. 1241 *pc* vg sy^s.hmg sa bo^Pt; Or^lat. The weight of external evidence therefore favours ὁ πατὴρ αὐτοῦ over Ιωσήφ, which must be judged a scribal attempt to ease the difficulty of a reading that seems to compromise the sense of the virginal conception of Jesus.

3.   See Plummer, *Critical Commentary*, p. 70.

to proclaim in a way hitherto unheard the scope of the salvation God is working in Jesus.

Interpreting Judgment: Luke 2.34-35

In v. 34, Simeon who in v. 28 blessed God blesses the parents. The narrator therefore has him offer a blessing which moves in two directions; and just as in v. 28 his blessing was a recognition of God's role in the unfolding drama, so now in v. 34 it is a recognition of the role of the parents in the same drama.[1] Unexpectedly he then turns to Mary, with Joseph vanishing from the narrative once more, since in what follows the narrator is keen to dramatize more of what faith involves, and in that dramatization throughout the infancy narrative Mary is the key figure and Joseph plays no part at all.

Throughout the oracle the accent is not so much on Jesus in himself as on the reactions to him and the consequences of these reactions. Therefore in v. 34 he is αὐτοῦ (in the phrase 'his mother' [ἡ μήτηρ αὐτοῦ], which relates him to Mary) and οὗτος ('this one'), and in v. 35 he is not mentioned at all.[2] It is also significant that Simeon blesses not the child but the parents, which contrasts with the apocryphal accounts where Simeon not only blesses the child but actually worships him.[3] Rather than focus upon the newborn child in himself, the narrative focuses upon the reactions to him in the future and the consequences of these reactions for both Jesus (rejection as 'a sign spoken against' [σημεῖον ἀντιλεγόμενον]) and 'the many' (οἱ πολλοί); the rise of some, the fall of others, the disclosure of hidden thoughts for all.

---

1.   The role of the parents is clearly different from the role of God, but the repetition of εὐλόγειν makes the link between the two, stressing the part the parents play as collaborators with God. They *become* part of the divine visitation.

2.   It is not even clear where he is. In v. 28 and presumably through the Nunc Dimittis he was in the arms of Simeon; but then in v. 34 Simeon blesses the parents, which if it involved gesture of some kind would have the child back with his parents. Certainly in Lk. 24.50 Jesus is shown lifting up his hands in blessing human characters; and in Gen. 48.17 blessing is also accompanied by gesture. So too the (Aaronic) priestly blessing was accompanied by uplifted hands (on which see H. Beyer, 'εὐλόγειν', *TDNT*, II, p. 760). In Mk 10.16 (though not in the parallel Lk. 18.15-17), Jesus blesses the children with gesture. In the end, it is hard to know where exactly Jesus is, as it will be when Anna appears on the scene.

3.   In the *Gospel of Pseudo-Matthew* 15.2 Simeon first prostrates himself before the child, then having taken him in mantle, adores him again and kisses his feet.

The language of the oracle is again Isaian, though more obliquely so than in the Nunc Dimittis;[1] and if in the Nunc Dimittis the Isaian language allowed the narrator to shape a vision of a messiah for all peoples, now in the oracle of vv. 34-35 it allows the narrator to add a second element to the revelation which comes through the Holy Spirit and Simeon—the vision of a messiah who is rejected.[2] This is in contrast to the royal language of the oracle of Gabriel in 1.30-35, of Zechariah in the Benedictus[3] and the angels in 2.11-14. There the note was triumphant, but now it is not: 'this one is destined for the fall and rising of many in Israel and to be a sign spoken against' (οὗτος κεῖται εἰς πτῶσιν καὶ ἀνάστασιν πολλῶν ἐν τῷ Ἰσραὴλ καὶ εἰς σημεῖον ἀντιλεγόμενον).

What is remarkable about the oracle is that it is the first hint in the infancy narrative of trouble of any kind, let alone rejection. In his oracle to Zechariah (1.13-17), Gabriel said nothing of rejection; and the same is true of his oracle to Mary (1.30-35). The Magnificat and Benedictus are wholly jubilant, as are the angelic proclamation and chorus in 2.10-14. For both characters and readers, then, this announcement is news. For once, the narrator does not allow the readers a position of privilege. With the characters, readers must grapple with the novelty and opacity of what Simeon prophesies.

The possibility it raises is that Mary has been deceived by heaven, in the sense that she has been led to speak her word of submission in 1.38 without knowing all the facts—especially the sombre fact now revealed. She has come to the point where there can be no turning

---

1. See Miyoshi, 'Jesu Darstellung', pp. 98-100, where he pays special attention to Isa. 51.17-23 as background to vv. 34-35. Other commentators (for example Plummer, Brown, Schürmann, Bovon, Danker, Marshall, Nolland, Muñoz Iglesias) see Isa. 8.14 and/or 28.16 underlying the announcement that Jesus is set εἰς πτῶσιν καὶ ἀνάστασιν πολλῶν, and a further suggestion (for example Lagrange, Bovon, Marshall, Fitzmyer) is that the sign of the prophet and his sons in Isa. 8.18 underlies the description of Jesus as σημεῖον ἀντιλεγόμενον.

2. D.L. Bock notes the way in which the evangelist draws upon Isaian texts to shape a Servant-christology which looks to the Servant as ultimately victorious and which therefore complements the earlier regal messianic texts, but which also includes suffering and rejection as part of the journey to victory (*Proclamation from Prophecy and Pattern: Lucan Old Testament Christology* [JSNTSup, 12; Sheffield: JSOT Press, 1987], pp. 85-88).

3. Though there the royal language of the first section (vv. 68-75) was qualified in the second section (vv. 76-79) with its vision of salvation as forgiveness.

back: the child is born and the die is cast. Moreover, the tone of the oracle suggests that there can be no averting the fate it foretells. This is all the more disturbing after the very positive interpretation of the messiah's coming in the Nunc Dimittis. In elaborating further the epistemology of the infancy narrative, therefore, the narrator now reveals that the decision to believe is not based upon possession of all the facts. Once the decision is made, as in Mary's case, there is much to be discovered; and some of that may prove daunting.

The consequences of the messiah's coming sketched in the oracle are both public and personal. The universalist vision of the Nunc Dimittis disappears, and the public dimension of the oracle focuses on the division within Israel which the messiah's coming will mean.[1] Jesus will bring to light the true divisions within Israel, not only the overt and predictable divisions between Jew and Gentile or 'righteous' (δίκαιος) and 'sinner' (ἁμαρτωλός) which the Lukan narrative will consistently overturn,[2] but the more covert and unpredictable divisions lying at the level of what the oracle calls 'thoughts' (διαλογισμοί).[3] There will be a division within Israel; but now the division will be between those who accept Jesus and those who reject him.

Simeon foretells that Jesus will be 'a sign spoken against' (σημεῖον ἀντιλεγόμενον), though he does not specify what kind of sign he will

---

1.   G.B. Caird (*St. Luke* [Harmondsworth: Penguin Books, 1963], p. 64) and J. Jeremias ('λίθος', *TDNT*, IV, p. 277, but revised in 'πολλοί', *TDNT*, VI, p. 541) have proposed that the πτῶσιν καὶ ἀνάστασιν of the oracle refer to the same group of people, as in Mic. 7.8. But this is hard to see, given that the oracle speaks of judgment, and given the pervasiveness of the theme of acceptance–rejection in the Lukan narrative.

2.   On the overturning of the division between Jew and Gentile, see texts from the Gospel narrative such as Lk. 3.6; 4.24-27; 7.1-10; 10.29-37; 17.11-19; 20.9-18; 24.45-49—which flower in the narration of the mission to the Gentiles so central to Acts. On the overturning of the division between δίκαιος and ἁμαρτωλός, see texts from the Gospel narrative such as Lk. 5.27-32; 7.29-30; 7.36-50; 8.26-39; 15.1-32; 18.9-14; 19.1-10; 23.39-43.

3.   Plummer (*Critical Commentary*, p. 155), Lagrange (*Evangile*, p. 89) and Creed (*St. Luke*, p. 43) understand διαλογισμοί to include thoughts both positive and negative. Yet whatever the case in OT usage (on which see Muñoz Iglesias, *Evangelios*, III, p. 192) every other use of διαλογίσμος in the NT is in some way negative; and this is clearly true of Lukan texts such as 5.22; 6.8; 9.46, 47; 24.38. To understand διαλογισμοί in the same way here presents no particular problem.

be.[1] This uncertainty typifies the oracle, which conveys a general sense of menace and foreboding but provides little detail. The reference to Jesus as 'a sign spoken against' implies that right interpretation of the sign cannot be taken for granted—that some will read the sign of Jesus wrongly and therefore reject him. The key question therefore concerns the right interpretation of the ambivalent sign. Simeon appears as a paragon of right interpretation; and the fall of some and the rise of others in Israel looks to the narrative of Luke–Acts in which some will accept Jesus (interpret the sign rightly) and others reject him (interpret the sign wrongly). Those who interpret rightly will rise, and those who interpret wrongly will fall—and all of this as part of the divine plan, as is implied by the divine passive 'is set' (κεῖται). God sends a messiah who is 'glory for your People, Israel' (δόξα λαοῦ σου Ἰσραήλ), but whose coming brings not only peace and salvation to the world, but also division and judgment to Israel.

In v. 10, the angel made it clear that the birth of the messiah in such inauspicious circumstances was no misadventure, but was the way chosen by God. Simeon has made the same thing clear in the hymn: God has chosen to intervene through a messiah born to parents of modest means. The more dramatic point to emerge now is that the messiah will be rejected, and—still more remarkably—that his rejection, far from falling outside the scope of God's plan or even thwarting it, is part of God's plan.[2] This will prove crucially important for the

1. The Nunc Dimittis says *what* the messiah will signify, indeed what he signifies *already*: εἰρήνη and σωτήριον (φῶς, δόξα). But it does not say *how* this is so in the present or *how* it will be so in the future. Muñoz Iglesias (*Evangelios*, III, p. 189) addresses the philological question of whether σημεῖον here looks to the Hebrew אות (sign, portent) or נס (banner, standard), but admits that such considerations cannot decide the issue of what kind of sign. J. Winandy ('La prophétie de Siméon [Lc, II, 34-35]', *RB* 72 [1965], pp. 321-51) argues that what is meant is the sign of Isa. 7.14, and makes the connection with v. 35a in claiming that the sword that will pierce Mary is contestation of the virginal conception of Jesus, though there is no hint of this in the narrative. Brown (*Birth of the Messiah*, p. 461) makes the link with Isa. 7.14, but does not share Winandy's more doubtful conclusions. In the end, the inability of the critics to decide the issue suggests that we are dealing here with 'le flou prophétique' (on which see Bovon, 'Effet du réel et flou prophétique', pp. 355-58), and that the focus here is less upon what kind of sign Jesus will be than upon how others respond to him.
2. Implied here and stated more clearly in the prophecies of the passion (9.22; 9.44; 18.31-33), the point emerges with absolute clarity in texts such as 24.26 (οὐχὶ

whole of the Lukan narrative; and that Simeon speaks under the influence of the Holy Spirit leaves no room for doubt that such an interpretation might simply be the work of human invention.

Having prophesied that by God's decision Jesus will be 'a sign spoken against', Simeon switches suddenly to Mary in v. 35a. She is the addressee of the entire oracle, since she is the character who throughout the infancy narrative embodies the process of recognition and who as part of that process is faced with the need to deal with a new and daunting revelation. But now Simeon speaks not only to Mary but about her. He turns to Mary immediately after he has prophesied that Jesus will be 'a sign spoken against'—which might be taken to indicate that the sword of which Simeon speaks is a metaphor for the pain Mary will experience as a result of her son's rejection; and there has been no shortage of commentators to read v. 35a in such terms.[1] By this reckoning, the sword is an image of shared pain.[2]

Yet a survey of the image's biblical background suggests other possibilities. The most illuminating of these in the context is the sword as metaphor of divine judgment.[3] To this point, the perspective of the oracle has been a perspective of divine judgment—a judgment that will bring about division within Israel. This favours an interpretation of the sword as a metaphor of judgment rather than pain. To understand the sword in this way would mean that in turning from Israel to Mary Simeon, turning from nation to individual, prophesies that the

---

ταῦτα ἔδει παθεῖν τὸν χριστόν) and Acts 2.23 (τοῦτον τῇ ὡρισμένῃ βουλῇ καὶ προγνώσει τοῦ θεοῦ ἔκδοτον διὰ χειρὸς ἀνόμων προσπήξαντες ἀνείλατε).

1. For a convenient listing of the various interpretations of the sword—both patristic and more recent—see Brown, *Birth of the Messiah*, pp. 462-63.

2. Bovon (*Evangelium*, p. 146) speaks of '[eine] Parallelisierung von Mutter und Sohn' in vv. 34-35, and sees this as recalling Elizabeth's speech in 1.42, where he claims that mother and son are similarly linked.

3. On ῥομφαία as a sword of judgment, see Brown (*Birth of the Messiah*, pp. 463-64), where he notes a range of texts from Ezekiel (5.1-2; 6.8-9; 12.14-16; 14.17) in which the sword is an image not just of destruction, but of discrimination; and this fits the context of v. 35 well. Of the Ezekiel texts, 14.17 (ῥομφαία διελθάτω διὰ τῆς γῆς) stands closest to v. 35, with its mention of both sword and piercing. See also Rev. 1.16; 2.12, 16; 19.15, 21, where it refers to the discriminating word of judgment spoken by Jesus; but see also Heb. 4.12 where μάχαιρα, which almost always in the LXX has an exclusively destructive sense, has this connotation.

divine judgment which comes in Jesus will have dimensions both public and personal.

For Israel the criterion of judgment will be whether or not the sign of Jesus is rightly interpreted; and if this same criterion applies to the judgment to which Mary will be subject, it means that she will not be exempt from the challenge of right interpretation of the sign of her son. That she is shown eventually in Acts 1.14 as among those awaiting the fulfilment of Jesus' promise means that Mary, like those with whom she waits, has succeeded in the task of interpretation.

This stress on Mary as interpreter fits what has been and will continue to be the characterization of her in the infancy narrative's second phase. Twice already Mary has been shown as astonished by the signs of God's action (vv. 18, 33), and once as pondering the different pieces of the picture she now has in the attempt to see the larger pattern (v. 19). In the following episode, she will again be shown as astonished (v. 48), uncomprehending (v. 50) and yet prepared to grapple with puzzlement (v. 51b). To understand the sword as a metaphor of pain links her more to the sign to be interpreted: she stands *with* Jesus sharing the pain of his rejection. But to read the sword as a metaphor of judgment understands Mary more as interpreter, as one who stands before the sign of Jesus and indeed all the signs of God's action in the process of interpretation.

This also accords with the narrative's dominant interest in the human response to God's action, in the narration of which Mary has been the protagonist from the second episode until now. In the first phase of the infancy narrative she was the prime example of faith, its ground and its effects. To this point in the second phase, as the signs of fulfilment have become more abundant and perplexing, she has appeared as the prime example of the believer grappling with puzzlement as God's action grows more overt. Now in v. 35a she appears as the believer who, faced with the supreme sign of her own son and in the process of grappling with the puzzlement he will provoke, will herself be subject to the divine judgment proclaimed by Simeon in vv. 34-35. Faith does not confer exemption from that.

An interpretation such as this suggests that Mary appears in v. 35a not so much as the embodiment of Israel,[1] but more as paradigm of

---

1. As argued by P. Benoit ('Et toi-même, un glaive te transpercera l'âme! [Lc 2, 35]', *CBQ* 25 [1963], pp. 251-61), Laurentin (*Structure*, pp. 89-91) and Legrand (*L'annonce*, p. 226).

the believer.[1] There is a kind of parallel between the experience of Israel and the experience of Mary, but this does not mean that she is an embodiment of the nation. Nor is it that Mary shares the fate of Jesus,[2] but that she shares the fate of all believers who in the process of interpretation demanded by faith must grapple with the puzzling sign of Jesus and run the risk of wrong interpretation.

In v. 32a, the effect of the messiah's coming was described as 'a light for the revelation of the Gentiles'; and now the purpose of the sword of judgment which will pass through both Israel and Mary is described: 'that thoughts out of many hearts may be revealed' (ὅπως ἂν ἄποκαλυφθῶσιν ἐκ πολλῶν καρδιῶν διαλογισμοί). In both cases we are dealing with a revelation, but revelations of a quite different kind. On the one hand, the effect of the messiah's coming is described horizontally in terms of geographical spread, reaching out to embrace the Gentiles. On the other hand, it is described vertically in terms of an inner penetration, reaching the depths of the hidden 'thoughts' (διαλογισμοί). The coming of the messiah, then, means a revelation which goes both out and down. No corner of the world and no corner of the human heart lies beyond its reach.

Why the Prophetess? Luke 2.36-38

The narrator decides to report nothing of the parents' reaction to Simeon's oracle. At a point where they might be expected to be even more astonished and perplexed than in v. 33, the narrator turns instead to the figure of Anna. The effacement of the parents is reinforced by the fact that Anna never mentions them or averts to them;[3] and this is because she, like the narrator, is less interested in the parents and their reaction than in the meaning of God's action in Jesus. Simeon himself, after a long and crucial appearance, simply vanishes from the narrative.[4] He has performed his interpretative function.

---

1. See 8.21 and 11.27-28 which also associate the mother of Jesus with the believer.
2. As Winandy, among many others, claims ('La Prophétie de Siméon', p. 349).
3. Compare the *Arabic Infancy Gospel* 6.2 which has Anna congratulate Mary.
4. Danker (*New Age*, p. 37) has Anna appear on the scene as Simeon is pronouncing the oracle of vv. 34b-35. 'Yet', he remarks, 'her faith remains firm'. But the impression in the narrative is that Simeon has fallen silent before Anna appears, and there is no indication of whether Simeon is present or not during Anna's prophecy.

Anna offers the second prophecy of the episode, although the text of her speech is not given. This is one of a number of differences between Simeon and Anna—differences enough to make it clear that we are dealing with a Lukan reprise rather than with repetition. Other differences are these:

1. Where Simeon has been introduced with almost no personal detail, the narrator introduces Anna with a flurry of personal detail in vv. 36-37. We are told of her name, her prophetic ministry, her family background, her age, her marital status and her exceptional piety. This is all very external when compared to the information we were given about Simeon. In his case, we were told of the private workings of the Holy Spirit in his life and in particular of the private revelation he had received from the Holy Spirit; and when he comes to the Temple, Simeon speaks only to the parents, which gives to his discourse as to the introduction of him an essentially private character. By contrast, all that we are told about Anna is strictly public knowledge. Her name, family background, age, marital status and piety are all in the public realm; and that she is immediately given the title 'prophetess' (προφῆτις) suggests that hers is a publicly recognized ministry. It is specifically said of Simeon (three times) that he is under the influence of the Holy Spirit, but Anna, though introduced as 'prophetess', is not said explicitly to be under the influence of the Holy Spirit. As befits the more public presentation of her, Anna appears as a more institutional character. Moreover, where Simeon comes from his private place to the public space of the Temple, Anna has no private place and inhabits the public space of the Temple. And then when she speaks hers is public rather than private discourse: she speaks not just to the parents, but 'to all who were looking for the redemption of Jerusalem' (πᾶσιν τοῖς προσδεχομένοις λύτρωσιν Ἰερουσαλήμ). In having both Simeon and Anna appear, the narrator shows the Holy Spirit stirring both publicly and privately to prompt right recognition of the messiah; and worlds both public and private converge at the point of right recognition.

2. Simeon speaks of the effects of the messiah's coming with regard to himself, all peoples, Israel and Mary; but Anna speaks of the effects only with regard to the nation.[1] She does not specify what the

---

1. The difference between λύτρωσις Ἰερουσαλήμ here and παράκλησις τοῦ Ἰσραήλ in v. 25 should be neither overstated nor ignored. Fitzmyer (*Luke*, p. 432) judges the two to be synonymous. Yet the focus of Ἰερουσαλήμ is sharper; and

messiah's coming means for her personally, and identifies her fate wholly with the fate of the nation in a way that accords with her function as a more public character than Simeon.

3. Simeon is male and Anna female.

4. The narrator reports a reaction at least to the Nunc Dimittis if not to the oracle of vv. 34-35, but there is no report of any reaction to Anna's speech. It is not even clear whether the parents hear the prophecy, and in contrast to the previous two episodes there is nothing to indicate how those who hear the prophecy react or what they do with the news.

5. Simeon sees the child and holds him in his arms, but there is no report of Anna either seeing or holding the child.

Yet for all the differences in the way they are characterized, there is much that Simeon and Anna share in common:

1. They are both introduced as pious Jews.

2. They are both presented as waiting for the fulfilment of a divine promise in which they have put their faith ('the consolation of Israel' in the case of Simeon and 'the redemption of Jerusalem' in the case of Anna).

3. They are both cast in a prophetic mould. Like Simeon, Anna recognizes and proclaims the truth of Jesus' identity and therefore the truth of God's action despite the puzzling signs. For her, as for Simeon, Jesus is not 'a sign spoken against', but a sign seen and rightly interpreted. In that sense, both Simeon and Anna are among the first to rise as the ἀνάστασις of v. 34 foretold.

4. They are both shown as praising God (εὐλόγησεν of Simeon in v. 28 and ἀνθωμολογεῖτο of Anna in v. 38).

This is enough to suggest that we are dealing not with a repetition, but with a reprise which implies complementarity—and a complementarity which anticipates much of what will follow in the Lukan narrative. The key OT text that the narrator will have Peter use to interpret the moment of Pentecost in Acts 2.17-21 will be Joel 2.28-32, in which the promise is that the Holy Spirit will be poured out on all flesh and that all will therefore prophesy—male and female, young

given the exceptional role that Jerusalem will continue to play in the Lukan narrative, the mention of it here establishes in the narrative a link between the proclamation of God's action in Jesus and the city itself. The paradox which the Gospel narrative will work out is that Jerusalem, ἡ ἀποκτείνουσα τοὺς προφήτας (13.34), will kill the one in whom its long-awaited redemption comes.

and old. The vision is one of potentially unimagined comprehensiveness. The first glimmer of fulfilment of the prophecy has been narrated in earlier episodes, as Elizabeth and then Zechariah prophesied. Now fulfilment gains momentum as Simeon and Anna in their different but complementary ways prophesy; and their prophecies look to the final fulfilment the beginning of which will be narrated in Acts 2.

It is no accident that in the infancy narrative, the specifically prophetic figures are all pious Jews and that they are male and female characters. It is also not by chance that the two prophecies of the first phase of the infancy narrative are located in the house of Zechariah, whereas the two prophecies of the second phase are located in the Temple. Nor it is accidental that in the first phase the two prophecies come in separate episodes, whereas in the second phase they come in the same episode: as God's action grows more overt, the prophetic manifestations grow more public and more intense. It appears already that the new gift of prophecy, which will come to full flower at Pentecost, rises within the world of Jewish religion and as its fulfilment; it appears in ways different but complementary; it is denied to no place, since it embraces space both sacral and secular; it is denied to no person, since man and woman prophesy; it is denied to no time, since it sounds now as it did in the past and as it will in the future.

Like the Nunc Dimittis, Anna's prophecy is theocentric.[1] The narrator says of Anna initially: 'she gave thanks to God' (ἀνθωμολογεῖτο τῷ θεῷ); and in what follows, Jesus is referred to simply as αὐτοῦ in a situation that creates an ambiguity[2] which the Lukan narrator would normally resolve by using the character's name.[3] The decision not to name Jesus is governed by the desire to control focus at this point. The phrase 'she gave thanks to God' implies an address of God;[4] and

1. As with Simeon earlier, the *Gospel of Pseudo-Matthew* 15.3 has Anna worship Jesus.
2. Laurentin (*Les Evangiles*, p. 252) notes the ambiguity that this introduces: does the αὐτοῦ here refer to Jesus or to God? He sees the ambiguity as part of a wider strategy by the narrator to create in the narrative an 'identification ambiguë manifeste' between Jesus and God. Yet the αὐτοῦ here is more simply explained as a move by the narrator to control the focus at this point by looking away from Jesus in himself to God as prime mover and redemption as the effect of his action.
3. On which see Aletti, *L'art de raconter*, p. 40.
4. ἀνθωμολογέω is a *hapax legomenon* in the NT, and as suggested by Marshall (following O. Michel, 'ὁμολογέω', *TDNT*, V, p. 213) suggests 'the ideas of recognition, obedience and proclamation which occur in praise rendered publicly

in this Anna is like Simeon in the Nunc Dimittis. Yet in two important ways her prophecy is different from Simeon's hymn and oracle; and these differences show further why the narrator decides to introduce the figure of Anna.

1. In v. 38b she turns from God to others, as did Simeon in vv. 34-35; but, as we have seen, Anna turns to a wider circle. She speaks not to the parents, but 'to all who were looking for the redemption of Jerusalem'.[1] In that sense, her role is to spread the news of the messiah's coming and its effect beyond the bounds of the family.[2] It is hard to know to whom exactly she speaks, with 'to all' (πᾶσιν) here as much an exaggeration as 'the whole multitude of the People' (πᾶν τὸ πλῆθος τοῦ λαοῦ) in 1.10, since it is hardly likely that Anna managed to contact all who were awaiting the redemption of Jerusalem, no matter how often or continuously she spoke. But the use of πᾶσιν stresses the scope of Anna's prophecy and sends her word beyond the physical confines of the Temple precincts. In that sense, it is an image of how the news spreads.[3] This is in keeping with the way the narrator presents her as a more public character than Simeon. It also looks to the rest of the Lukan narrative: Anna announces the 'what' of God's action, prompting in the minds of those who hear the question of 'how', which the rest of the Lukan narrative will address.

2. In having Anna focus on the fulfilment of the promise of a redeemed Jerusalem as the meaning of what God is doing in Jesus, the narrator sets the menacing oracle of vv. 34-35 between two jubilant proclamations of salvation. What this implies is that, although there are dark nuances to the divine visitation, its ultimate meaning is light. This again looks to the broader sweep of the Lukan narrative in which

---

to God in return for his grace' (*Gospel*, p. 124); and BAGD (p. 67) adds the nuance of 'to give thanks'. Michel notes the link with the piety of the Psalter which associates prayer to God with witness to human beings.

1. Here again the voice of Second Isaiah sounds in the echo of Isa. 40.2; 52.9. Some witnesses (A D L Θ Ψ 053. 0130 *f* [13] 𝔐 sy[h]) read ἐν Ἰερουσαλήμ, and others (1216 *pc* a r[1] vg[cl] bo[ms]) Ἰσραήλ. Both of these are corrections intended to expand the scope of the salvation proclaimed by Anna, which was felt to be too restrictive. This is true *a fortiori* of the *Arabic Infancy Gospel* 15.3, which has Anna proclaim the salvation of the world.

2. See Fitzmyer, *Luke*, p. 423.

3. The imperfect ἐλάλει suggests that Anna's proclamation was more than a brief and isolated event, on which see Plummer, *Critical Commentary*, p. 73, and Fitzmyer, *Luke*, p. 431.

rejection and persecution will appear as the very things that give new impetus to the divine plan in its trajectory through time.

The Return to Nazareth: Luke 2.39-40

Fulfilling the Law: Luke 2.39
Just as there was no report of the parents' reaction after Simeon's oracle in vv. 34-35, neither is there now after Anna's prophecy. The inner world of the characters remains closed to the readers, with the narrator holding firmly to the external mode of narration he has used throughout, with the sole exception of v. 33 where in stereotyped terms he reported the astonishment of Mary and Joseph.

In the previous episode, nothing was said of the implementation of the imperial decree of the census. Mentioned at the start, it was never mentioned again. Not so now with the demands of the law however. The narrator makes a point of underlining that, for all the surprises in the Temple, Mary and Joseph fulfilled the prescriptions of the law—which is called here not simply 'the law' or 'the law of Moses' but 'the law of the Lord'. The link with God is explicitly stated; and it emerges at the end as at the beginning of the episode that the law and prophecy of the kind narrated are in no way opposed. Both are of God. The demands of the law in no way inhibit the spirit of prophecy, and the spirit of prophecy in no way inhibits obedience to the law. Indeed, given the inclusion formed by the mention of the law in v. 39, the law emerges as the frame within which the interpretative word of prophecy is both spoken and heard. This was not true of the imperium in the previous episode.

Verse 39 completes a narrative arc which began in 2.4 with Joseph and Mary leaving for Bethlehem. The narrative has moved from Nazareth to Nazareth, with the narrator in 2.4 reporting that Joseph and Mary went 'from Galilee from the city of Nazareth' (ἀπὸ τῆς Γαλιλαίας ἐκ πόλεως Ναζαρέθ), and in v. 39 that parents and child return 'into Galilee to their own city, Nazareth' (εἰς τὴν Γαλιλαίαν εἰς πόλιν ἑαυτῶν Ναζαρέθ). The inclusion seals the narrative arc and, with its redundant mention of Galilee and Nazareth, serves to emphasize the secular space after the consistent emphasis on the sacral space through the episode. Jerusalem and the Temple have dominated the narration to the point where in shifting from sacral to secular space there is a need to stress the secular, lest it be obscured and the effect of the narrative's tactic of moving between worlds be correspondingly diminished.

The Growth of the Child: Luke 2.40

The narration becomes more elliptical than ever in v. 40, as the single verse narrates the twelve years lying between this and the following episode. We are told that the child grew in wisdom (σοφίᾳ) and grace (χάρις θεοῦ ἐπ' αὐτό),[1] but we are not told what the signs of this wisdom and grace might have been. That will come in the following episode.

Verse 39 has made it apparent that the divine plan unfolds not only in dramatic moments such as the encounters filling the last two episodes, but also in the ordinariness, indeed the hiddenness of Nazareth. Now v. 40 makes it plain that the divine plan also unfolds in the slow, undramatic rhythms of a child's growth.[2]

Conclusion

The narrator has presented in this episode two complementary figures, who contrast sharply with but also complement the shepherds in the previous episode—not only in their character and background, but also in the way revelation comes to them. For the shepherds, it was through the angel; and for Simeon and Anna, it is through the Holy Spirit. In one way, this reproduces the pattern of the first phase of the infancy narrative, where the angel first appeared to Zechariah and Mary, and then the Holy Spirit inspired Elizabeth and Zechariah. Yet in another way the movement of the first phase has been reversed: the narrative has moved from the shepherds (of whose piety nothing is said and who have expected nothing) to Simeon and Anna (whose piety is noted and who have expected salvation), whereas earlier it moved from Zechariah (whose piety was noted and who had asked for

---

1. The report of Jesus' growth here is fuller and more specific than the report of John's growth in 1.80. There it was reported simply that John ἐκραταιοῦτο πνεύματι. In v. 40, however, the action of God is more explicit, as is the wisdom theme which recalls the messianic Isa. 11.2 and prepares for the following episode.

2. Compare again the apocryphal gospels (especially *the Infancy Gospel of Thomas*) with their extraordinary accounts of Jesus' boyhood, accounts which Plummer describes as 'unworthy inventions' (*Critical Commentary*, p. 74).

a son) to Mary (of whose piety nothing is said and who has asked for nothing).

The same crossover effect is evident in the way the narrator has handled space. Where in the first phase the narrative began in the sacral space of the Temple and then moved to the secular space of Nazareth and Zechariah's house, now the narrative has moved from the secular space of Bethlehem (and surrounds) to the Temple: the movement is again reversed. As the revelation of Jesus grows more public, the Temple serves a function similar to that in 1.5-25. It is not only the sacral space, but also the public space where the people gather, and is therefore the ideal place for the kind of convergence the episode narrates and the spreading of the news such as Anna's prophecy ensures. The people at the Temple hear from Anna the interpretation they did not hear from the dumbstruck Zechariah in the first episode; and in that sense it is Anna's prophecy rather than Jesus' blessing in 24.50 which completes 1.5-25.

The infancy narrative, then, moves in a large arc from 1.5-25 to 2.22-40—from Jewish piety to Jewish piety, from Temple to Temple. The first episode narrated the failure of one pious Jew (Zechariah) to believe a divine promise and the failure of other pious Jews (the People) to interpret rightly the signs of fulfilment.[1] In this episode, however, the narrator has shown the triumph of Jewish piety, as two pious Jews believe a divine promise and rightly interpret the signs of fulfilment.

The difference is that now the Holy Spirit is abroad and active in a way not true of the first episode. It would seem, then, that it is the Holy Spirit that brings Jewish piety to the point of full and right recognition of the divine visitation. This emerged in a preliminary way in Elizabeth and Zechariah, who prophesied earlier in the seclusion of their own house. It emerges climactically now in Simeon and Anna, who prophesy in the public space of the Temple. Instead of Zechariah's silence in the Temple we now have their proclamation.

Simeon and Anna rightly interpret the signs of fulfilment in Jesus despite the gap between the 'what' of the promise ('the consolation of Israel' and 'the redemption of Jerusalem') and the 'how' of its fulfilment (a newborn child brought to the Temple by parents of modest means). Simeon at least comes to the recognition that Jesus is God's

---

1.   Elizabeth does better in interpreting the signs of fulfilment, but that is not part of the central action in theTemple.

salvation not only for Israel but for all peoples, as the Nunc Dimittis has declared in terms clearer than anything earlier in the infancy narrative. Yet the paradox is that he will be rejected—and this not by misadventure but as part of God's plan. This is news to both characters and readers; and the question now is, how and why will this happen?

Once again God has seized the initiative in unexpected ways. According to the law, the parents had brought the child to the Temple to present him to God; but God instead has intervened according to the Holy Spirit to present the child through prophetic figures to Mary and Joseph but also 'to all who were looking for the redemption of Jerusalem'. The pattern of surprise is by now so well established in the narrative that we may expect that whatever answer to the question 'how?' the narrator may provide, it will be surprising enough to test the interpretative powers of both characters and readers.

Chapter 8

JESUS AS INTERPRETER IN LUKE 2.41-52

Climax or Anticlimax ?

'Is this scene the most important of the infancy narrative,' asks Bovon, 'or the onset of an apocryphal weakening, the first sign of a collapse?'[1] Certainly it is an episode that has drawn different judgments. Plummer describes it as 'a supplement',[2] and Brown as a secondary addition unbalancing the original diptych of the infancy narrative.[3] Van Iersel claims that '[i]n order to understand it the reader need not be acquainted with the preceding parts of the Birth-Stories';[4] and Fitzmyer is more emphatic in his judgment that it is 'an independent unit, which does not depend on anything that precedes in the infancy narrative and which could be dropped without any great loss to the narrative'.[5] Not all would agree, however;[6] and the general claim of this chapter is that from a narrative point of view 2.41-52 is not an independent unit,[7] and that it could not be dropped without

1. Bovon, *Evangelium*, p. 155.
2. Plummer, *Critical Commentary*, p. 6.
3. Brown, *Birth of the Messiah*, pp. 251-52.
4. B. van Iersel, 'The Finding of Jesus in the Temple: Some Observations on the Original Form of Luke II.41-51a', *NovT* 4 (1960), p. 164.
5. Fitzmyer, *Luke*, p. 435. In the same vein he claims elsewhere that 'it is ill-suited to the rest of the two chapters at the beginning of this Gospel' (p. 434), and that '[it] is only loosely connected with what precedes' (p. 435). See too the similar view of Hendrickx, *Infancy Narratives*, p. 112.
6. For more favourable judgments, see for example R. Laurentin, *Jésus au Temple: Mystère de Pâques et foi de Marie en Luc 2, 48-50* (Paris: Gabalda, 1966), p. 93, and Schürmann, *Lukasevangelium*, p. 133, where he comments that '[d]er "Nachtrag" 2,41-52 wird... zum mächtigen Finale des ganzen Präludiums Lk 1-2'.
7. This does not imply any attempt to tackle the question of sources, which has been treated at great length though without great conclusiveness in many historical-critical studies of the pericope.

substantial loss to the infancy narrative.

From a narrative point of view the episode may not be an independent unit, but still there are things that distinguish it from previous episodes. For the first time in the narrative, Jesus acts and speaks as a free agent; there is no hint of either angels or the Holy Spirit;[1] the OT citations and echoes dwindle to almost nothing;[2] and in general the language of the episode is less heavily semitized.[3] These are interrelated phenomena which call not just for observation but for explanation.

Commentators have been slow to agree on a focus of the episode. Bultmann favours a double focus[4] which includes (1) the exceptional wisdom of the child Jesus,[5] and (2) his decision to stay in the Temple as revelation of his destiny.[6] Others point to the christological revelation of v. 49 as the episode's centre of gravity.[7] The range of opinion suggests that the episode, though brief, is not straightforward, and that

---

1.   Hence Marshall's remark that 'the story is a natural one, and does not include any supernatural features' (*Gospel*, p. 126)

2.   On which, see the comments of Nolland, *Luke*, p. 128.

3.   A. Schlatter, *Das Evangelium nach Lukas* (Stuttgart: Calwer Verlag, 1960), p. 205; Laurentin, *Structure*, p. 142; Brown, *Birth of the Messiah*, p. 480; Fitzmyer, *Luke*, p. 435. But see also H. Sahlin, *Der Messias und das Gottesvolk* (Uppsala: Alqvist, 1945), pp. 308-11, where he notes the clear semitisms that remain.

4.   Bultmann, *History of the Synoptic Tradition*, p. 300.

5.   Bultmann notes (*History of the Synoptic Tradition*, p. 301) the similarities between the story of Jesus' display of precocious intelligence in this episode and stories found in Josephus and Philo about Moses, in Herodotus about Cyrus, in Plutarch about Alexander, in Philostratus about Apollonius of Tyana—describing the episode as 'a legend' formed under such influences. Laurentin (*Jésus au Temple*, pp. 135-41) sees Jesus' display in this episode as connected to divine Wisdom (Sir. 24.1-12). For quite different reasons, then, both give the wisdom motif a centrality denied by most (on which see Fitzmyer, *Luke*, pp. 436-37).

6.   H. De Jonge, 'Sonship, Wisdom, Infancy: Luke II.41-51a', *NTS* 24 (1977–78), p. 339, describes the episode as 'a textbook case of "concentric symmetry"', with vv. 46b-47 the centre and μέσῳ the 85th of the pericope's 170 words. He concludes by hedging his bets: 'Luke ii.41-51 has its climax, or at least one of its climaxes, in the encounter of Jesus and the doctors'.

7.   Among many, van Iersel, 'The Finding of Jesus'; Schürmann, *Lukasevangelium*, p. 133; Lagrange, *Evangile*, p. 93; Bovon, *Evangelium*, p. 154; Brown, *Birth of the Messiah*, p. 490; Fitzmyer, *Luke*, p. 437; Räisänen, *Die Mutter Jesu*, p. 134; J.F. Jansen, 'Luke 2.41-52', *Int* 30 (1976), pp. 400-404.

it may be worth testing the contending claims by posing the questions of narrative criticism.

The claim in this chapter is that the episode is the climax of the infancy narrative and therefore 'the most important of the infancy narrative'—at least in narrative terms. This is because it recounts the moment when Jesus appears in the narrative for the first time as *interpreter of himself*. In earlier episodes, other characters have interpreted Jesus, his identity and role. Now he interprets himself and his action; and at that point leadership in the interpretative task passes to Jesus, with whom it will remain throughout the Third Gospel. It is in this sense that 'the converging trajectories' discerned by Laurentin in the previous episode are more apparent and, in narrative terms, more decisive in this episode.

The Need for Interpretation: Luke 2.41-45

A Conventional World: Luke 2.41-42

The narrator begins by evoking a conventional world; and he does so in ways that establish in the episode two related contexts. First, he stresses that the Passover pilgrimage to Jerusalem[1] is made in conformity to custom. In v. 41 we have 'each year' (κατ᾽ ἔτος), and in v. 42 'according to custom' (κατὰ τὸ ἔθος), both of which evoke the rhythms of religious practice, though without mentioning the element of obligation .[2] The Temple-piety which marked the parents in the previous episode is shown to be an enduring part of their life. The first context evoked in the episode, then, is religious.

---

1.   Brown (*Birth of the Messiah*, p. 485) and L. Legrand ('Deux voyages: Lc 2,41-50; 24,13-33', in F. Refoulé (ed.), *A Cause de l'Evangile* [Paris: Cerf, 1985], pp. 409-29) see this first journey from Galilee to Jerusalem as an anticipation of Jesus' journey to Jerusalem in the Gospel narrative, with both journeys bringing Jesus to Jerusalem at Passover time. Yet in vv. 42-43 nothing is said of Jesus journeying to Jerusalem. What is said in v. 43 is that Jesus *remained* in Jerusalem, and it is there that the narrative focuses. This tells against the claim of Brown and Legrand.

2.   It is clear from Deut. 16.16 that adult males were supposed to go to Jerusalem for the Passover, though it is difficult to know how widely the practice was observed in the first century. It is also difficult to know whether women and children made the pilgrimage (see Str–B II, p. 142). But the real question lies less at the level of historicity than at the level of narrative strategy: why include the notice, whether historical or not?

Secondly, the language is strongly familial. Mary and Joseph are referred to as 'his parents' (οἱ γονεῖς αὐτοῦ), which again defines them not in themselves but in relation to Jesus, and so stresses the bond of family. It is the parents who take the initiative, with the sole reference to Jesus being the mention of his age in v. 42. The child is backgrounded in a way that again underscores the bond of family. The second context evoked is therefore familial.

As the episode begins, Jesus is wholly passive as he was in the previous two episodes. Yet there is a difference, since he is now presented as a boy of twelve, a character therefore who though still a child stands on the threshold of adult life and the independent action that implies.[1] Jesus is reintroduced by the narrator at a point of transition—but a transition, it would seem, that will unfold within a context shaped by the conventions of religion and family evoked in the opening verses of the episode.

A world shaped by such conventions is a world that demands compliance rather than interpretation of any kind. Insofar as Jesus remains within such a world, he will remain the child who simply follows his parents, and his parents will remain pious Jews and dutiful parents who do not face the challenge of interpretation. The need for interpretation would only arise when and if the conventions evoked should be disrupted.

As in earlier episodes the fulfilment of the prescriptions—in this case the celebration of the Passover—is never narrated. This conforms to a pattern in the infancy narrative. In 1.5-25, it was the incense-burning which went unnarrated; in 1.57-80 it was the circumcision; in 2.1-21 it was the census and circumcision; in 2.22-40 it was the purification and presentation; and now it is the Passover festival, which is mentioned twice in the first two verses but never narrated. It provides both the starting point and the context of the action which the episode will recount, but the focus is not on the Passover itself. The action of God and the human response to it with which the episode is concerned are neither at odds with the Passover

---

1. For an extended discussion of the significance of the age of twelve and why Luke chooses to have Jesus at that age, see De Jonge, 'Sonship, Wisdom, Infancy', pp. 317-24. He concludes that 'Luke presents Jesus as still immature, not fully developed either spiritually or rationally, in order to make his wisdom appear all the more clearly' (p. 322).

nor identical with it. This is as it has been earlier with the forms of both Jewish religion and Roman hegemony included in the narrative.

Jesus in Jerusalem: Luke 2.43

Preferring to leave the Passover festival buried in the silence between vv. 42 and 43, the narrator moves immediately to its aftermath. Again the parents appear simply as 'his parents', which underscores again the family bond and therefore the parents' role and responsibility in caring for their child. The reader is told that Jesus remained in Jerusalem, but the narrator says nothing of why.[1] The silence imposes the question, 'why?', and so begins to build a suspense which will be resolved only in v. 49.

For all that Jesus' motive is unclear, one thing is sure—that his stay in Jerusalem disrupts the patterns of convention evoked in vv. 41-42; and at that point his action demands interpretation. Readers and characters are situated differently as they begin the task of interpretation. From v. 43 onwards, the question for the readers is, 'why has Jesus stayed in Jerusalem?'; but for the parents the question will become in v. 45, 'where is Jesus?' At this point, then, the readers remain privileged over the parents, who are left to deduce in v. 45 what the readers are told in v. 43. Yet despite the reader-privilege, both parents and readers must grapple in their different ways with an enigma.

The Beginning of Interpretation: Luke 2.44-45

In v. 44, the narrator begins the narration of interpretation, and he does so by turning to the parents. They are faced with a fact—the absence of Jesus—and therefore with a question which comes only slowly: where is he? Their first interpretation of the fact and answer to the question is that Jesus is 'in the travelling party' (ἐν τῇ

---

1. Various reasons have been suggested. K. Bornhäuser (*Die Geburts- und Kindheitsgeschichte Jesu* [Gütersloh: Bertelmanns, 1930], p. 127) suggests that the parents left early and that Jesus remained piously in order to complete the celebrations. F.C. Hamlyn ('The Visit of the Child Jesus to the Temple', *ExpTim* 27 [1915], pp. 43-44) counters with the suggestion that Jesus stayed because he knew that he, like Samuel, had to live in the sanctuary; and J.R. Gray ('Was Our Lord an Only Child? Luke II, 43-46', *ExpTim* 71 [1959], p. 53) claims that the parents overlooked Jesus because they were caring for their other children. None of these finds any warrant in the narrative itself.

συνοδίᾳ)—which the well-informed readers know to be wrong. On the basis of this first interpretation, they proceed a day's journey before eventually seeking Jesus among the company. They are then faced with a second fact—that Jesus is not 'in the travelling party'. At that point, they realize with the readers that their first interpretation was wrong; and with that realization, their question, 'where is Jesus?' grows more urgent. As it does, the effect of suspense gains momentum.

In v. 45, the narrator has the parents return to Jerusalem, a second action which presumes a second interpretation—that Jesus, if not 'in the travelling party', must have remained in Jerusalem.[1] At that point, the parents move towards the knowledge given to the readers in v. 43. Yet without the aid of an omniscient narrator they can only suppose what the readers know with certainty. They again 'suppose' (νομίσαντες) as they did at the start of v. 44. Still, the fact that they move towards the readers' knowledge means that the narrator is building a *rapprochement* between parents and readers.

These two verses have shown the parents very much on the move— and not only physically. Theirs is also a journey of interpretation and discovery. Their itinerary may be traced in four steps:

1. A first supposition ('supposing him to be in the travelling party' [νομίσαντες αὐτὸν εἶναι ἐν τῇ σονοδίᾳ]).
2. A first action prompted by the supposition ('they sought him among their relatives and acquaintances' [ἀναζήτουν αὐτὸν ἐν τοῖς συγγενεῦσιν καὶ τοῖς γνωστοῖς]).
3. The realization that the first supposition was mistaken ('not finding him' [μὴ εὑρόντες]).
4. A second supposition which prompts a second action ('they turned back to Jerusalem in search of him' [ὑπέστρεψαν εἰς Ἰερουσαλὴμ ἀναζητοῦντες αὐτόν]).

For them at this stage the question remains, 'where is Jesus?' For the readers who follow the parents in their journey of discovery, the question remains, 'why has Jesus remained in Jerusalem?'; and to this

---

1. As with Jesus in v. 43, the narration remains external, with the parents' motivation clear, but with no indication of their inner reaction once they realize Jesus is gone, which means that conjectures such as Muñoz Iglesias offers (*Evangelios*, III, p. 245) go beyond what the narrative allows. In characteristic style, the narrator will leave the disclosure of their inner reaction until later in the episode when Mary will give voice to it.

there is now added the further question of whether the parents will find him and, if so, how?

Brown claims that v. 44 'could be omitted with no loss of logic. The loss would be one of drama'.[1] Yet in an episode which, like the entire infancy narrative, stresses cognition rather than action, with the governing interest in human response that this implies, it is more than a question of drama in an incidental sense as Brown implies. The two verses work together to show patterns of human response to a puzzling fact. Here as throughout the infancy narrative the response is a process which builds slowly and by way of peripateia to a moment of revelation, and it is a response which evolves differently for characters and readers. If the episode were simply a plot of action, then Brown's claim would be valid; but in an episode which is rather a plot of discovery the two verses serve an important function which makes Brown's claim seem less valid. It is not only a question of the logic (and drama) of human action, but also and more especially a question of the pattern (and drama) of human response.

The Interpretation of Jesus: Luke 2.46-49

Among the Teachers: Luke 2.46-47

Between vv. 45 and 46 the narrator decides for another silence, with nothing said of what happened to either Jesus or the parents in the three days mentioned early in v. 46.[2] The style of narration is more elliptical than ever, but here as earlier in the infancy narrative the more elliptical the narration the more intense the focus; and in this episode the ellipses build to the focal point of v. 49.

The ellipses in vv. 46-47 are substantial. First, nothing is said of

---

1. Brown, *Birth of the Messiah*, p. 486 n. 25.
2. Some uncertainty surrounds the three days. As Muñoz Iglesias notes: 'en el texto no aparece si los tres días se han de contar desde que Jesús se perdió, desde que José y María emprenden el regreso a Jerusalén, o desde que empiezan su búsqueda en la Ciudad' (*Evangelios*, III, p. 247). J. Dupont ('L'Evangile de la Fête de la Sainte Famille [Lc 2,41-52]', *AsSeign* 14 [1961], pp. 24-43), Laurentin (*Jésus au Temple*, pp. 101-102) and J.K. Elliott ('Does Luke 2.41-52 Anticipate the Resurrection?', *ExpTim* 83 [1971], pp. 87-89) claim that the three days anticipate the three days between Jesus' death and resurrection. For convincing counter-arguments, however, see Muñoz Iglesias, *Evangelios*, III, p. 249, and De Jonge, 'Sonship, Wisdom, Infancy', pp. 324-27, who insists upon the formulaic character of the phrase and favours a general translation such as 'only after several days'.

how the parents react when they find Jesus—the effect of which is to leave the parents in the background for the moment, with Jesus in the foreground. Secondly and more importantly, there is no report of the exchange between the teachers and Jesus such as we find in the apocryphal accounts.[1] The effect of the silence is to focus upon Jesus rather than upon the content of his replies to the teachers or upon the teachers themselves. The narrator's decision not to report any exchange between Jesus and the teachers also suggests that this is not where the episode's centre of gravity is to be found.

The elision of the teachers continues in the phrase 'all who heard' (πάντες οἱ ἀκούοντες), which includes the teachers but does not focus upon them. At the same time, it is hard to know who exactly is included in the group of 'all who heard'. As in 2.18 it would seem to include the parents among those who are amazed at Jesus' display of intelligence; and the elision of the subject in v. 48 seems to support this.[2]

The phrase 'all who heard' (πάντες οἱ ἀκούοντες) is reminiscent of 1.66 (πάντες οἱ ἀκούσαντες, referring to those in the Judaean hills who hear the news of John's birth and its circumstances) and 2.18 (πάντες οἱ ἀκούσαντες, referring to those at the birth scene who hear the shepherds' tale). Yet here we are dealing with the Lukan technique of reprise, since the two instances, though similar, are not identical. In 1.66, the news passes from the birth scene into the hills through the neighbours who have witnessed the birth, been part of the drama of naming and heard Zechariah's cry of praise. In 2.18, however, the news passes from the angels through the shepherds to those at the birth scene. The involvement of heaven is more overt and direct, and the news comes from countryside to birth scene rather than from birth scene to countryside as in 1.66. Now in v. 47 it is

---

1. Compare the report in *Ta Paidika Tu Kyriu* 19.2 which has Jesus discussing at length questions of astronomy, medicine, physics and metaphysics. See also the *Arabic Infancy Gospel* 50.2-3 which has him engaged in a debate anticipating the debate in 20.41-44 concerning the messiah's provenance.

2. On the elision of the subject, Brown notes that 'Luke is simply careless' (*Birth of the Messiah*, p. 475). This may be so, but given how careful Luke is usually in the way he styles his characters (especially in situations such as this where there is an ambiguity), it seems more likely that here he deliberately elides the subject in order to leave the focus on Jesus and to identify the parents with those (including the readers) who must make sense of Jesus' presence in the Temple among the teachers.

Jesus who is heard rather than Zechariah and the neighbours or the angel and the shepherds. Where in the previous two instances there was a source (Zechariah and the angel) and a mediation (the neighbours and the shepherds), now source and mediation converge in Jesus. This means that the focus in vv. 46-47 is less on the process and content of the communication and more on the communicator himself: Jesus. In 1.66 and 2.18 it was clear to the readers what exactly was heard; but in this third instance it is less clear what exactly Jesus says. This sharpens the focus on him rather than on what he says.

In 2.18, the parents, with 'all who heard', were confronted by an extraordinary message conveyed by unlikely messengers. Now in v. 47, again with 'all who heard', they are confronted by an extraordinary display of 'understanding' (σύνεσις) from an unlikely source. There is again a gap between what is said and who is saying it; and hence the amazement of all. Yet the questions are different for the different characters. The parents' question, 'where?', is now answered; and both their supposition (that Jesus, if he is not in the travelling party, must be in Jerusalem) and their later supposition implied if not expressed in the narrative (that Jesus must or might be in the Temple) are shown to be right. But the answer to one question prompts another. The question 'where?' now becomes the question 'why?', as will appear when Mary speaks in v. 48. For the readers, the question 'why?' persists, though now in different terms. Since v. 43 the readers' question has been, 'why has Jesus remained in Jerusalem?'; but now, learning that Jesus is not just in Jerusalem but in the Temple among the teachers, the question becomes, 'why here?' With the parents, the readers ask whether Jesus left his family simply to engage the teachers in discussion? The readers have learnt with the parents that Jesus is in the Temple among the teachers. At that point, reader-privilege is undermined and both parents and readers face the same question. The two journeys of discovery begin to converge as the episode builds to the moment of revelation in v. 49.

The intensification of focus on Jesus and his authority in vv. 46-47 moves in three steps—from 'hearing' (ἀκούοντα) to 'questioning' (ἐπερωτῶντα) to 'answering' (ἀποκρίσεσιν).[1] He who begins by

---

1. Brown (*Birth of the Messiah*, p. 474) rightly cautions against making too much of Jesus sitting in the midst of the teachers as if he had become the teacher of the teachers. As Brown notes, the seated position could equally be the position of the disciple (e.g. Acts 22.3). Lagrange (*Evangile*, p. 96) goes too far in imagining the

listening becomes more active in the act of questioning, and more active still as he answers questions put to him—and answers in a way that draws amazement. Yet there is no indication that the understanding (σύνεσις) displayed by Jesus is the result of a divine inspiration or revelation of any kind. The knowing readers, like the parents, are not surprised that one who is Son of God should display such unusual understanding. As interpreters, the readers are able to judge that it is because he is Son of God that Jesus displays such understanding. For parents and readers the surprise is that Jesus should have separated himself from his parents in order to enter into discussion with the teachers. The apparent motive seems hardly to justify the action. For the other characters, who know nothing of Jesus' identity, the surprise is that the child should display such precocious intelligence, so that for them the question is, 'whence this understanding?' This implies the question, 'who is this child?', which is different from the question of parents and readers. For the moment, Jesus' identity prompts him to speak wondrously of issues and questions debated by the teachers. But the episode will come to its true focus when he speaks wondrously of himself.

In his dialogue with the teachers, Jesus is able to meet them on their own ground and on their own terms, accepting their premises, moving within the bounds of their logic, and speaking their language. The display is exceptional enough to evoke amazement but it is not unique, since similar displays of human precocity, if uncommon, are not unknown now nor were they in the ancient world.[1] At this point, Jesus might be judged yet another precociously intelligent child giving signs of future greatness. Yet the readers and the parents know him to be much more, as he himself will declare in v. 49. In vv. 46-47, the narrator has Jesus engage the teachers in an astonishing way as one indication of what his identity enables. But this is not an end in itself, since it prepares for v. 49 where, in turning to interpret himself, Jesus' interpretative word will appear more stark and enigmatic, evoking not astonishment but perplexity, and will appear as a word which casts his future greatness in a quite different light.

teachers inviting the intriguing child into their elite circle.

1.   On spectacular displays of precocious wisdom in the lives of famous men, see the examples mentioned in my earlier note. See too the further examples detailed by Brown, *Birth of the Messiah*, pp. 481-82.

The Voice of Convention: Luke 2.48

Between vv. 47 and 48 the narrator sets another of the silences that punctuate the episode. Nothing is said of what happens to the teachers and others of 'all who heard', who simply disappear from the scene.[1] As he moves to what will be the climactic moment of both interpretation and revelation, the narrator retires from the public to the private arena, narrowing the focus from 'all who heard' to the parents alone. Nor is anything said of when Jesus realizes that his parents have arrived on the scene and how he reacts to the realization, since the focus now is not upon his recognition of them, but on his recognition of himself and the need they have to follow him in that recognition.

Verse 48 however offers an inside view of the parents (ἐξεπλάγησαν), and also makes it clear that it is not only hearing Jesus (ἀκούοντες) that provokes their astonishment, but also seeing him (ἰδόντες). The vocabulary suggests that they are even more astonished by where he is (ἐξεπλάγησαν) than by what he says (ἐξίσταντο).[2] This is not surprising, given what they know of his identity. It is more puzzling to them (as to the readers) that Jesus' identity as messiah and Son of God should mean that he do what he has done than that he display extraordinary understanding.

Puzzled by his disappearance, the parents are astonished by where they find him. More than ever, the strange action of Jesus demands interpretation; and it is Mary's question that voices the demand. The narrator styles her 'his mother' (ἡ μήτηρ αὐτοῦ) in a way that underscores anew the family bond. To the same end, the narrator also has Mary refer to Jesus as 'child' (τέκνον), thus emphasising his relationship to his parents, and to Joseph as 'your father' (ὁ πατήρ

---

1. Compare again the apocryphal accounts which have the teachers ask Mary if she is the mother of this child and, when she has said she is, bless both her and her son (*Infancy Gospel of Thomas* 19.4; *Arabic Infancy Gospel* 53; *Ta Paidika Tu Kyriu* 19.4).

2. Laurentin (*Jésus au Temple*, pp. 33-34) seems right in claiming that ἐξεπλάγησαν has a stronger sense than ἐξίσταντο in the previous verse, though the claim is queried by Brown, *Birth of the Messiah*, p. 475. The verb ἐξεπλάγησαν contrasts not only with ἐξίσταντο, but also with θαυμάζειν, since this is the first time the verb ἐκπλήσσεσθαι has been used in the infancy narrative to describe astonishment or amazement. In previous episodes, we had different forms of θαυμάζω: ἐθαύμαζον (1.21), ἐθαύμασαν (1.63), ἐθαύμασαν (2.18), θαυμάζοντες (2.33). The change of verb suggests that there *is* something different about this reaction, whether or not it be in this case a difference of intensity.

σου). Joseph is silent throughout, but he is given pride of place in Mary's expression, 'your father and I' (ὁ πατήρ σου κἀγώ), which as De Jonge notes is an unusual word order.[1] The effect of the word order is to stress the phrase 'your father' in reference to Joseph in order to prepare for what Jesus will say in v. 49 in reference to God. The play on the word 'father' and the stress on the family bond in what Mary says prepare for what Jesus will say in v. 49, where the question of belonging will be cast in a quite different light. Joseph's paternity is emphasized in v. 48 in order to prepare for its transcendence in v. 49.

In what Mary says, we learn the inner reaction of the parents to the disappearance of Jesus, as the narrator has her provide the inside view that he himself did not provide earlier. The reaction is twofold: there is both bafflement ('Why have you done this to us?' [τί ἐποίησας ἡμῖν οὕτως;]) and anguish ('fretfully' [ὀδυνώμενοι][2]). There is nothing surprising in such a reaction: it is completely conventional. What matters more from a narrative point of view is that the narrator allows the character to articulate the reaction that he himself has not reported earlier.

For the first time since 1.34 the narrator has Mary ask a question. There the question was 'how?' (πῶς . . . ;), and now it is 'why?' (τί . . . ;). The question 'how can the child be born?' becomes the question 'why has the child done this?' In 1.34, Mary's question served to accentuate the strangeness of what was promised, and in v. 48 her question serves to accentuate the strangeness of what has happened. In both cases, her question provokes an enigmatic word of explanation—from Gabriel earlier and now from Jesus; and here, as from the mouth of Gabriel earlier, it will be a revelation of the identity of Jesus which focuses upon him as Son of God.

It is difficult to establish with certainty the tone of Mary's question;[3]

---

1.   De Jonge, 'Sonship, Wisdom, Infancy', pp. 330-31.
2.   The verb ὀδύνασθαι occurs only in Luke in the NT, and refers to acute distress of either mind or body. In Lk. 16.24-25 and Acts 20.38 it refers to distress in the face of mortal threat —a nuance read here by Laurentin, who takes ὀδυνώμενοι ('mot paroxystique') to be an anticipation of Mary's distress at the death of her son and an initial fulfilment therefore of Simeon's prophecy in 2.35 (*Les Evangiles*, pp. 109-10, 116). This strains the narrative (and the word) to breaking point.
3.   Indicative of which is the disagreement among commentators who have tackled the question. For example, R. Pesch ('Kind, warum hast du so an uns

but what is clear is that it pursues the line and logic of human convention which began in vv. 41-42, and demands an explanation of something that has clearly infringed that line and logic. The question is
both reasonable and natural for a mother whose twelve-year-old son
has been missing for some days. It focuses upon the family bond; it
implies that Jesus has acted not as a result of some coercion but on his
own initiative (ἐποίησας, with Jesus the subject); it recognizes how
extraordinary Jesus' action has been; it expresses bafflement as to what
its motive might have been.

Faced with the fact of Jesus in the Temple among the teachers,
Mary cannot find her way to right interpretation. How can who he is
and what he has done be reconciled? For the parents and the readers
to answer that question, Jesus himself must speak for the first time in
the Lukan narrative. In the previous two episodes, the human characters have needed heavenly intervention to come to right interpretation.
Now they need the intervention of Jesus.

Enigmatic Interpretation: Luke 2.49
If Mary's question seems reasonable and natural, Jesus' reply by
contrast seems unreasonable and unnatural, even priggish or imperti-
nent—hardly designed to draw the admiration which his earlier
performance among the teachers drew. In that sense, it is a surprising
first word from the character who will dominate the Gospel narrative
and who will often speak in surprising ways.

Jesus meets his mother's question with two questions of his own
which are at best an oblique reply. The answer to his first question
('Why did you seek me?' [τί ὅτι ἐζητεῖτέ με;]) is obvious—at least
according to the logic voiced by Mary in her question. What emerges,
however, is that Jesus is speaking from a different logic, that he and
his parents are at cross-purposes in a way that was not true of Jesus
and the teachers. He met the teachers on their own ground and on
their own terms; but he does not meet his parents on the ground and
terms set forth in Mary's question. His words in v. 49 disrupt the
logic of convention which has held sway to this point and to which
Mary's question gave voice. In order to answer her own question or

getan?', *BZ* 12 [1968], pp. 245-48), Brown (*Birth of the Messiah*, p. 489),
Fitzmyer (*Luke*, p. 443) and Muñoz Iglesias (*Evangelios*, III, p. 254) detect a note
of reproach; but Laurentin (*Jésus au Temple*, p. 36) detects instead a note of
deference and affection.

to understand the answer Jesus gives, Mary must again move ground on her journey of discovery.

The narrator has Jesus offer an interpretation of both his absence from the company and his presence in the Temple—the interpretation which neither his parents nor the readers, left to their own devices, have been able to supply. In v. 43 the narrator said nothing of why Jesus remained in Jerusalem, preferring to leave the revelation of motive until now when he can place it on the lips of Jesus himself.

In v. 10, the angel revealed to the shepherds that the odd circumstances of the messiah's birth were the will of God; in vv. 29-35, the Holy Spirit revealed to Simeon that it was part of God's plan that the messiah appear as just another child born to parents of modest means and, more paradoxically still, that he become eventually 'a sign spoken against'. Now Jesus reveals that he has left his parents and installed himself in the Temple not simply because of an irresistible penchant for theological discussion, but because he is the Son of God: 'I must be in the things of my father' (ἐν τοῖς τοῦ πατρός μου δεῖ εἶναί με). Not that he refers to himself explicitly as Son of God: he leaves to others the task of naming him Son of God as foretold by Gabriel in 1.32 (υἱὸς ὑψίστου κληθήσεται) and 1.35 (κληθήσεται υἱὸς θεοῦ). This is an instance of the indirect christology of the Lukan narrative, in which the narrator will have Jesus point the way but leave it to the characters and readers to follow.[1]

It is hardly accidental that in the last of the infancy narrative's episodes the title that the narrative implies is Son of God, the title most prominent in Gabriel's oracle in 1.32, 35, and the title implied in Jesus' last word in the Gospel narrative (24.49, where he refers to God again as 'my father'). This is the primary 'what', the christological ground of the Lukan narrative, which in this episode receives its primary 'how', the specification of a distinctively Lukan christology which has Jesus as prime interpreter of himself as Son of God. In

---

1. On the indirect christology of the Lukan narrative, see Aletti, *L'art de raconter*, pp. 42 and 203, where he writes of Jesus' function in the narrative as the one who reveals himself: 'Sa christologie reste indirecte, pour laisser à ses auditeurs le soin de percevoir, grâce aux signes surtout, son identité prophétique et messianique'. It is also true that Gabriel's statements in 1.32 (υἱὸς ὑψίστου κληθήσεται) and 1.35 (κληθήσεται υἱὸς θεοῦ) are foreshadowings of such an indirect christology, since Gabriel does not himself name Jesus as Son of God but foretells that others will name him thus.

1.30-35, Gabriel revealed (to Mary and the readers at least) Jesus' identity as Son of God; but now Jesus himself reveals that his identity as Son demands action, and action which may seem strange. What is difficult for Mary and the readers is to discover the coherence between Jesus' identity and his action. Yet the form of his reply ('Did you not know. . . ?' [οὐκ ἤδειτε;]) implies that a grasp of this coherence is the knowledge which enables right interpretation and which both parents and readers are expected to share.

If it is now clear that Jesus has remained in the Temple among the teachers because he is Son of God, it remains unclear what exactly he means by the oblique and enigmatic statement that he must be 'in the things of my father' (ἐν τοῖς τοῦ πατρός μου).[1] Commentators have sought to show that the enigmatic phrase must mean either 'in the affairs of my father' (i.e. action)[2] or 'in the house of my father' (i.e. place),[3] with the weight of opinion favouring the second rendering. Certainly the phrase can have that sense; but that is not to say that it can have only that sense. Moreover, as De Jonge notes, 'if Luke had only wanted to say "I must be in my Father's house", he expressed himself in an unnatural and even extraordinary manner'.[4] Given that elsewhere he refers to the house of God as οἶκος,[5] Luke might simply have written ὁ οἶκος τοῦ πατρός μου.[6] Furthermore, the expression τὰ τοῦ with the genitive of a noun is never found in the NT with the sense of 'the house of'.[7] Yet this is not to say that it cannot have this

---

1. As the history of interpretation well testifies. For a full account of the solutions that have been proposed from patristic to modern times, see Laurentin, *Jésus au Temple*, pp. 38-72.

2. For a listing of commentators who have favoured this translation in the last hundred years, see Sylva, 'The Cryptic Clause', p. 134.

3. For the much longer roll-call of those who have supported this translation, see again Sylva, 'The Cryptic Clause', p. 133.

4. De Jonge, 'Sonship, Wisdom, Infancy', p. 332. This is not unlike what we saw in 2.14 where the Lukan narrator had simply εὐδοκίας rather than the εὐδοκίας αὐτοῦ one might have expected if he were referring solely to the favour of God.

5. See Lk. 6.4 (Mk 2.26); 9.51 (where οἶκος is used for the sanctuary itself in a context where Matthew uses ναός [Mt. 23.35]); 19.46 (Mk 9.17); Acts 7.47.

6. As he does in 16.27 where we read εἶπεν δέ· ἐρωτῶ σε οὖν πάτερ ἵνα πέμψῃς αὐτὸν εἰς τὸν οἶκον τοῦ πατρός μου .

7. See Mk 8.33 ('the things of God'); Mt. 22.21 ('the things of Caesar. . . the things of God'); 1 Cor. 2.11 ('the thoughts of a man'); 1 Cor. 7.32, 34 ('the things

sense in 2.49, since evidence from outside the NT suggests that it can.[1]
Still, that does not answer the question, why if he wanted to say no
more than that did Luke choose so odd an expression?

De Jonge offers four reasons in support of the claim that the phrase
cannot mean only 'in my father's house':

1. The δεῖ looks comprehensively to all that will be involved in
   the unfolding of God's plan. Its sweep is too broad to allow
   so restrictive an understanding.

2. Having just said that he must be ἐν τοῖς τοῦ πατρός μου,
   Jesus leaves the Temple in 2.51 and retires to Nazareth,
   which implies that he is as much ἐν τοῖς τοῦ πατρός μου in
   Nazareth as he was in the Temple. Location is not decisive.

3. The incomprehension of the parents is the result not just of
   the play on the word 'father', as Laurentin claims,[2] but of the
   enigmatic character of Jesus' entire pronouncement. That the
   narrator has the parents perplexed immediately after the
   pronouncement suggests that he wants to underscore the
   ambiguity of what Jesus has said. Their perplexity would be
   hard to explain if the narrator had meant Jesus simply to say
   that he must be 'in the house of my father'.

4. The question οὐκ ἤδειτε ὅτι ἐν τοῖς τοῦ πατρός μου δεῖ
   εἶναί με; presumes a positive answer from the parents. Yet
   they cannot have been expected to know that Jesus was in the
   Temple. What they might have been expected to know, however, is that Jesus as God's son must take his unique place in
   the unfolding divine plan.

Taken together, these are persuasive enough to suggest that 'in the
house of my father' is one of several meanings that the narrator
gathers together in the ambiguity of ἐν τοῖς τοῦ πατρός μου—an
ambiguity best caught in a literal and unspecific translation such as
'the things of my father'. The effect of the ambiguity is to leave the
readers sharing the parents' perplexity and asking what it might mean

of the Lord'); 1 Cor. 13.11 ('the things of a child').
    1. See LXX Job 18.19; Tob. 6.2; Esth. 7.9. See too the evidence from the
papyri presented by J.H. Moulton, *Einleitung in die Sprache des Neuen Testaments*
(Heidelberg: Winter, 1911), p. 167, and from the Greek authors (including the
Fathers) presented by Laurentin, *Jésus au Temple*, pp. 58-61.
    2. Laurentin, *Jésus au Temple*, p. 78.

to be 'in the things of my father'?[1]—which question will be answered in the course of the entire Lukan narrative. At this early point of the narrative, what matters is not that the question be answered, but that it be made clear to both characters and readers that, however perplexing his actions may be, Jesus always acts as Son of God and therefore in obedience to the will of the God he calls 'my father'.[2] In this episode and in a way proleptic of the Gospel narrative, Jesus has acted in obedience to the divine will. Again something which seems at odds with any conventional understanding of what God might want is interpreted as the result of the divine will;[3] and this again looks to the Lukan narrative as a whole, which will spell out the detail of the obedience proclaimed by Jesus and thus illumine the enigma created by the ambiguity of v. 49b.

As Jesus comes to the point of revelation in v. 49, there emerges a distinctively Lukan christology which has Jesus as prime interpreter of himself. The narrator has him assume the leadership in the interpretative task as the one who reveals the coherence between his identity and his action; and this is a role he will retain throughout the Third Gospel.

A christology such as this has its roots in the OT christology which has dominated the infancy narrative to this point, but which has its own originality—particularly in the way it focuses upon Jesus as interpreter.[4] As the initiative passes to Jesus, the OT citations and

1.   De Jonge, 'Sonship, Wisdom, Infancy', pp. 331-37. See also Sylva, 'The Cryptic Clause', where he argues for an understanding of the phrase as a *double entendre*, though along different lines than does De Jonge.

2.   On the connection between Jesus as Son of God and obedience to the Father, see the remarks of O. Cullmann, *The christology of the New Testament* (Philadelphia: Westminster Press, 1959), p. 270. In the Temptation scene (4.1-13), it is precisely as Son of God that Jesus will be tested (vv. 3, 9) and as Son of God will show himself wholly obedient to God.

3.   At the same time, Jesus does not say why God might have wanted him to do something which by any ordinary reckoning is odd; nor does he specify what God wants except in the vaguest terms. This continues the interplay of revelation and concealment.

4.   Such a christology will take a crucial step forward in Lk. 4.16-30 (on which see Aletti, *L'art de raconter*, pp. 39-61) and come to full flower finally in Lk. 24.13-49 (on which see Aletti, *L'art de raconter*, pp. 177-98). In both episodes, Jesus appears as he does already in this episode in the role of 'l'unique herméneute' (Aletti, *L'art de raconter*, p. 42).

echoes dwindle to almost nothing, and the language becomes less heavily semitized. As Jesus comes to a language of his own, the language of the past becomes more muted. To this point, Jesus has been interpreted by other characters using the language of the OT, but now he interprets himself using a language of his own. Now it is to him that both characters and readers must listen. In a narrative which has been so absorbed by the human response to God's action, it is not surprising that we find a christology which includes the element of response, which displays 'a dominance of the cognitive'.

If it is unclear exactly what Jesus' statement means, it is still less clear how he has come to the knowledge of God's will which allows him to become the interpreter he is shown to be in v. 49. In 2.1-21, right interpretation came about through the exchange between the angel and the shepherds: the shepherds were able to interpret rightly because of the angelic revelation. In 2.22-40, right interpretation was the result of the influence of the Holy Spirit upon Simeon and Anna: they were able to interpret rightly because of the impulse of the Holy Spirit. But now nothing is said of either angelic revelation or the Holy Spirit's impulse, with the result that whatever has passed between God and Jesus seems more direct and more hidden. Where in the earlier episodes the narrator introduced both heavenly agents and human characters, now in this episode Jesus appears as both heavenly agent and human character, as the point at which divine visitation and human recognition, theology and epistemology converge. Again we see how the episode serves as a point of convergence in the narrative.

The absence of any special heavenly prompting suggests that Jesus has acted freely and independently in a way true of neither the shepherds nor Simeon and Anna. Similarly, 'he remained' (ὑπέμεινεν) in v. 43 and 'have you done' (ἐποίησας) in v. 48, both with Jesus as subject, suggest that it is Jesus who has taken the initiative; and to have him at the age of twelve puts him at the age of discretion at which he is capable of independent action.[1] It appears, then, that the narrator is keen to underscore that Jesus has acted in free obedience to what he has come to recognize as God's will.

At the same time, the δεῖ ('it is necessary') of v. 49 reintroduces into the narrative's presentation of the divine plan the dynamic of necessity which appeared first in 1.5-25. This is the first of the many

---

1. On which see Brown, *Birth of the Messiah*, p. 473.

appearances of the Lukan δεῖ;[1] and here as often throughout the Lukan narrative it implies subjection to an already declared divine plan which seeks human collaboration but is not thwarted by human rejection. In 1.5-25, the narrator began to orchestrate the paradox of divine necessity and human freedom; and in the last episode of the infancy narrative he returns to the same theme in a different key. The paradox now is that Jesus freely recognizes and collaborates with a divine plan which has its own dynamic of necessity.

Jesus has come to a knowledge of what God asks of him and of the necessity that imposes on him—a knowledge which enables right interpretation and which is the fruit of neither heavenly revelation nor precocious human intelligence. It comes instead from the peculiar relationship with God which Jesus proclaims in v. 49. He describes his relationship with God as a father–son relationship; and it is this that is implied as the source of the knowledge that enables his interpretation.[2]

---

1.   δεῖ occurs 18 times in Luke and 24 times in Acts—enough to make it a distinctively Lukan expression when compared to its frequency in other NT writings (Matthew 8 times; Mark 6 times; John 10 times; Pauline Letters 16 times; Pastorals 9 times; Hebrews 3 times; 1 Peter once; 2 Peter once; Revelation 8 times). It can refer to fulfilment of the prescriptions of the law (Lk. 13.14) or even norms of human conduct (Lk. 15.32); but it refers more frequently and distinctively in the Lukan narrative to Jesus' proclamation of the kingdom of God and his sharing of the fate of the prophets in Jerusalem. See further C.H. Cosgrove, 'The Divine ΔEI in Luke–Acts: Investigations into the Understanding of God's Providence', *NovT* 26 (1984), pp. 168-90; J. Dupont, 'Jésus retrouvé au temple', *AsSeign* 11 (1970), pp. 46-47; and De Jonge, 'Sonship, Wisdom, Infancy', pp. 350-51, where he concludes that 'the verb δεῖ refers in the first place to the necessity with which God's intention, once revealed, must be fulfilled; and only in the second place does it refer to the duty which God laid upon Jesus, and which Jesus took upon himself' (p. 351). Laurentin claims that the Lukan δεῖ is 'l'expression-clé pour signifier le Mystère pascal' (*Jésus au Temple*, p. 102), restricting its meaning to Jesus' return to the Father through his death and resurrection. He thus reads the words of Jesus in 2.49 as a foreshadowing of Jesus' return 'chez mon Père' by way of the paschal mystery. There is no doubt that the Lukan δεῖ does have this connotation at times, especially in Jesus' predictions of his death and resurrection. But it has other connotations as well, which Laurentin seems not to admit. The Lukan δεῖ looks not just to the paschal mystery, but to the entire sweep of God's plan, the heart of which is of course the paschal mystery, but the ramifications of which extend further. Laurentin is too restrictive in his interpretation.

2.   If Jesus' peculiar knowledge in this episode does look back to his peculiar conception (and hence his peculiar relationship with God), then the claim of, for

Jesus may proclaim his dependence upon the God he calls ὁ πατήρ μου, yet it works the other way as well. God is seen to depend upon Jesus—at least in the narrative.[1] Until now, God has not been mentioned at all in the episode. This is in contrast to the previous episode where God was mentioned repeatedly by both narrator and characters.[2] In this episode, however, the narrator holds the mention of God until he can have Jesus speak of God and for God. For the first time, therefore, God enters the narrative through Jesus.

Interpreting the Enigma: Luke 2.50-52

The Puzzlement of the Parents: Luke 2.50

In turning from Jesus to the parents, the narrator has them make no reply. Unable to come to the right interpretation to which Jesus has come and which he has passed on,[3] they are reduced to a silence which contrasts with the proclamation he has made as fruit of his own recognition. With the parents reduced to silence by their incomprehension, the narrator infringes his rule of external narration and offers an inside view of the characters, speaking for them since they cannot speak for themselves.

There is much that Mary and Joseph know, but as the unfolding of

instance, J.A. Fitzmyer ('The Virginal Conception of Jesus in the New Testament', *TS* 34 [1973], p. 552; *Luke*, p. 435) that after 1.26-38 the virginal conception of Jesus has no influence on the narrative looks less than wholly convincing.

1.   Just as Mary with her ὁ πατήρ σου κἀγώ in v. 48 speaks for both Joseph and herself, Jesus with his ἐν τοῖς τοῦ πατρός μου δεῖ εἶναί με speaks for both God and himself.

2.   God is mentioned by the narrator nine times (vv. 22, 23 [twice], 24, 26, 28, 38, 39, 40) and once by Simeon (v. 29). On this see Laurentin, *Les Evangiles*, p. 240.

3.   Neither the *Infancy Gospel of Thomas* nor *Ta Paidika tu Kyriu* mentions any incomprehension on the part of the parents—presumably because they felt it inappropriate that Mary in particular should be shown as having anything less than full knowledge and comprehension of her son's divinity. So too Laurentin (*Jésus au Temple*, p. 184) denies that the reference is to any lack of understanding of Jesus' divine filiation (but see the rejection of the claim by Brown, *Birth of the Messiah*, p. 484 n. 19). For a detailed account of the many attempts to exonerate Mary from any hint of incomprehension, see Muñoz Iglesias, *Evangelios*, III, pp. 261-67, where he concludes: 'Pienso que a la base de todas estas interpretaciones forzadas de Lc 2,50 hay un presupuesto mariológico que se da por inconcluso y que no es tan cierto' (p. 265).

the divine plan becomes more enigmatic there is another interpretation to which they must come. It is not that they did not know that Jesus must be 'in the things of my father'; what is puzzling is that for him to be 'in the things of my father' should mean the kind of thing he has done.[1] Throughout the Third Gospel, Jesus will be shown as consistently 'in the things of my father', but often in enigmatic ways, most especially in the Passion narrative. But here for the first time, and in ways proleptic of the whole, a gap is set between the 'what' and the 'how' of Jesus' being 'in the things of my father'. The 'what' is no problem: 'I must be in the things of my father'. The problem is the 'how', since in the Third Gospel for Jesus to be 'in the things of my father' will often involve—as it has in this episode—actions and situations far removed from conventional perceptions of 'the things of God'.

Jesus has come to a right interpretation of what it means for him to be 'in the things of my father', however strange it may seem. In that sense, he has come to an understanding (σύνεσις) surpassing the understanding (σύνεσις) which drew such amazement in v. 47. There his questions and answers were understood and admired on that basis; but now his questions and answers, which voice a different understanding, are not understood and draw no admiration. Yet this new understanding is the understanding to which the characters and readers must come if they are to understand how Jesus is always 'in the things of my father'.

1. Commentators have identified in different ways what exactly it was that puzzled the parents. Laurentin (*Jésus au Temple*, pp. 174-76) claims that Mary in particular is puzzled by the hidden reference to the paschal mystery in Jesus' words; F. Spadafora ('"Et ipsi non intellexerunt" [Lc 2,50]', *Divinitas* 11 [1967], pp. 55-70) has the parents puzzled by the fact that Jesus should make them suffer so; E. Burrows (*The Gospel of the Infancy and Other Biblical Essays* [London: Burns, Oates & Washbourne, 1940], pp. 1-58) claims that Jesus remained at the Temple in levitical service because the redemption price had not been paid in the previous episode and that it was this the parents failed to understand; J.B. Cortes and F.M. Gatti ('Jesus' First Recorded Words [Lk 2,49-50]', *Marianum* 32 [1970], pp. 404-18) claim that Jesus had said something to his parents before they set out on the return journey and that it was this, had they understood it, which would have enabled them to comprehend what had happened; and finally, M.A. Power ('Who Were They Who 'Understood Not'?', *ITQ* 7 [1922], pp. 261-81, 444-59) cuts the Gordian knot by claiming that αὐτοί in v. 50 refers not to the parents, but to those standing around (οἱ διδάσκαλοι). None of these is satisfactory from a narrative point of view.

The initiative in the interpretative task passes at this point from angels and inspired human characters to Jesus. This is another way of saying that it passes from God to Jesus, since though he has chosen to work through angels and the Holy Spirit it has been God who held the initiative. But now, with no mention of either angels or the Holy Spirit, the initiative passes to Jesus. From now on, to interpret rightly the signs of God's action both characters and readers will need to listen to Jesus.[1]

Action as Interpretation: Luke 2.51a

At first sight it seems strange that Jesus, having just announced that he must be 'in the things of my father', should return to Nazareth with Joseph and Mary. Having proclaimed his allegiance to his heavenly father, Jesus returns to the town of the man who appears to be his father. This immediately expands the sense of what it means for him to be 'in the things of my father'. It means not only that he stay unexpectedly in Jerusalem or the Temple, but also that he return with Joseph and Mary to Nazareth. Clearly, then, it is not location that decides what it might mean for Jesus to be 'in the things of my father'.

What is decisive is that wherever he is Jesus be obedient to the will of his heavenly father; and it appears that the will of his heavenly father now is that he be obedient to the will of his parents, as is suggested by 'he was subject to them' (ἦν ὑποτασσόμενος αὐτοῖς), which may be read as a divine passive.[2] To return with them does not imply a return to the logic of convention voiced in Mary's question nor an immediate revision of the different logic implied in Jesus' reply. If he returns to Nazareth with his parents, it is within the context established by v. 49. Again we find a convergence of God's will (ἦν ὑποτασσόμενος) and his own free decision ('he went down'

---

1.   This will be said explicitly by the voice from heaven in 9.35: οὗτός ἐστιν ὁ υἱός μου ὁ ἐκλελεγμένος, αὐτοῦ ἀκούετε. It is not however said in the Lukan version of the Baptism (3.21-22). But this is because it has already been shown in a preliminary way in 2.41-52 and will be shown quite fully and explicitly in 4.16-30. This is an instance of the Lukan narrator's preference for showing over telling.

2.   The stress on Jesus' obedience here contrasts with the *Gospel of Pseudo-Matthew* 13.1-2, where Jesus so dominates the life of the family that all seem subject to him. Compare too the *Arabic Infancy Gospel* 53.2, which stresses how completely Jesus pleased his parents in everything—presumably to compensate for the pain he has caused them in this episode.

[κατέβη], with Jesus the subject). His obedience to the will of God may entail a transcendence of parental authority, but this does not mean a rejection of parental authority. This is as we have seen it with both imperial and Mosaic authority in the previous two episodes.

No sooner has Jesus come enigmatically to centre stage than the narrator decides to remove him until he reappears years later in 3.21, with only the second growth-report in v. 52 between now and then. Jesus may disappear from centre stage and John may reappear in 3.2, but for all the comings and goings of the key characters the plan of God will remain at centre stage. Indeed what emerges is that their comings and goings are part of God's unfolding plan.

The Remembering of Mary: Luke 2.51b
In v. 51b, the narrator offers a new inside view of Mary, and one that looks back to both 1.66 and 2.19. In the two earlier instances, the report implied three things:

1.   Words are heard which are not understood.
2.   The words have mysterious and portentous implications for the future of the one spoken about.
3.   The act of storing in the heart implies not only incomprehension, but also an openness to clarification in the future, a preparedness to live with unclarity in the belief that clarity will come in time.

The same is true in this third instance, though as in 2.19 it is not only the words spoken which are puzzling, but also the events witnessed.[1] In the three instances the words spoken and the one speaking them are different, but the pattern is the same, as is the purpose of the remembering. In 2.19, it was what the shepherds said of Jesus which was puzzling and portentous, but here it is what Jesus says of himself. By placing the report of Mary's remembering after the report of her incomprehension, the narrator makes it clear that her remembering relates to the way in which she deals with incomprehension. This is as it was in 2.19, where we saw that the question was not whether faith and incomprehension were compatible, but how faith handles incomprehension.

The narrator has Mary ponder not only what she hears from Jesus,

---

1.   This is again to understand τὰ ῥήματα as 'things' in the sense of events rather than simply as 'words'.

but also the odd juxtaposition of his statement in the Temple that he must be 'in the things of my father' and his return to Nazareth in subjection to his parents. The narrator might well have chosen to place the report of Mary's remembering immediately after the report of her incomprehension, at the start of v. 51. But he chooses instead to insert between the reports of Mary's incomprehension and remembering the report of Jesus' return to Nazareth in subjection to his parents. This implies that it is not only Jesus' enigmatic words which call for pondering, but also his return to Nazareth and his subjection to his parents. Like the readers, Mary must ponder what it might mean for Jesus to be 'in the things of my father', given that it can mean both his puzzling stay in Jerusalem and his less puzzling return to Nazareth. In her remembering, Mary begins to traverse the gap between the 'what' and the 'how' of Jesus being 'in the things of my father'. She grapples with the enigma of what it means for Jesus to be Son of God.

The Growth of Jesus: Luke 2.52
In another example of the Lukan technique of reprise, the two growth-reports of vv. 40 and 52 are similar but not identical, as the following schematic presentation helps to see:

	Verse 40	Verse 52
1.	'But the child'	'And Jesus'
	τὸ δὲ παιδίον	καὶ Ἰησοῦς
2.	'grew and became strong'	'increased'
	ηὔξανεν καὶ ἐκραταιοῦτο	προέκοπτεν
3.	'filled with wisdom'	'in wisdom and stature'
	πληρούμενον σοφίᾳ	ἐν τῇ σοφίᾳ καὶ ἡλικίᾳ
4.	'and the grace of God	'and in grace
	was upon him'	with God and human beings'
	καὶ χάρις	καὶ χάριτι
	θεοῦ ἦν ἐπ' αὐτό	παρὰ θεῷ καὶ ἀνθρώποις

A number of differences are worth noting. First, in v. 52 the narrator names Jesus absolutely for the first time in the infancy narrative. Earlier in this episode, where named at all, he has been 'the boy Jesus' (Ἰησοῦς ὁ παῖς)—from the narrator in v. 43—and 'child' (τέκνον)—from Mary in v. 48); and in the previous episodes he was 'this child' (τοῦ παιδίου τούτου, 2.17), 'the child Jesus' (τὸ παιδίον Ἰησοῦν, 2.27) and 'the child' (τὸ παιδίον, 2.40). But now as he becomes for the first time an independent agent in the narrative, he becomes simply 'Jesus' ('Ιησοῦς).

Secondly, the addition of 'to human beings' (ἀνθρώποις) gives the sense of Jesus as one who has entered the public arena and who is becoming increasingly the object of human attention, as the episode has indeed shown. Where in v. 40 there was the sense that things were between Jesus and God, in v. 52 there is more the sense that things are between Jesus, God and human beings, as they have been in this last episode.

A third difference is that the phrase 'the grace of God was upon him' (χάρις θεοῦ ἦν ἐπ' αὐτό) in v. 40 conveys a more passive sense than does 'in grace with God and human beings' (χάριτι παρὰ θεῷ καὶ ἀνθρώποις) in v. 52. The movement in v. 40 is from God to Jesus, where the movement in v. 52 is more from Jesus to God and human beings. This is again appropriate at a point where Jesus has become for the first time an independent agent in the narrative.

Conclusion

In the previous two episodes, other characters, both heavenly and human, have interpreted the strange ways of fulfilment of the divine promise emerging in Jesus. In this final episode, the unfolding fulfilment of Gabriel's promise is again shown to be strange as Jesus leaves his parents and stays in Jerusalem; and the question is, who will interpret what Jesus has done? Earlier it was visionary shepherds and inspired prophets who had rightly perceived the coherence between the 'what' of the promise (who Jesus is) and the 'how' of fulfilment (how Jesus appears). In this episode however there has been no mention of either angels or the Holy Spirit. It is Jesus himself who becomes the interpreter of himself and his action, the one who reveals the coherence between who he is and what he has done. In v. 49, it becomes apparent that Jesus has separated himself from his parents and stayed in Jerusalem not simply because of a penchant for theological debate, but because he is Son of God and therefore in filial obedience to God's will. For all that it may seem strange, what Jesus has done is what God wants. In having him make that revelation, the narrator has Jesus assume the leadership in the interpretative task.

In the final episode of the infancy narrative divine visitation and human recognition, theology and epistemology, converge to produce a

distinctively Lukan christology which will remain decisive through
the whole of the Third Gospel. In this sense, the infancy narrative
which begins as theology and epistemology becomes christology. At
that point Jesus becomes prime mover in the narrative, now fully
qualified to play the unique role which will be his in the Gospel
narrative.

The christology that emerges has its roots in the OT christology
which has dominated the infancy narrative to this point, but which has
its own originality in the way it focuses upon Jesus as interpreter of
himself. As this christology is born, the voice of the OT falls silent
and it is the voice of Jesus, speaking in accents of his own, which is
heard. In a narrative which has been so absorbed by the human
response to God's action it is not surprising that we find a christology
which includes the element of response, which displays 'a dominance
of the cognitive'.

Yet the interpretation that Jesus offers in v. 49 is so enigmatic that
it prompts at least as many questions as it answers. The ambiguity of
v. 49 leaves both characters and readers asking what the phrase 'in the
things of my father' might mean. The question becomes more perplexing with Jesus' return to Nazareth in obedience to Mary and
Joseph; and it is the question that the entire Lukan narrative will set
itself to answer. What the programmatic statement of v. 49 implies is
that, however strange the words and deeds of Jesus may seem in the
narrative which follows, he is always speaking and acting as Son of
God and therefore in obedience to the God he calls 'my father'.
Throughout the Third Gospel, therefore, it is Jesus himself who in
word and action will answer the question his own words and actions in
this episode have stirred.

Step by step through the episode the narrator has brought the parents and the readers to a point of convergence. From vv. 43-46 the
readers are in a position of privilege, which means that they and the
parents face different questions: the latter ask 'where is Jesus?', the
former ask, 'why in Jerusalem?' At v. 46, however, parents and
readers learn together that Jesus is in the Temple among the teachers.
In v. 48, Mary formulates the question shared by the parents and the
readers—'why?' Parents and readers listen together to Jesus' reply in
v. 49, and both find it puzzling. This means that from now on in the
Gospel narrative the readers, though knowing more than most of the
characters, must listen to Jesus as much as any of the characters. In

that sense, it is not only a distinctively Lukan protagonist who is born in this episode, but also a distinctively Lukan reader.

As Jesus comes finally to centre stage in the narrative, both God and the narrator become more discreet than ever. God is not mentioned at all until he appears as 'my father' in v. 49, and then it is Jesus rather than the narrator who mentions him. Both God and the narrator pass the word to Jesus. The style of narration becomes still more elliptical, with the narrator punctuating the episode with large silences and for the most part holding to an external mode of narration.[1] At no point are the readers offered an inside view of Jesus nor is anything said of what might have passed between God and Jesus. In that sense, Jesus is both revealed and concealed; and from now on in the Third Gospel, it will be he rather than either God or the narrator who will control the interplay of revelation and concealment.

---

1. In vv. 44 (νομίσαντες), 48 (ἐξεπλάγησαν), 50 (οὐ συνῆκαν) and 51 (διετήρει. . . ἐν τῇ καρδίᾳ αὐτῆς), the narrator offers inside views of the parents; but in the crucial v. 48 it is Mary herself who speaks.

Chapter 9

THE NARRATIVE BORN

At the end of the path traced by the art of the Lukan narrator through the infancy narrative, we are in a position to formulate conclusions—first at the point of narrative strategy and then at the point of narrative statement.

Narrative Strategy: The Ways of the Midwife

The study has brought to light a range of techniques by means of which the narrator has shaped his vision of the divine visitation and human recognition of it; and in that sense it has shown how the narrator functions as midwife in bringing the narrative to birth.[1] The work of the narrator as midwife consists in establishing patterns of relationship between, first, the narrator, God, the characters and the readers, and, secondly, the various elements of the narrative (episodes, characters, times, places, worlds).

Narrator, God, Characters, Readers
Narratorial Discretion. It has emerged that the narrator prefers a discretion which shows itself in a variety of ways. For the most part, the narration is external, with the few inside views shallow and stereotyped. The Lukan narrator prefers to let the characters speak for themselves, especially at key moments of revelation, evaluation and interpretation. In broader terms, this amounts to a preference for

---

1. In many of the apocryphal accounts of the birth of Jesus, the midwife appears as a key character: she enters the narrative tradition at a later point to meet what was perceived to be a need. So too with the Lukan narrator: he enters the narrative tradition at a later point to meet a perceived need. In the apocryphal accounts the midwife assists at the birth of Jesus; and the Lukan narrator plays a key role in bringing the Lukan narrative to birth.

showing over telling. In effacing himself and allowing the characters to speak for themselves, the narrator appears as one who is keen to show the characters grappling with the divine visitation, to have them show rather than him tell the readers.

Yet for all that the narration is external, the narrator appears as one who enjoys omniscience. This is all the more striking after the claim of the prologue (1.3): 'it seemed good to me also, having followed all things closely, to write an orderly account for you' (ἔδοξε κἀμοὶ παρηκολουθηκότι ἄνωθεν πᾶσιν ἀκριβῶς καθεξῆς σοι γράψαι). Sternberg charges that '[Luke's] practice flatly contradicts his empirical undertaking and terms of reference'.[1] Sternberg insists upon 'the sharp line drawn (by the OT) between limited and omniscient discourse'[2] and the difference (scrupulously respected by the OT narrators but not by Luke) between 'the two models of narrative, the inspirational and the empirical'.[3] Sternberg sees the Lukan narrative as moving clumsily from the empirical in the prologue to the inspirational in the narrative proper.

Yet in the infancy narrative the line between the two models of narrative is not as sharp as Sternberg implies. First, it is not certain that the prologue amounts to the clear choice of empirical narration and therefore the 'virtual' refusal of omniscience that Sternberg notes. It is a question of how to read the phrase: 'having followed all things closely' (παρηκολουθηκότι ἄνωθεν πᾶσιν ἀκριβῶς). Sternberg takes it to mean an 'empirical undertaking', as if 'all things' (πᾶσιν) referred to the facts in an empirical sense. Yet πᾶσιν could be understood less empirically to include a survey of the existing narratives mentioned in v. 1 and an assessment of the pastoral need that prompts the Lukan composition. On this understanding, the prologue would mean that the narrator, having surveyed existing narratives and the situation of the narratee, decides that the existing narratives are not designed to confer the desired sense of well-foundedness (ἀσφάλεια) and therefore sets himself to compose a different kind of narrative which will.

Secondly, the narrative which begins at v. 5 does not display the same kind of omniscience as the OT narrator. This is because the Lukan narrator's omniscience is limited in three ways: first, his inside

1. Sternberg, *Poetics*, p. 86.
2. Sternberg, *Poetics*, p. 86.
3. Sternberg, *Poetics*, p. 87.

views are few, shallow and stereotyped; secondly, he has access to the earthly effects of God's decisions, but no access to the process of heavenly decision-making, that is, no access to the mind of God in the way of the OT narrator; and thirdly, it is the heavenly messengers rather than the narrator who display omniscience with regard to what God has decided.

What we have in the Lukan narrative, then, is a blurring of the sharp line upon which Sternberg insists. Sternberg suggests as an explanation for this either inadvertence, greed or carelessness on the Lukan narrator's part, and claims that this leads to a wobbling point of view very different from the OT narrator's mastery of point of view. Yet if the Lukan narrator is moving from a different ideological matrix (that is, an ideology of incarnation,[1] using 'ideology' here in Sternberg's sense), then the blurring of the line may be read less as a clumsy wobble than as a ploy by a narrator looking to stage a God whose action in Jesus blurs the sharp line between heaven and earth upon which OT narrative insists. As God works in history, the narrator works in the narrative. This looks to the narrative as a rhetorical correlate of God's action.

What the Lukan narrator's omniscience involves is a full knowledge of both the workings of heaven on earth and the response of the human characters to this—though on both counts he displays little knowledge of motivation, that is, why God acts in this way or why the characters respond as they do. In a way denied to the human characters, the narrator has access to all the earthly arenas of the action. This is a knowledge he must have if he is to show the whole of the divine visitation and human recognition of it in a way that might provide the promised sense of well-foundedness (ἀσφάλεια).[2] The alternative is that he fall prey to the partial vision which makes the characters' journey to recognition less than straightforward. In the Lukan narrator, therefore, we have a relative omniscience which does not align him completely with either God or the heavenly messengers, but which does separate him from the human characters and so enables him to perform the task he sets himself in the prologue.

The narrator's discretion shows itself too in the way he handles

---

1.   Which is not to imply that the infancy narrative voices a Johannine theology of the incarnation of the pre-existent Word, on which see Fitzmyer, *Luke*, p. 340.

2.   On the the connection between a showing mode and narratorial omniscience, see Aletti, *L'art de raconter*, p. 223.

Scripture. In contrast to Matthew, the Lukan narrator does not cite Scripture explicitly or signal how specific biblical promises have been fulfilled.[1] Scripture is ubiquitous in the infancy narrative—in echo, allusion, indirect citation, images, vocabulary; yet it is not once cited explicitly.[2] Scripture is understood as promise in its entirety, and the narrator is keen to stage the fulfilment of the biblical promise. But he prefers to show the fulfilment rather than tell the reader in the explicit and magisterial way preferred by Matthew.

The Privileged Readers. In the first phase of the infancy narrative, the readers are beneficiaries of the narrator's omniscience and as such are consistently privileged over the characters, who learn what the readers already know. A knowledge gap is set between readers and characters in a way that opens two quite different epistemological paths in the narrative. From the position of privilege granted by the narrator, the readers may follow the responses of the various characters, and so see what it is that makes for right or wrong recognition of God's visitation.

In the second phase, however, the situation changes, as on a number of occasions the readers learn belatedly with the characters. The angelic revelation in 2.12, Simeon's prophecy in 2.34-35, and Jesus' statement in 2.49 are all moments where the readers learn at the same time as the characters. This is in contrast to the first phase where the readers learn before the characters. By the end of the infancy narrative reader-privilege has been undermined if not abolished, as the readers find themselves wondering with the parents first why Jesus has disappeared and then why God should want it this way. The tactic makes it clear that there is a point where the readers, though privileged, must also listen to Jesus as prime interpreter.

Revelation and Concealment. Throughout the infancy narrative, there is an interplay between revelation and concealment.[3] However much is revealed to readers or characters, there are things (and often important

1. For the contrast, see the formula quotations of Mt. 1.22; 2.15; 2.17-18; 2.23.

2. In the Third Gospel Scripture is cited explicitly only once—by Jesus (not by the narrator) in 22.37. On four other occasions it is again Jesus who mentions explicitly the fulfilment of Scripture in the events taking place (4.21; 18.31; 21.22; 24.44). On this, see Aletti, *L'art de raconter*, pp. 194-95.

3. On which see Aletti, *L'art de raconter*, p. 77.

things) that remain unrevealed. There are things that the characters are not told (especially at the point of 'how') or told only belatedly; and there are things not told the readers (especially at the point of 'how') or things of which they learn belatedly with the characters. Gabriel, for instance, in the first two episodes announces 'what' but little of 'how'; the 'why' of God's action is never disclosed (why this time, this place, these characters?); the narrative remains silent at vital moments such as the conception of Jesus; the inner world of the characters remains for the most part closed to the readers, with the result that their motivation is often obscure.

The interplay of revelation and concealment serves the narrative's understanding of both revelation and recognition as process; and process means that there will be an element of concealment until the end when all will be revealed and recognized. In the meantime, the interplay of revelation and concealment in the narrative provides the dynamic of the reading process: it ensures that the readers read on.

The Role of Mary. Mary is unique among the characters for a number of reasons. For one thing, she is privileged over all other human characters in what she knows. She knows more of the identity of her son; yet strangely this becomes a problem, since it aggravates the sense of incoherence between his identity and the circumstances of his appearance. For Mary, then, unique privilege means unique pondering.

She is also the one character to straddle both phases of the infancy narrative; and as such she embodies the processes of both divine visitation and human recognition of it. God first makes the promise; and Mary then conceives, gives birth to and nurtures Jesus. Here we have the process of promise and fulfilment in the divine visitation. To this there corresponds the process of faith and interpretation: Mary reads the Scripture aright, believes the promise, comes to praise, but then must grapple with the puzzling signs of fulfilment which seem at odds with the promise. Three times in the second phase she is said to be astonished, and never more so than at the end of the last episode, where it is said explicitly that she does not understand the meaning of what Jesus has said and done. Her puzzlement means that she must reconsider what she has heard and seen, engage in 'a rereading of the series of signs'[1] such as is implied in the references to her pondering

---

1.   Aletti, *L'art de raconter*, p. 189.

in 2.19 and 2.51b. Faced with the interplay of revelation and concealment, the readers must read on; faced with the same interplay, Mary is committed to a process of rereading the signs of God's action.

In her initial act of faith in the promise and in her grappling with the signs of fulfilment, Mary is the character in whom the narrator provides an answer to the question insinuated in the first episode: what does Abrahamic faith look like now? The question was discreetly put and the answer is discreetly given. Rather than tell the readers what the answer might be, the narrator prefers to show Abrahamic faith in Mary, and to do so not quickly but step by step in a process which begins in 1.26-38 and which remains unfinished even at the end of the infancy narrative.

Throughout the infancy narrative, Mary is cast in a receiving mode. Others take the initiative and she responds: Gabriel comes to her bearing the promise; an inspired Elizabeth speaks first in 1.39-56; the shepherds come with their announcement; Simeon and Anna do the same; and it is Jesus who takes the initiative in the final episode. It is also true that Mary is never responsible for the transmission of the news she receives: in that sense, she never proclaims. This might suggest that Mary is a wholly passive character; yet this is not so. From 1.26-38 until the end of the infancy narrative, there is in her a paradoxical interaction of the active and passive. Her activity is primarily at the point of epistemology, much of which is inward though no less active for that. This suggests that it is epistemology rather than mariology which provides the key for understanding how Mary functions in the narrative.

Subversive Patterning

Every birth involves a kind of death, a separation from the world of the womb. So it is with the birth of Lukan christology. The narrator uses a variety of techniques to pattern the elements of his narrative: episodes, characters, times, places, worlds; and these techniques serve to subvert an old world in order that it may appear in the narrative that both a new world and a new mode of recognition come to birth in Jesus. The birth of the Lukan narrative means the severing of the umbilical cord; and this is the condition for the birth of new worlds, new convergences, new horizons such as we find in Luke 1–2. Narrative technique lies in service of that.

A Deliberate Dissonance. From the first, the narrator opens a gap between the 'what' of God's promise and the 'how' of its fulfilment, setting into the narrative a seeming incoherence which as the narrative unfolds is revealed as coherence.[1] In 1.5-25, it is strange that the promise of the messianic precursor is made to an elderly and childless couple, and also to a priest who fails to believe and is (again strangely) struck dumb. Yet despite all that tells against it the narration of fulfilment begins without delay as Elizabeth conceives. Only with John's birth in the fourth episode (1.57-80) does the full coherence of the 'what' of God's promise and the 'how' of its fulfilment appear in the narrative; and it is only then that Zechariah appears in the narrative as one who has come to discover the coherence lying beyond the seeming incoherence.

The sense of a seeming incoherence grows stronger in the second episode as the promise is made to an unwed woman of undistinguished provenance that she will virginally conceive the messiah. Unlike Zechariah, however, the woman finds her way to faith in the promise, that is, to a perception of the coherence lying beyond the seeming incoherence; and her faith will be vindicated by the events which the narrative recounts, as she gives birth to the messiah, albeit in surprising circumstances.

In these first two episodes many prophecies are made, and it is worth tracing their fate in the narrative. In 1.5-25, Gabriel promises that Elizabeth will conceive and the promise is fulfilled within the episode itself; the same is true of the angel's promise that Zechariah will be silent. A number of prophecies are made concerning the future ministry of John. One is fulfilled in 1.39-56—the promise of v. 15 that John will be filled with the Holy Spirit from his mother's womb, though the effect of the Spirit's impulse is to have John acclaim not the messiah but the messiah's mother as believer. Other prophecies are fulfilled in the account of John's ministry in 3.1-20—'he will be great before the Lord'; 'he will turn many of the sons of Israel to the Lord their God' and 'the hearts of the fathers to their children and the disobedient to the wisdom of the just'. The fulfilment of the prophecy that John 'will go before the Lord in the spirit and power of Elijah' is harder to see, given that it is Jesus rather than John who is cast in the

---

1. It is this which Aletti, in *L'art de raconter*, describes as a process of 'véridiction', a term that is felicitous in the French but does not pass easily into English. 'Verification' is a reasonably accurate if somewhat clumsy rendering.

mould of Elijah (4.25-26). At least one of Gabriel's prophecies concerning John is never fulfilled, since there is no hint in the narrative that John lived as a Nazarite.

In vv. 26-38, Gabriel prophesies that Mary will conceive, as she does—though we are never told when the Holy Spirit overshadows her. Concerning Jesus, Gabriel prophesies that he will be great, which is confirmed in the narrative, albeit in enigmatic ways. It is also said that God will give him the throne of his father, David, and that there will be no end to his reign; but when or how this happens is never said in the narrative. Gabriel announces that Jesus will be called Son of God; but it is not until Paul's proclamation in Acts 9.20 that we have a character actually call Jesus Son of God. Again the patterns of fulfilment are various and unpredictable; and they remain so throughout the infancy narrative's first phase, as Zechariah in the Benedictus makes a series of prophecies about the ministry of both his son and the messiah which are fulfilled in various and unpredictable ways in the ensuing narrative.

In the infancy narrative's second phase, as the focus turns little by little to Jesus, the dissonance becomes more precisely a gap between the 'what' of his identity as messiah and Son of God and the 'how' of his actual appearance and action. This prepares for the moment in which Jesus appears in the narrative as the one who, in offering the interpretation which discloses the coherence between who he is and what he has done, bridges the gap.

In 2.1-21 the promised child is born, but in poor circumstances which are strange after the grandeur of Gabriel's promise. Through the angel, heaven intervenes to reveal that, however strange it may seem that he who is the Davidic messiah and Son of God be laid in a manger, this is the way God wants it. The coherence between the 'what' of the promise and the 'how' of its fulfilment is revealed to the shepherds, who believe what they hear and so assume leadership in the interpretative task as they go to the birth scene.

In 2.22-40, the Davidic messiah and Son of God is brought to the Temple; and again the circumstances are puzzling. First, there is nothing exceptional about the child's appearance in the Temple: he comes as one among many born to parents of modest means. Nonetheless, the inspired Simeon and Anna recognize that this is the one through whom will come not only 'the consolation of Israel' and 'the redemption of Jerusalem', but also 'light for the revelation of the

Gentiles'. As inspired interpreters, Simeon and Anna recognize and proclaim the coherence between the child's identity and the circumstances of his appearance in the Temple. For the parents and the readers, the unexpected erupts in Simeon's oracle of vv. 34-35 where he looks to a future far stranger than anything in the present. In contrast to Gabriel whose oracles in 1.26-38 were wholly jubilant, Simeon foretells that the Davidic messiah and Son of God will become 'a sign spoken against', that he will bring judgment and will suffer rejection— and this as part of God's plan (reading 'he is set' [κεῖται] in v. 34 as a divine passive). The juxtaposition of the two oracles of Simeon—one jubilant, the other menacing—reveals a future in which the gap between the 'what' of Jesus' identity and the 'how' of his fate will grow much wider, making the task of interpretation correspondingly more difficult and the need for interpretation correspondingly more urgent. But it also implies that then as now there will be a coherence to be discovered by those who have ears to hear the interpretation which reveals the coherence.

In 2.41-52, what is puzzling is that the boy Jesus should leave his family and the company and install himself in the Temple among the teachers. It emerges eventually in the episode that Jesus has done this not because of an irresistible penchant for theological discussion, but because his identity as Son of God demands it. Yet what is strange (as the parents' reaction recognizes) is precisely that his identity as Son of God should demand such an action. As he reveals the coherence between his identity and his action in 2.49, leadership in the interpretative task passes from visionary shepherds and inspired prophets to Jesus. At that point, Jesus is born in the narrative as prime interpreter, and in that sense he assumes the role he will retain to the very end of the Third Gospel where he will be shown first on the road to Emmaus (24.25-27) expounding the Scriptures in a way that reveals the coherence between his messianic identity and the death he has suffered, and then in 24.44-47 performing a similar function among the apostles to whom leadership in the interpretative task will pass in Acts.

Throughout, then, the pattern of narration is clear. First, there is set into the narrative a seeming incoherence between the 'what' and the 'how' of God's action; secondly, the narrator begins a process of narration which reveals the coherence lying beyond the seeming incoherence; thirdly, as part of this process he introduces human characters who in various ways (and like the narrator himself) succeed in recognizing the coherence between the 'what' and the 'how' of God's action. These characters are Mary, Elizabeth, Zechariah, the shepherds, Simeon and Anna, and climactically of course Jesus.

Within this process of recognition by the human characters, the three hymns that the narrator sets into the narrative play a special role. Tracing the movement from one to the other, we trace the increasingly precise recognition by the characters of the shape of God's action. In the Magnificat, Mary celebrates the God who has always shown himself a saviour; in the Benedictus, Zechariah celebrates John as the one who will prepare for the climactic saving act now promised; and in the Nunc Dimittis Simeon celebrates Jesus as the embodiment of God's salvation. From hymn to hymn the focus shifts from God through John to Jesus; and this prepares for the moment when it will shift wholly to Jesus who will not only embody God's salvation but interpret its surprising ways; that is, interpret himself.

The Use of Reprise. Both in the detail of the narration and in the larger construction of the infancy narrative, there appears a technique of reprise which is quite different from the repetition it may at times seem to be. To offer a few of the many examples: the John–Jesus parallelism; the various modes of divine visitation (when, where, to whom and through whom); the various modes of human recognition (Zechariah, the People, Elizabeth, Mary, John, the crowd of neighbours and relatives, the shepherds, Simeon and Anna, the teachers and the parents); the different modes of praise in the three hymns; the similar structures of 1.5-25 and 1.26-38 and 2.1-21 and 2.22-40; the three scenes in the Temple.

In each case, elements already introduced are treated in a different way or set in a different context. This undermines any sense of repetition; and the roots of the technique lie in the narrative's conviction that the story now unfolding, though it may seem to repeat the past, in fact gathers up the past and brings it to a new point of fulfilment. The story of the Lukan narrative appears as a reprise of the story of Israel. This builds into the narrative a dynamic of retrospection and prospection. Insofar as familiar elements are re-introduced, the narrative is retrospective; and insofar as they are handled differently or joined to new elements the narrative becomes prospective.

The Handling of Time. The interplay of retrospection and prospection is clearest in the way the narrator handles time. Given the dynamic of promise-fulfilment and faith-interpretation which undergirds the narrative, there is a constant interplay between past, present and future, subverting any sense of the readers adrift in a present with no past and no future. The past is never simply 'back there'; nor is the future simply 'out there'. The narrator has past and future converge to create the present.

The narrative begins in 1.5-25 with clear echoes of the past, which sound in the infancy narrative until the final episode where they fall silent in order to focus wholly on the figure of Jesus. Until then, the echoes of the past become the promises which set the narrative in motion, all of them looking to a future fulfilment, the narration of which consumes most of the narrative's energies.

Of such a narrative, Rimmon-Kenan notes that '[p]rolepses. . . replace the kind of suspense deriving from the question 'What will happen next? by another kind of suspense, revolving around the question "How is it going to happen?"'[1] In Luke 1–2 however there is not only a question of how it is going to happen, but more importantly still a question of how human beings respond to what happens. This means that in the infancy narrative there is a stress upon cognition rather than action.[2] The narrator wants to establish the 'what' and the 'how' of the divine visitation, but he is more interested still in establishing the 'what' and the 'how' of the recognition this requires of the human being.

Moving between Worlds. The narrator moves not only in time, but also between worlds—for example between public and private, between sacred and secular—in order to stage their meeting. The narrative subverts dichotomies and posits relationships where there may have seemed to be none. At times, he simply juxtaposes two quite different worlds (for example the sway of Caesar and the sway of God in 2.1-21) without ever specifying exactly how he understands the

---

1. Rimmon-Kenan, *Narrative Fiction*, p. 48. See too Sternberg's comments which might be applied to the Lukan narrative: 'the Bible makes the most of this enforced shift from 'what' to 'how' hypotheses about the future by multiplying the adventures of meaning and experience en route to the predetermined end' (*Poetics*, p. 278).

2. Aletti, *L'art de raconter*, p. 37.

relationship between the two. At other times, he uses odd juxtapositions (for example Gabriel and Mary, Jesus and the manger, the angel and the shepherds), the effect of which is a defamiliarization underscoring the gap between the 'what' and the 'how' of the narrative.

Related to the defamiliarizing effect of such juxtapositions is the narrator's technique of the sudden switch (for example from Jerusalem to Nazareth, from the birth scene to the shepherds, from the parents and child to Simeon and Anna). In each case we have a switch from one world to another, in a way that not only highlights the diversity and comprehensiveness of the divine action, but also stages a meeting of worlds made possible only by the divine action.

A similar effect is achieved by the way in which the narrator stages the convergence of seemingly divergent paths. Initially, God is shown as working in different worlds which are made to converge. The first two episodes show a convergence of heaven and earth; those two episodes come to a point of convergence in the third; the separate stories of Caesar and God and of the shepherds and the parents converge in 2.1-21, as do the separate stories of the parents, Simeon and Anna in 2.22-40; and in the final episode the separate stories of the parents and Jesus converge. In each case, a physical convergence looks to a larger convergence of worlds.

Dissolving Symmetries. The opposite to the patterns of convergence are the dissolving symmetries appearing in the narrative. The symmetries, like the seeming repetitions, are shown to be more apparent than real; and this looks to the pervasive tendency of the infancy narrative to play with the difference between what is and what appears to be.

In the infancy narrative there are three levels:

1. There is first a superficial symmetry, with the order and coherence it implies. This is embodied in the narrative in such things as the John–Jesus parallelism and the dynamic of promise-fulfilment.
2. At another level, however, there is a deeper asymmetry, even incoherence and disorder, which emerges in the narrative as a seeming non-fulfilment of promises made. Between the 'what' of the promise and the 'how' of fulfilment there is consistently a gap; and figures such as Abraham and Zechariah, superficially so similar, emerge as quite dissimilar—as do the first two episodes for all that they seem alike.

3.   At a still deeper level, however, the infancy narrative brings
to light a coherence rooted in the plan of God, a coherence
lying beyond both superficial symmetry and apparent asymmetry. Only in the light of God's plan is this coherence
discovered; and it is at this level that the promised sense of
well-foundedness (ἀσφάλεια) may be found.

Transcending Horizons. Throughout the infancy narrative the narrator establishes horizons in order to transcend them in the narration,
and this as a way of establishing the new horizon which emerges in
Jesus. The OT horizon is established immediately but is transcended
more and more as the narrative moves to focus upon Jesus in the final
episode. Zechariah and Mary in their questions establish what in the
circumstances seem fixed horizons (sterility and virginity), only to
have them transcended by God's promise. In the final episode, the
narrator uses the technique four times: conventional piety (vv. 41-42),
human wisdom (vv. 46-47), Joseph's paternity (v. 48) and the Temple
as 'the things of my father' (v. 49) are all set in the narrative as
horizons which are transcended in the episode itself.

Moreover, in five of the infancy narrative's seven episodes, the
stated human purpose—in each case commanded by an external
authority—is never narrated: the incense-burning in 1.5-25, circumcision in 1.57-80, the census and circumcision in 2.1-21, the presentation and purification in 2.22-40, and the Passover in 2.41-52. This
amounts to the transcendence of a horizon which establishes a new
kind of authority: the authority of God emerging in Jesus.

Narrative Statement: The Birth of a Christology

At the level of narrative statement, this study has shown how a
dynamic of promise-fulfilment is basic to the narration of the divine
visitation in the infancy narrative. It has also shown how at the point
of human recognition of the divine visitation there is a corresponding
dynamic of faith-interpretation—faith in the promise and interpretation of the first signs of fulfilment.

Faith appears as the recognition of a coherence between the past
signs of God's fidelity and the present promise he is shown to make in
the narrative itself. Interpretation then appears as the recognition of a
coherence between the 'what' of God's new promise and the 'how' of
its fulfilment, the beginning of which is recounted in the infancy

narrative. The study has shown finally how in the infancy narrative the narrator brings the lines of narration to a point of convergence in 2.41-52, where leadership in the interpretative task passes to Jesus. At that point, the infancy narrative brings to birth (1) a distinctively Lukan christology, (2) Jesus as protagonist of the Lukan narrative, and (3) the Lukan narrative itself.

The First Phase: Deploying The Elements
In the first phase, the narrator deploys the elements of the narrative at the point of both divine visitation and human recognition of it. In doing so, he constructs a grammar of the divine visitation and right recognition of it which may be represented as follows:

Promise	←→	Fulfilment
Hearing	←→	Seeing
Faith	←→	Interpretation
Praise	←→	Proclamation

1. God is shown to work according to a dynamic of promise-fulfilment, with both the promise he makes and its fulfilment in some way strange.
2. The promise is spoken by the heavenly messenger, heard by the human character; and its fulfilment produces signs which are seen and heard by the characters.
3. The key promise is the promise of a Davidic messiah who will also be Son of God in an extraordinary way. The first signs of fulfilment of this promise will come only in the narrative's second phase.
4. The human characters are expected to believe the promise they hear (on the basis of their reading of the past signs of God's fidelity) and interpret the signs of fulfilment they see. Given that both promise and fulfilment are in some way strange, both faith and interpretation are cast as a challenge.
5. The prime fruit of faith is praise of God; and the prime fruit of right interpretation of the signs of fulfilment is a proclamation to human beings (which includes both prophecy of what God will do and proclamation of what God has done).
6. The divine visitation has about it a necessity which paradoxically does not abolish human freedom; and human recognition of it also combines freedom and necessity, as human characters at times speak and act under the influence of the Holy Spirit and at other times not.

The whole of the first phase moves from separation to convergence. In the first two episodes, Mary (as exemplar of faith) and Elizabeth (as exemplar of right interpretation) are separate characters in separate episodes; the two women then meet in a single episode and their meeting entails the meeting of praise (as the fulness of faith) and prophecy (as the fulness of interpretation); then in the fourth episode, faith and interpretation, praise and prophecy converge not only in a single episode but in the single voice of Zechariah. The move from separation to meeting to convergence shows that faith and interpretation, praise and proclamation are parts of a single process of human recognition of the divine visitation and that within the process there is a ceaseless oscillation between the two.

The first phase is essentially theocentric, with the narrator presenting an array of christological elements drawn from the OT as the raw material of a distinctively Lukan christology, but focusing on God rather than the messiah. God is presented as prime mover, and human characters respond to what God says and does through his intermediaries. In the first three episodes human characters meet, but they neither learn from each other nor share their knowledge with each other. They learn directly from heaven, and they turn to heaven in praise rather than to each other to transmit information. This begins to change in 1.57-80, where for the first time human characters (the crowd of neighbours and relatives) learn from other human characters (Elizabeth and Zechariah), and the crowd in turn share their knowledge with 'all who heard' in the hill-country. But until then it is God who reveals, and it is God to whom the human characters turn in praise.

In the decision to begin with God rather than Jesus, the Lukan narrative shows itself different from the other Gospels.[1] In contrast to both Matthew and Mark, Luke is inductive rather than deductive in his approach.[2] The other synoptic evangelists begin with Jesus and move

---

1.   God is named 20 times in the Lukan infancy narrative as θεός (13 times in ch. 1, 7 times in ch. 2). God is also named 25 times as κύριος, with and without the article (16 times in ch. 1, 9 times in ch. 2). In Matthew's much briefer infancy narrative the word θεός appears once only in the translation of 'Εμαννουήλ in 1.23, and κύριος appears 4 times (3 times in reference to the angel [1.24; 2.13; 2.19] and once in reference to the word of Scripture [2.15]).

2.   Matthew begins his narrative with βίβλος γενέσεως 'Ιησοῦ Χριστοῦ υἱοῦ Δαυὶδ υἱοῦ 'Αβραάμ, and does not mention God until 1.20 where the angel first

to God, with the implication that if one wishes to know God, then one must first know Jesus. Luke, however, begins with God and moves to Jesus, implying that if one wishes to know Jesus, then one must first know God or at least God as Luke presents him. Yet the Lukan narrative, in keeping with narrative conventions of the time of its composition, presents God through a variety of intermediaries[1]—which means that the readers must know them. In the context of the infancy narrative, this means that in order to understand how Jesus functions in the last episode there is a need to look at how God's intermediaries function in the earlier episodes. Trajectories beginning in the earlier episodes converge in 2.41-52.

The Second Phase: Creating Convergence
In the second phase, the narrator brings the elements he has deployed in the first phase to a point of convergence. The promise made by Gabriel of the birth of the Davidic messiah who would be Son of God is fulfilled, but from the first the signs of fulfilment are stranger than they were in the first phase. This means that the gap between the 'what' of the promise and the 'how' of its fulfilment grows wider in the second phase, and right interpretation of the signs of fulfilment grows correspondingly more challenging. This appears especially in the figure of Mary, who in the first phase moved serenely enough through puzzlement to faith, but who in the second phase struggles with signs of fulfilment which seem at odds with the promise she has heard from Gabriel and which she has believed. As the task of interpretation becomes more challenging, the need for an interpreter

intervenes to instruct Joseph. Mark begins his narrative with ἀρχὴ τοῦ εὐαγγελίου Ἰησοῦ Χριστοῦ (υἱοῦ θεοῦ), with the reference to God textually uncertain. Either way, it is clear that Mark begins with Jesus. John is harder to assess with his opening ἐν ἀρχῇ ἦν ὁ λόγος, καὶ ὁ λόγος ἦν πρὸς τὸν θεόν, καὶ θεὸς ἦν ὁ λόγος. But see F.J. Moloney, 'Johannine Theology', in R.E. Brown, J.A. Fitzmyer and R.E. Murphy (eds.), *New Jerome Biblical Commentary* (London: Geoffrey Chapman, 1990), pp. 1417-26, where he writes: 'despite appearances, John really is not a story about Jesus but a story about what God has done in Jesus' (pp. 1420, 18).

1.   Where in OT narrative God often enough appears on the stage and speaks a good deal, in later narrative texts (for example the intertestamental literature) God never appears on the stage of the narrative nor speaks. The closest he comes to it is in cases such as the baptism and transfiguration scenes in the Third Gospel where the unnamed voice from heaven sounds.

becomes more acute; and Jesus is introduced in the last episode as the one who meets the need.

In a number of ways through the first six episodes of the infancy narrative the narrator has prepared for the point of climax which comes in the last episode as Jesus appears as prime interpreter.

1. In consistently passing the word to the characters at points of revelation, interpretation and evaluation, the narrator has prepared for the moment in which the word of interpretation and revelation will pass to Jesus, with whom it will remain through the Gospel narrative. Narratorial discretion, therefore, serves the christology that emerges in the last episode.

2. The same is true of the narrator's choice of a 'showing' mode of narration throughout the infancy narrative. Rather than simply tell the reader that Jesus will function as prime interpreter of himself and his action, the narrator prefers to show the process whereby Jesus emerges as prime interpreter and then to show him actually in the act of interpretation. This is related to the indirect christology that emerges, where Jesus implies that he is Son of God but leaves it to others to name him as such. Like the narrator, Jesus appears as one who prefers a showing mode: rather than simply tell others that he is Son of God, he will in his words and deeds throughout the Gospel narrative show not only that he is Son of God but also how he is Son of God.

3. In focusing less upon what happens and more upon how human characters respond to it, the narrator prepares for the emergence of a christology which has Jesus as prime interpreter and which therefore focuses less upon what happens and more upon how Jesus interprets it.

4. The narrator prepares for the moment in which Jesus emerges as prime interpreter by showing a series of characters, both heavenly and human, who succeed in the act of interpretation. The procession of interpreters includes characters as diverse as Gabriel, the People in the Temple, Elizabeth, Mary, John, Zechariah, the neighbours and relatives, the angels, the shepherds, Simeon and Anna—all of whom in varying degrees and in different ways successfully interpret the action of God. In the first six episodes, the human characters struggle in the act of interpretation unless aided by heaven. Heaven therefore intervenes through either an angel or the Holy Spirit to enable human recognition of what God is doing. All of this looks to the moment in which Jesus, without any hint of heavenly assistance, successfully

interprets his own action as part of God's plan. At the end of the procession comes the character in whom both heavenly and human interpreters converge.

5. In the way he uses Scripture the narrator also prepares for the christology that emerges in the last episode. Through the first six episodes the OT, though never cited directly, is ubiquitous in allusion, echo and reminiscence. The readers are not told explicitly, but are shown how the OT functions as prime interpretative resource. As Jesus assumes his role as prime interpreter in the last episode, the echoes and allusions of the OT dwindle to almost nothing. The language of the OT gives way to the language of Jesus. It is no longer the OT that is the prime interpretative resource as it has been through the first six episodes. The readers are shown instead how the prime interpretative resource from now on is Jesus himself.

6. In building into the narrative from the first a paradoxical combination of divine necessity and human freedom, the narrator also prepares for the moment in which Jesus reveals that he has acted under the impulse of the Lukan δεî—yet this in an episode where evidence suggests that he has freely decided to remain in the Temple among the teachers on the understanding that this is what he means for him now to be 'in the things of my father'.

7. The same is true of the paradoxical combination of revelation and concealment which the narrator builds into the narrative from the first. In what he says in 2.49, Jesus reveals why he has remained in the Temple among the teachers; and yet his words remain deeply enigmatic—all the more so when, having justified his stay in Jerusalem with the claim that he must always be 'in the things of my father', Jesus returns to Nazareth with his parents. His words and actions in the last episode reveal and conceal in about equal proportion; and this comes as the climax of a strategy which has pervaded the infancy narrative.

The shift enacted from the first to the last episode and from the first to the second phase is a shift from theology to christology. In that sense, it is better to say that the infancy narrative becomes christocentric as theology gives way to christology rather than that it is from the first christocentric.[1] As God gives way to Jesus, human recognition

---

1. In the light of this, there is a need to modify some of the many claims made for the infancy narrative as christology. Fitzmyer, for example, claims that '[w]hen one considers the Lucan infancy narrative as a whole, one sees that its main purpose

shifts from response to what God says and does through his intermediaries to response to what Jesus says and does. Angels and the
Holy Spirit are nowhere to be found in the final episode: as in the
transfiguration episode, 'when the voice had spoken Jesus was found
alone' (ἐν τῷ γενέσθαι τὴν φωνὴν εὑρέθη Ἰησοῦς μόνος, 9.36).
Other voices, both heavenly and human, have sounded throughout the
infancy narrative, but in the end it is the voice of Jesus alone which
sounds as prime interpreter. Or at least Jesus is the sole character
whose voice sounds, since the voice of the narrator is also heard. The
paradox of this is that the narrator offers an interpretation of Jesus
which establishes Jesus as prime interpreter. Who then is the prime
interpreter? In fact, the narrator—but a narrator who is determined
to efface himself in order that Jesus appear in the narrative as prime
interpreter.

The Lukan ἀσφάλεια

In 1.4, the narrator promises the narratee a new sense of well-
foundedness (ἀσφάλεια), and we are in a position now to see more of
what this might mean.[1] The prologue's statement of the narrative's

is . . . to make christological affirmations about him from the beginning of his
earthly existence' (*Luke*, p. 446). Yet the infancy narrative does more than make
christological affirmations about Jesus in the sense of applying traditional titles to
him (messiah, Son of God, Saviour and so on) from the first. As narrative, it is a
process by which a christology is slowly brought to birth, and a process that eventually shows Jesus exercising the interpretative role which will be his through the
Gospel narrative, but which was not his 'from the beginning of his earthly existence'. Fitzmyer also claims that 'the Lucan infancy narrative knows only a
'christology from above' (*Luke*, p. 447; similarly Laurentin [*Structure*, pp. 146-
47]). Here the problem is the 'only', since the narrator also shapes a christology
'from within' (i.e. from within the narrative itself). The same may be said of
Brown's claim that '[t]he addition of these stories to the Gospel proper
is . . . intelligible as part of a christological process' (*Birth of the Messiah*, p. 31):
the process is not only behind the narrative, but also within the narrative. Brown
again: 'the Lukan birth story [is] dominated by a christology centered on Jesus'
conception and birth' (*Birth of the Messiah*, p. 478). Yet it is more particularly a
christology centred on the emergence in the narrative of Jesus as interpreter.
Laurentin reads the infancy narrative as 'la Révélation du Christ' (*Les Evangiles*,
p. 135): true, and in particular of the role he will play in the Gospel.
    1.   The last phrase of the prologue has drawn a variety of interpretations, on
which see Fitzmyer, *Luke*, pp. 300-301, and R.J. Dillon, 'Previewing Luke's
Project from his Prologue (Luke 1:1-4)', *CBQ* 43 (1981), pp. 224-27.

purpose ('that you may know the well-foundedness of what you have been taught' [ἵνα ἐπιγνῷς περὶ ὧν κατηχήθης λόγων τὴν ἀσφάλειαν]) assumes that the narratee has been informed of the 'what' of God's visitation, which is mentioned in only very oblique terms in the prologue ('the things which have been fulfilled' [τὰ πεπληροφορημένα πράγματα] and 'what you have been taught' [οἱ κατηχήθης λόγοι]). The need for reassurance therefore is at the point of 'how' rather than 'what'; and the ἀσφάλεια works at the level of the 'how' of both divine visitation and human recognition of it. In Jesus who is Son of God, God does visit his people but in surprising ways. At the same time, these ways are not so surprising that recognition of the divine visitation lies beyond human ken. Still, recognition is a challenge, and the infancy narrative sets out what is required in order to meet the challenge. By the end of the infancy narrative it appears that the prime requirement is to follow Jesus through the Gospel narrative as in word and action he interprets himself as the one in whom God visits his people.

In the prologue, the narrator claims that it will be his ordering of the narrative that will confer the sense of ἀσφάλεια (ἔδοξε κἀμοί...καθεξῆς σοι γράψαι), and it is a question of what kind of ordering he means. The infancy narrative shows an ordering which makes fulfilment follow promise and which makes faith the reply to the promise and right interpretation the reply to the first signs of fulfilment; and given that both promise and fulfilment are made in some way strange it is an order that emerges only in the midst of what seems to be disorder. By the end of the infancy narrative, the ordering appears more precisely as a revelation of the coherence between Jesus' identity and action—which is again a coherence revealed in the midst of what seems to be incoherence.

These conclusions have resorted to the expedient of distinguishing strategy and statement, narrative and christology. Yet finally, as this study has argued, they are inseparable. The infancy narrative brings to birth not only a christology, but also a protagonist, a narrator and readers, and an interaction between all of these. This is simply to say that it is narrative; and it is from the womb of narrative that Christology comes forth.

By the end of Luke 1–2, the Lukan narrative is born—but only born. Much more will unfold before Gabriel's grand promises are shown to be fulfilled. That which is born will grow, and in unexpected ways. Yet the readers may read on confident that, whatever twists and turns may lie ahead, the Lukan narrative will confirm the truth of Wordsworth's claim that 'the child is father of the man'.[1]

1.   W. Wordsworth, *My Heart Leaps Up*.

BIBLIOGRAPHY

Abrams, M.H., *A Glossary of Literary Terms* (New York: Holt, Rinehart & Winston, 1971).

Adams, D.R., 'The Suffering of Paul and the Dynamics of Luke–Acts' (PhD dissertation, Yale University, 1979).

Ades, J.I., 'Literary Aspects of Luke', *Papers on Language and Literature* 15 (1979), pp. 193-99.

Aichele, G., 'Literary Fantasy and the Composition of the Gospels', *Forum* 5 (1989), pp. 42-60.

—*The Limits of Story* (Atlanta: Scholars Press, 1985).

Aletti, J.-N., 'Jésus à Nazareth (Lc 4,16-30): Prophétie, écriture et typologie', in F. Refoulé (ed.), *A Cause de l'Evangile* (Paris: Cerf, 1985), pp. 431-51.

—'Luc 24,13-33: Signes, accomplissement et temps', *RSR* 75 (1987), pp. 305-20.

—'Mort de Jésus et théorie du récit', *RSR* 73 (1985), pp. 147-60.

—*L'art de raconter Jésus Christ: L'écriture narrative de l'évangile de Luc* (Paris: Seuil, 1989).

Alter, R., 'Biblical Narrative', *Commentary* 61 (1976), pp. 61-67.

—*The Art of Biblical Narrative* (New York: Basic Books, 1981).

—*The Pleasures of Reading in an Ideological Age* (New York: Simon & Schuster, 1989).

Ankersmit, F.R., *Narrative Logic: A Semantic Analysis of the Historian's Language* (The Hague, Boston and London: Mouton Publishers, 1983).

Audet, J.P., 'Autour de la théologie de Luc 1–2', *ScEccl* 11 (1959), pp. 409-18.

—'L'annonce à Marie', *RB* 63 (1956), pp. 346-74.

Auerbach, E., *Mimesis: The Representation of Reality in Western Literature* (trans. W. Trask; Garden City, NY: Anchor Books, 1957).

Auffret, P., 'Note sur la structure littéraire de Lc 1,68-79', *NTS* 24 (1978), pp. 248-58.

Aune, D.E., *The New Testament in its Literary Environment* (Philadelphia: Westminster Press, 1987).

Austin, J.L., *How to Do Things with Words* (London and New York: Oxford University Press, 1962).

Bagwell, J.T., *American Formalism and the Problem of Interpretation* (Houston: Rice University Press 1986).

Bakhtin, M.M., *The Dialogic Imagination* (trans. M. Holquist; Austin: University of Texas Press, 1981).

Bal, M., *Narratology: Introduction to the Theory of Narrative* (trans. C. van Boheemen; Toronto and London: University of Toronto Press, 1985).

—'Tell-Tale Theories', *Poetics Today* 7 (1986), pp. 555-64.

—'The Narrating and the Focalizing: A Theory of the Agents of Narrative (trans. J.E. Lewin)', *Style* 17 (1983), pp. 235-69.

Baltzer, K., 'The Meaning of the Temple in the Lucan Writings', *HTR* 58 (1965), pp. 263-77.

Barfield, O., *Saving the Appearances* (New York: Harcourt Brace, 1957).

Barnouw, D., 'Critics in the Act of Reading', *Poetics Today* 1 (1980), pp. 213-22.

Barr, D.L., *New Testament Story: An Introduction* (Belmont: Wadsworth Publishing, 1987).

Barrett, C. K., *Luke the Historian in Recent Study* (London: Epworth Press, 1961).

Barton, J., 'Reading the Bible as Literature: Two Questions for Biblical Critics', *Literature & Theology* 1 (1987), pp. 135-53.

Bauer, J., 'πῶς in der griechischen Bibel', *NovT* 2 (1957), pp. 81-89.

Beavis, M.A., 'The Trial before the Sanhedrin (Mark 14:53-65): Reader Response and Greco-Roman Readers', *CBQ* 49 (1987), pp. 581-96.

Benoit, P., 'Et toi-même, un glaive te transpercera l'âme! (Lc 2,35)', *CBQ* 25 (1963), pp. 251-61.

—'L'enfance de Jean-Baptiste selon Luc I', *NTS* 3 (1956–57), pp. 169-94.

Berlin, A., 'Point of View in Biblical Narrative', in *A Sense of the Text: The Art of Language in the Study of Biblical Literature* (Winona Lake, IN: Eisenbrauns, 1982), pp. 71-113.

—*Poetics and Interpretation of Biblical Narratives* (Sheffield: Almond Press, 1983).

Bleich, D., 'Epistemological Assumptions in the Study of Response', in J.P. Tompkins (ed.), *Reader-Response Criticism: From Formalism to Post-Structuralism* (Baltimore and London: Johns Hopkins University Press, 1980), pp. 134-63.

Bock, D.L., *Proclamation from Prophecy and Pattern: Lucan Old Testament Christology* (JSNTSup, 12; Sheffield: JSOT Press, 1987).

Boomershine, T.E., *Story Journey: An Invitation to the Gospel as Storytelling* (Nashville: Abingdon Press, 1988).

Booth, W.C., *The Rhetoric of Fiction* (Harmondsworth: Peregrine Books, 1987).

Bornhäuser, K., *Die Geburts- und Kindheitsgeschichte Jesu* (Gütersloh: Bertelsmann, 1930).

Bossuyt, J., and J. Radermakers, *Jésus: Parole de la grâce selon S. Luc* (2 vols.; Brussels: Editions Institut d'Etudes Théologiques, 1983).

Bovon, F., 'Effet du réel et flou prophétique dans l'oeuvre de Luc', in F. Refoulé (ed.), *A Cause de l'Evangile* (Paris: Cerf, 1985), pp. 349-60.

—'L'importance des médiations dans le projet théologique de Luc', in *L'oeuvre de Luc: Etudes d'exégèse et de théologie* (Paris: Cerf, 1987), pp. 181-203.

—*Das Evangelium nach Lukas (Lk 1,1–9,50)* (Zürich: Benzinger Verlag/Neukirchener Verlag, 1989).

—'Le Dieu de Luc', in *L'oeuvre de Luc: Etudes d'exégèse et de théologie* (Paris: Cerf, 1987), pp. 221-42.

—*Luc le théologien: Vingt-cinq ans de recherches (1950–1975)* (Paris: Delachaux & Niestlé, 1978).

Braudy, L., *Narrative Form in History and Fiction* (Princeton: Princeton University Press, 1970).

Breech, J., *Jesus and Postmodernism* (Philadelphia: Fortress Press, 1989).

Brinker, M., 'Two Phenomenologies of Reading: Ingarden and Iser on Textual Indeterminacy', *Poetics Today* 1 (1980), pp. 203-12.

Brinkmann, B., 'Die Jungfrauengeburt und das Lukasevangelium', *Bib* 34 (1953), pp. 327-32.

Brombert, V., 'Opening Signals in Narrative', *New Literary History* 10 (1979), pp. 489-502.

Brooks, P., *Reading for the Plot: Design and Intention in Narrative* (New York: Vintage Books, 1984).

Brown, R.E., 'Gospel Infancy Narrative Research from 1976–1986: Part II (Luke)', *CBQ* 48 (1986), pp. 660-80.

—'Luke's Method in the Annunciation Narratives of Chapter One', in J.W. Flanagan and A.W. Robinson (eds.), *No Famine in the Land* (Missoula, MT: Scholars Press, 1975), pp. 179-94.

—*The Birth of the Messiah: A Commentary on the Infancy Narratives in Matthew and Luke* (Garden City, NY: Doubleday, 1977).

Brown, R.E., K.P. Donfried, J.A. Fitzmyer and J. Reumann (eds.), *Mary in the New Testament* (Philadelphia: Fortress Press; New York: Paulist Press, 1978), pp. 107-62.

Brown, S., 'Reader Response: Demythologizing the Text', *NTS* 34 (1988), pp. 232-37.

—*Apostasy and Perseverance in the Theology of Luke* (Rome: Biblical Institute Press, 1969).

Bultmann, R., *The History of the Synoptic Tradition* (trans. J. Marsh; Oxford: Basil Blackwell, 1963).

Burger, C., *Jesus als Davidssohn* (Göttingen: Vandenhoeck & Ruprecht, 1970).

Burrows, E., *The Gospel of the Infancy and Other Biblical Essays* (London: Burns, Oates & Washbourne, 1940).

Cadbury, H.J., 'Commentary on the Preface of Luke', in F. Foakes-Jackson and K. Lake (eds.), *The Beginnings of Christianity* (London: Macmillan, 1922), II, pp. 489-510.

—*The Making of Luke-Acts* (London: Macmillan, 1927).

—*The Style and Literary Method of Luke* (Cambridge, MA: Harvard University Press, 1920).

Cagnat, R. (ed.), *Inscriptiones Graecae Ad Res Romanas Pertinentes* (Paris: E. Leroux, 1906), III.

Caird, G.B., *St. Luke* (Harmondsworth: Penguin, 1963).

Carroll, J.T., *Response to the End of History: Eschatology and Salvation in Luke–Acts* (Atlanta: Scholars Press, 1988).

Carter, W., 'Zechariah and the Benedictus (Luke 1,68-79): Practicing what he Preaches', *Bib* 69 (1988), pp. 239-47.

Casalegno, A., *Gesù e il Tempio: Studio redazionale di Luca–Atti* (Brescia: Morcelliana, 1984).

Champion, J., 'The Poetics of Human Time: Paul Ricoeur's Time and Narrative, Volume 3', *Literature & Theology* 3 (1989), pp. 341-48.

Chatman, S., *Story and Discourse: Narrative Structure in Fiction and Film* (Ithaca, NY: Cornell University Press, 1980).

Cohn, D., *Transparent Minds: Narrative Modes for Presenting Consciousness in Fiction* (Princeton: Princeton University Press, 1978).

Collins, J.C., 'The Rediscovery of Biblical Narrative', *Chicago Studies* 21 (1981), pp. 45-58.

Conrad, E.W., 'Annunciation of Birth and the Birth of the Messiah', *CBQ* 47 (1985), pp. 656-63.

Conzelmann, H., *The Theology of St. Luke* (trans. G. Buswell; Philadelphia: Fortress Press, 1982).

Cortes, J.B., and F.M. Gatti, 'Jesus' First Recorded Words (Lk 2,49-50)', *Marianum* 32 (1970), pp. 404-18.

Cosgrove, C.H., 'The Divine ΔEI in Luke–Acts: Investigations into the Understanding of God's Providence', *NovT* 26 (1984), pp. 168-90.

Cotterell, P., and M. Turner, *Linguistics and Biblical Interpretation* (London: SPCK, 1989).

Crane, R.S., 'The Concept of Plot', in R. Scholes (ed.), *Approaches to the Novel: Materials for a Poetics* (San Francisco: Chandler Press, 1966), pp. 233-43.

Creed, J.M., *The Gospel according to St. Luke: The Greek Text with Introduction, Notes and Indices* (London: Macmillan, 1930).

Crossan, J.D., 'Literary Criticism and Biblical Hermeneutics', *JR* 57 (1977), pp. 76-80.

—'Waking the Bible: Biblical Hermeneutic and Literary Imagination', *Int* 23 (1978), pp. 269-85.

Culbertson, D., *The Poetics of Revelation: Recognition and the Narrative Tradition* (Macon: Mercer University Press, 1989).

Culler, J., 'Defining Narrative Units', in R. Fowler (ed.), *Style and Structure in Literature: Essays in the New Stylistics* (Ithaca, NY: Cornell University Press, 1975), pp. 123-42.

—'Literary Competence', in J.P. Tompkins (ed.), *Reader-Response Criticism: From Formalism to Post-Structuralism* (Baltimore and London: Johns Hopkins University Press, 1980), pp. 101-17.

—*On Deconstruction: Theory and Criticism after Structuralism* (Ithaca, NY: Cornell University Press, 1982).

—*The Pursuit of Signs* (Ithaca, NY: Cornell University Press, 1981).

Cullmann, O., *The Christology of the New Testament* (Philadelphia: Westminster Press, 1959).

Culpepper, R.A., *Anatomy of the Fourth Gospel: A Study in Literary Design* (Philadelphia: Fortress Press, 1983).

—'Commentary on Biblical Narratives: Changing Paradigms', *Forum* 5 (1989), pp. 87-102.

—'Story and History in the Gospels', *RevExp* 81 (1984), pp. 467-77.

Dahl, N.A., 'The Purpose of Luke–Acts', in *Jesus in the Memory of the Early Church* (Minneapolis: Augsburg, 1976).

Danby, H. (ed.), *The Mishnah* (Oxford: Clarendon Press, 1933).

Danker, F.W., *Jesus and the New Age according to St. Luke: A Commentary on the Third Gospel* (St Louis: Clayton Publishing House, 1972).

Daube, D., 'Evangelisten und Rabbinen', *ZNW* 48 (1957), pp. 119-20.

Davies, J.H., 'The Lucan Prologue (1–3): An Attempt at Objective Redaction Criticism', in E.A. Livingstone (ed.), *Studia Evangelica VI* (Berlin: Akademie-Verlag, 1973), pp. 79-85.

Davis, C.T., 'A Multidimensional Criticism of the Gospels', in R.A. Spencer (ed.), *Orientation by Disorientation: Studies in Literary Criticism and Biblical Literary Criticism* (Pittsburgh: Pickwick Press, 1980).

—'The Literary Structure of Luke 1–2', in D.J.A. Clines, D.M. Gunn and A.J. Hauser (eds.), *Art and Meaning: Rhetoric in Biblical Literature* (JSOTSup, 19; Sheffield: JSOT Press, 1982), pp. 215-29.

Dawsey, J.M., 'The Literary Unity of Luke–Acts: Questions of Style—A Task for Literary Critics', *NTS* 35 (1989), pp. 48-66.

—'What's in a Name? Characterization in Luke', *BTB* 16 (1986), pp. 143-47.

—*The Lukan Voice: Confusion and Irony in the Gospel of Luke* (Macon: Mercer University Press, 1986).

De Jonge, H.J., 'Sonship, Wisdom, Infancy: Luke II.41-51a', *NTS* 24 (1977–78), pp. 317-54.

Detweiler, R., 'After the New Criticism: Contemporary Methods of Literary Interpretation', in R.A. Spencer (ed.), *Orientation by Disorientation: Studies in Literary Criticism and Biblical Literary Criticism* (Pittsburgh: Pickwick Press, 1980), pp. 3-24.

Dibelius, M., *Aufsätze zur Apostelgeschichte* (ed. H. Greeven; Göttingen: Vandenhoeck & Ruprecht, 1951).

—'Jungfrauensohn und Krippenkind: Untersuchungen zur Geburtsgeschichte Jesu im Lukas-Evangelium', in G. Bornkamm (ed.), *Botschaft und Geschichte: Gesammelte Aufsätze von Martin Dibelius* (Tübingen: Mohr, 1953), pp. 19-22.

Dillon, R.J., 'Reviewing Luke's Project from his Prologue (Luke 1:1-4), *CBQ* 43 (1981), pp. 205-27.

—*From Eye-Witnesses to Ministers of the Word* (Rome: Biblical Institute Press, 1978).

Dodd, C.H., *According to the Scriptures: The Sub-Structure of New Testament Theology* (London: Nisbet, 1952).

Doeve, J.W., *Jewish Hermeneutics in the Synoptic Gospels and Acts* (Assen: Van Gorcum, 1954).

Dömer, H., *Das Heil Gottes: Studien zur Theologie des lukanischen Doppelwerks* (Bonn: Peter Hanstein, 1978).

Dornisch, L., 'Ricoeur's Theory of Mimesis: Implications for Literature and Theology', *Literature & Theology* 3 (1989), pp. 308-18.

Drury, J., 'Luke', in F. Kermode and R. Alter (eds.), *The Literary Guide to the Bible* (Cambridge, MA: Belknap/Harvard University Press, 1987), pp. 418-39.

—*Tradition and Design in Luke's Gospel* (London: Darton, Longman & Todd, 1976).

Du Plooy, G.P.V., 'The Design of God in Luke–Acts', *Scriptura* 25 (1988), pp. 1-6.

Dupont, J., 'L'Evangile de la Fête de la Sainte Famille (Lc 2,41-52)', *AsSeign* 14 (1961), pp. 24-43.

—'Jésus retrouvé au temple', *AsSeign* 11 (1970), pp. 46-47.

—'Le Magnificat comme discours sur Dieu', *NRT* 102 (1980), pp. 321-43.

Easton, B.S., *The Gospel according to St. Luke: A Critical and Exegetical Commentary* (New York: Scribner's, 1926).

Eco, U., *The Role of the Reader: Explorations in the Semiotics of Texts* (Bloomington: Indiana University Press, 1984).

Edwards, O.C., *Luke's Story of Jesus* (Philadelphia: Fortress Press, 1981).

Egan, K., 'What is a Plot?', *New Literary History* 9 (1978), pp. 455-73.

Elliott, J.K., 'Does Luke 2:41-52 Anticipate the Resurrection?', *ExpTim* 83 (1971), pp. 87-89.

Ellis, E.E., *Prophecy and Hermeneutic in Early Christianity* (Tübingen: Mohr, 1978).

—*The Gospel of Luke* (London: Nelson, 1966).

Erbetta, M. (ed.), *Gli Apocrifi del Nuovo Testamento: Vangeli 1/2 (Infanzia e Passione di Cristo; Assunzione di Maria)* (Casale Monferrato: Casa Editrice Marietti, 1983), pp. 3-227.

Erdmann, G., *Die Vorgeschichten des Lukas- und Matthäusevangeliums und Vergils vierte Ekloge* (Göttingen: Vandenhoeck & Ruprecht, 1932).

Ernst, J., *Das Evangelium nach Lukas* (Regensburg: Pustet, 1977).

Eslinger, L., 'The Wooing of the Woman at the Well: Jesus, the Reader and Reader-Response Criticism', *Literature & Theology* 1 (1987), pp. 167-83.

Evans, C.F., *Saint Luke* (London: SCM Press; Philadelphia: Trinity Press International, 1990).

Farris, S., *The Hymns of Luke's Infancy Narratives: Their Origin, Meaning and Significance* (JSNTSup, 9; Sheffield: JSOT Press, 1985).

Feuillet, A., 'Le Sauveur messianique et sa Mère dans les récits de l'enfance de Saint Matthieu et de Saint Luc (Deuxième partie: Luc 1-2)', *Divinitas* 34 (1990), pp. 103-50.

—'Les hommes de bonne volonté ou les hommes que Dieu aime: Note sur la traduction de Luc 2,14b', *Bulletin de l'Association Guillaume Budé* 4 (1974), pp. 91-92.

Figueras, P., 'Siméon et Anne, ou le témoignage de la Loi et des prophètes', *NovT* 20 (1978), pp. 84-99.

Fisch, H., *A Remembered Future: A Study in Literary Mythology* (Bloomington: Indiana University Press, 1984).

—*Poetry with a Purpose: Biblical Poetics and Interpretation* (Bloomington: Indiana University Press, 1988).

Fish, S.E., 'Literature in the Reader: Affective Stylistics', in J.P. Tompkins (ed.), *Reader-Response Criticism: From Formalism to Post-Structuralism* (Baltimore and London: Johns Hopkins University Press, 1980), pp. 70-100.

—*Is there a Text in this Class? The Authority of Interpretive Communities* (Cambridge, MA: Harvard University Press, 1980).

Fitzmyer, J.A., 'The Virginal Conception of Jesus in the New Testament', *TS* 34 (1973), pp. 541-75.

—*Luke the Theologian: Aspects of his Teaching* (New York: Paulist Press, 1989).

—*The Gospel According to Luke* (AB 28, 28a; Garden City, NY: Doubleday, 1981, 1985).

Flender, H., *St. Luke: Theologian of Redemptive History* (Philadelphia: Fortress Press, 1967).

Fornara, C.W., *The Nature of History in Ancient Greece and Rome* (Berkeley, Los Angeles and London: University of California Press, 1988).

Forster, E.M., 'The Plot', in R. Scholes (ed.), *Approaches to the Novel: Materials for a Poetics* (San Francisco: Chandler Press, 1966), pp. 145-66.

Fowler, R.M., 'Postmodern Biblical Criticism', *Forum* 5 (1989), pp. 3-30.

—'Using Literary Criticism on the Gospels', *Christian Century* 99, 626-629.

—'Who is "The Reader" in Reader Response Criticism?', *Semeia* 31 (1985), pp. 5-23.

Franklin, E., *Christ the Lord: A Study in the Purpose and Theology of Luke–Acts* (Philadelphia: Westminster Press, 1975).

Freedman, W., 'The Literary Motif: A Definition and Evaluation', *Novel* 4 (1971), pp. 123-31.

Frei, H.W., 'The "Literal Reading" of Biblical Narrative: Does it Stretch or Will it Break?', in F. McConnell (ed.), *The Bible and the Narrative Tradition* (New York and Oxford: Oxford University Press, 1986), pp. 36-77.

—*The Eclipse of Biblical Narrative: A Study in Eighteenth and Nineteenth Century Hermeneutics* (New Haven and London: Yale University Press, 1974).

Freund, E., *The Return of the Reader: Reader-Response Criticism* (London and New York: Methuen, 1987).

Frey, J.-B., 'La signification du terme πρωτότοκος d'après une inscription juive', *Bib* 11 (1930), pp. 373-90.

Frye, N., *The Great Code: The Bible and Literature* (New York and London: Harcourt Brace Jovanovich, 1982).

Frye, R.M., 'A Literary Perspective for the Criticism of the Gospels', in D. Miller (ed.), *Jesus and Man's Hope* (Pittsburgh: Pittsburgh Theological Seminary, 1971), II.

—'Literary Criticism and Gospel Criticism', *TTod* 36 (1979), pp. 207-19.

Funk, R., *The Poetics of Biblical Narrative* (Sonoma, CA: Polebridge Press, 1988).

Gächter, P., *Maria im Erdenleben: Neutestamentliche Marienstudien* (Innsbruck: Tyrolia, 1955).

Gardner, H., 'Narratives and Fictions', in *In Defence of the Imagination* (Oxford: Oxford University Press, 1982), pp. 111-37.

Gaston, L., 'The Lucan Birth Narratives in Traditional Redaction', in G. MacRae (ed.), *Society of Biblical Literature Seminar Papers 1976* (Missoula, MT: Scholars Press, 1976), pp. 209-18.

Geldenhuys, N., *A Commentary on the Gospel of Luke: The English Text with Introduction, Exposition and Notes* (Grand Rapids: Eerdmans, 1951).

Genette, G., *Narrative Discourse: An Essay in Method* (trans. J.E. Lewin; Ithaca, NY: Cornell University Press, 1978).

—*Nouveau discours du récit* (Paris: Seuil, 1983).

George, A., 'La naissance du Christ Seigneur (Lc 2,1-20)', *AsSeign* 10 (1963), pp. 44-57.

—'La présentation de Jésus au Temple (Lc 2,22-40)', *AsSeign* 2 (1970), pp. 29-39.

—*Etudes sur l'oeuvre de St. Luc* (Paris: Gabalda, 1978).

Gerhart, M., 'The Restoration of Biblical Narrative', *Semeia* 46 (1989), pp. 13-29.

Gewiess, J., 'Die Marienfrage, Lk 1,34', *BZ* 5 (1961), pp. 221-54.

Gibbs, J.M., 'Mark 1,1-15, Matthew 1,1–4,16, Luke 1,1–4,30, John 1,1-51: The Gospel Prologues and their Function', in E.A. Livingstone (ed.), *Studia Evangelica VI* (Berlin: Akademie-Verlag, 1973), pp. 154-88.

Giblin, C.H., 'Reflections on the Sign of the Manger', *CBQ* 29 (1967), pp. 87-101.

—*The Destruction of Jerusalem* (Rome: Biblical Institute Press, 1986).

Glöckner, R., *Die Verkündigung des Heils beim Evangelisten Lukas* (Mainz: Mathias-Grünewald Verlag, 1975).

Godet, F., *Commentaire sur l'Evangile de saint Luc* (2 vols.; Paris: Librairie Fischbacher, 1888–89).

Goffman, E., *Frame Analysis: An Essay on the Organization of Experience* (Cambridge, MA: Harvard University Press, 1974).

Gooding, D., *According to Luke: A New Exposition of the Third Gospel* (Leicester: Inter-Varsity Press; Grand Rapids: Eerdmans, 1987).

Goppelt, L., *Typos: The Typological Interpretation of the Old Testament in the New* (trans. D.H. Madvig; Grand Rapids: Eerdmans, 1982).

Gordon, R.P., *1 and 2 Samuel* (OTG; Sheffield: JSOT Press, 1984).

Gottcent, J.H., *The Bible: A Literary Study* (Boston: Twayne Publishers, 1986).

Gowler, D.B., 'Characterization in Luke: A Socio-Narratological Approach', *BTB* 19 (1989), pp. 54-62.

Graff, G., *Literature against Itself: Literary Ideas in Modern Society* (Chicago: University of Chicago Press, 1979).

Gray, J.R., 'Was our Lord an Only Child? Luke II, 43-46', *ExpTim* 71 (1959), pp. 53.

Graystone, G., *Virgin of All Virgins: An Interpretation of Lk 1:34* (Rome: Tipografia Pio X, 1968).

Gregg, R.B., *Symbolic Inducement and Knowing: A Study in the Foundations of Rhetoric* (Columbia: University of South Carolina Press, 1984).

Gressmann, H., *Das Lukasevangelium* (Tübingen: Mohr, 1919).

Gros Louis, K.R.R., 'Different Ways of Looking at the Birth of Jesus', *Bible Review* 1 (1985), pp. 33-40.

—'The Jesus Birth Stories', in K.R.R. Gros Louis and J.S. Ackerman (eds.), *Literary Interpretations of Biblical Narratives*, II (Nashville: Abingdon Press, 1982), pp. 273-84.

Gros Louis, K.R.R., and J.S. Ackerman (eds.), *Literary Interpretation of Biblical Narratives* (2 vols.; Nashville: Abingdon Press, 1982).

Grundmann, W., *Das Evangelium nach Lukas* (Berlin: Evangelische Verlagsanstalt, 1961).

Gueuret, A., 'Sur Luc 1,46-55: Comment peut-on être amené penser qu'Elisabeth est sémiotiquement celle qui a prononcé le cantique en Luc 1,46', in *Centre Protestant d'Etudes et de Documentation* Supplément (1977), pp. 1-12.

—*L'engendrement d'un récit: L'évangile de l'enfance selon saint Luc* (Paris: Cerf, 1983).

—*La mise en discours: Recherches sémiotiques à propos de l'Evangile de Luc* (Paris: Cerf, 1987).

Güttgemanns, E., 'Narrative Analyse synoptischer Texte', *LB* 25 (1973), pp. 50-73.

Hadas, M., and M. Smith, *Heroes and Gods: Spiritual Biographies in Antiquity* (New York: Harper & Row, 1965).

Haenchen, E., *The Acts of the Apostles: A Commentary* (trans. B. Noble, G. Shinn, H. Anderson and R. Wilson; Oxford: Basil Blackwell, 1971).

Hamlin, C., 'Patterns of Reversal in Literary Narrative', in M.J. Valdes and O.J. Miller (eds.), *Interpretation of Narrative* (Toronto: Toronto University Press, 1978), pp. 61-77.

Hamlyn, F.C., 'The Visit of the Child Jesus to the Temple', *ExpTim* 27 (1915), pp. 43-44.

Hamm, D., 'Sight to the Blind: Vision as Metaphor in Luke', *Bib* 67 (1986), pp. 457-77.

Harnack, A. von, 'Zu Lk 1,34-35', *ZNW* 2 (1901), pp. 53-57.

Harrington, D.J., 'Birth Narratives in Pseudo-Philo's *Biblical Antiquities* and the Gospels', in M.P. Horgan and P.J. Kobelski (eds.), *To Touch the Text* (New York: Crossroad, 1989), pp. 316-24.

Harvey, W.J., *Character and the Novel* (Ithaca, NY: Cornell University Press, 1966).

Hauck, F., *Das Evangelium nach Lukas* (Leipzig: Deichert, 1934).

Hawkins, J., *Horae Synopticae* (Oxford: Clarendon Press, 1909).

Heil, J.P., 'Reader-Response and the Irony of Jesus before the Sanhedrin in Luke 22:66-71', *CBQ* 51 (1989), pp. 271-84.

Hendrickx, H., *The Infancy Narratives* (London: Geoffrey Chapman, 1984).

Hengel, M., *Zur urchristlichen Geschichtsschreibung* (Stuttgart: Calwer Verlag, 1979).

Henn, T.R., *The Bible as Literature* (New York: Oxford University Press, 1970).

Herbert, M., and M. McNamara (eds.), *Irish Biblical Apocrypha: Selected Texts in Translation* (Edinburgh: T. & T. Clark, 1989).

Higgins, A.J.B., 'Luke 1–2 in Tatian's Diatessaron', *JBL* 103 (1984), pp. 193-222.

Holtz, T., *Untersuchungen über die alttestamentlichen Zitate bei Lukas* (Berlin: Akademie-Verlag, 1968).

Holub, R.C., *Reception Theory: A Critical Introduction* (London and New York: Methuen, 1984).

Hubbard, B., 'Commissioning Stories in Luke–Acts: A Study of their Antecedents, Form and Content', *Semeia* 8 (1977), pp. 103-26.

Iersel, B. M. van, *Reading Mark* (trans. W. Bisscheroux; Edinburgh: T. & T. Clark, 1989).

Iersel, B. van, 'The Finding of Jesus in the Temple: Some Observations on the Original Form of Luke II.41-51a', *NovT* 4 (1960), pp. 161-73.

Ingarden, R., *The Cognition of the Literary Work of Art* (trans. R. A. Crowley and K. Olson; Evanston: Northwestern University Press, 1973).

—*The Literary Work of Art: An Investigation on the Borderlines of Ontology, Logic and the Theory of Literature* (trans. G.G. Grabowicz; Evanston: Northwestern University Press, 1973).

Isaacs, M.E., 'Mary in the Lukan Infancy Narrative', *The Way* Supplement 25 (1975), pp. 80-95.

Iser, W., 'Indeterminacy and the Reader's Response in Prose Fiction', in J. Hillis Miller (ed.), *Aspects of Narrative* (New York: Columbia University Press, 1971), pp. 1-45.

—'The Reading Process: A Phenomenological Approach', in J.P. Tompkins (ed.), *Reader-Response Criticism: From Formalism to Post-Structuralism* (Baltimore and London: Johns Hopkins University Press, 1980), pp. 50-69.

—*The Act of Reading: A Theory of Aesthetic Response* (Baltimore and London: Johns Hopkins University Press, 1980).

—*The Implied Reader: Patterns of Communication in Prose Fiction from Bunyan to Beckett* (Baltimore and London: Johns Hopkins University Press, 1978).

James, H., *The Art of the Novel: Critical Prefaces by Henry James* (ed. R.P. Blackmur; New York and London: Charles Scribner's Sons, 1962).

Jansen, J.F., 'An Exposition of Luke 2:42-52', *Int* 30 (1976), pp. 400-404.

Jasper, D. (ed.), *Images of Belief in Literature* (London: Macmillan, 1984).

Jasper, D., *The New Testament and the Literary Imagination* (Atlantic Highlands: Humanities Press International, 1987).

Jauss, H.R., *Toward an Aesthetic of Reception* (Minneapolis: University of Minnesota Press, 1982).

Jeremias, J., 'ΙΕΡΟΥΣΑΛΗΜ/ΙΕΡΟΣΟΛΥΜΑ', *ZNW* 65 (1974), pp. 273-76.

—*Die Sprache des Lukasevangeliums: Redaktion und Tradition im Nicht-Markusstoff des dritten Evangeliums* (Göttingen: Vandenhoeck & Ruprecht, 1980).

Jervell, J., *Luke and the People of God: A New Look at Luke–Acts* (Minneapolis: Augsburg, 1972).

Johnson, L.T., *The Literary Function of Possessions in Luke–Acts* (Missoula, MT: Scholars Press, 1977).

Josipovici, G., *The Book of God: A Response to the Bible* (New Haven and London: Yale University Press, 1988).

Juel, D., *Messiah and Temple* (Missoula, MT: Scholars Press, 1977).

Karris, R.J., 'The Gospel According to Luke', in R.E. Brown, J.A. Fitzmyer and R.E. Murphy (eds.), *New Jerome Biblical Commentary* (London: Geoffrey Chapman, 1990), pp. 675-721.

—*Luke: Artist and Theologian: Luke's Passion Account as Literature* (Mahwah, NJ: Paulist Press, 1985).

Kaut, T., *Befreier und befreites Volk: Traditions- und redaktionsgeschichtliche Untersuchung zu Magnifikat und Benediktus im Kontext der vorlukanischen Kindheitsgeschichte* (Frankfurt: Anton Hain, 1990).

Kearney, R., *Dialogues with Contemporary Continental Thinkers: The Phenomenological Heritage* (Manchester: Manchester University Press, 1984).

Kelber, W.H., 'Gospel Narrative and Critical Theory', *BTB* 18 (1988), pp. 130-37.

—*Mark's Story of Jesus* (Philadelphia: Fortress Press, 1979).

Kennedy, G.A., *New Testament Interpretation through Rhetorical Criticism* (Chapel Hill: University of North Carolina Press, 1984).

Kermode, F., *The Genesis of Secrecy: On the Interpretation of Narrative* (Cambridge, MA: Harvard University Press, 1979).

—*The Sense of an Ending: Studies in the Theory of Fiction* (London and New York: Oxford University Press, 1967).

Kilgallen, J.J., 'Luke 2,41-50: Foreshadowing of Jesus Teacher', *Bib* 66 (1985), pp. 553-59.

Kilpatrick, G.D., 'ΛΑΟΙ at Luke II.31 and Acts IV.25,27', *JTS* 16 (1965), pp. 127.

Kingsbury, J.D., *Matthew as Story* (Philadelphia: Fortress Press, 1986).

Klemm, D.E., 'Ricoeur, Theology, and the Rhetoric of Overturning', *Literature & Theology* 3 (1989), pp. 267-84.

Klostermann, E., *Das Lukasevangelium* (Tübingen: Mohr, 1975).

Kort, W.A., 'Narrative and Theology', *Literature & Theology* 1 (1987), pp. 27-38.

—*Narrative Elements and Religious Meaning* (Philadelphia: Fortress Press, 1975).

—*Story, Text and Scripture: Literary Interests in Biblical Narrative* (University Park: Pennsylvania State University Press, 1988).

Krieg, R.A., *A Story-Shaped Christology: The Role of Narratives in Identifying Jesus Christ* (Mahwah, NJ: Paulist Press, 1988).

Kugel, J.L., 'On the Bible and Literary Criticism', *Prooftexts* 1 (1981), pp. 217-36.

Kurz, W.S., 'Luke–Acts and Historiography in the Greek Bible', in P.J. Achtemeier (ed.), *Society of Biblical Literature Seminar Papers 1980* (Chico, CA: Scholars Press, 1980), pp. 283-300.

—'Narrative Approaches to Luke–Acts', *Bib* 68 (1987), pp. 195-220.

Kysar, R., *John's Story of Jesus* (Philadelphia: Fortress Press, 1984).

Lagrange, M.-J., *Evangile selon Saint Luc* (Paris: Gabalda, 1921).

Lategan, B.C., and W.S. Forster, *Text and Reality: Aspects of Reference in Biblical Texts* (Atlanta: Scholars Press; Philadelphia: Fortress Press, 1985).

Laurentin, R., *Jésus au Temple: Mystère de Pâques et Foi de Marie en Luc 2,48-50* (Paris: Gabalda, 1966).

—*Les Evangiles de l'Enfance: Vérité de Noël au-delà des mythes* (Paris: Desclée, 1982).

—*Structure et théologie de Luc 1-2* (Paris: Gabalda, 1957).

LaVerdiere, E., *Luke* (Dublin: Veritas Publications, 1984).

Leaney, A.R.C., *A Commentary on the Gospel according to St. Luke* (London: A. & C. Black, 1958).

Legrand, L., 'Deux voyages: Lc 2,41-50; 24,13-33', in F. Refoulé (ed.), *A Cause de l'Evangile* (Paris: Cerf, 1985), pp. 409-29.

—'L'évangile aux bergers: Essai sur le genre littéraire de Luc 2,8-20', *RB* 75 (1968), pp. 161-87.

—'The Christmas Story in Lk 2,1-7', *IndTS* 19 (1982), pp. 289-317.

—*L'annonce à Marie (Lc 1,26-38): Une apocalypse aux origines de l'Evangile* (Paris: Cerf, 1981).

Leisegang, H., *Pneuma Hagion* (Leipzig: Hinrichs, 1922).

Leitch, T.M., *What Stories Are: Narrative Theory and Interpretation* (University Park: Pennsylvania State University Press, 1986).

Leitch, V.B., *American Literary Criticism from the Thirties to the Eighties* (New York: Columbia University Press, 1988).

Lohfink, G., 'Weinachten und die Armut', *GL* 35 (1962), pp. 401-405.

Loisy, A., *L'Evangile selon Luc* (Paris: E. Nourry, 1924).

Longman, T., *Literary Approaches to Biblical Interpretation* (Grand Rapids: Zondervan, 1987).

Lotman, J.M., 'Point of View in a Text', *New Literary History* 6 (1975), pp. 339-52.

—*The Structure of the Artistic Text* (trans. G. Lenhoff and R. Vroon; Ann Arbor: University of Michigan Press, 1977).

Lubbock, P., *The Craft of Fiction* (New York: Viking Press, 1963).

Lyonnet, S., 'χαῖρε κεχαριτωμένη', *Bib* 20 (1939), pp. 131-41.

Maddox, R., *The Purpose of Luke–Acts* (Edinburgh: T. & T. Clark, 1982).

Mailloux, S., 'Rhetorical Hermeneutics', *Critical Inquiry* 11 (1985), pp. 620-41.

—'Reader-Response Criticism?', *Genre* 10 (1977), pp. 413-31.

Malbon, E.S., 'Disciples/Crowds/Whoever: Markan Characters and Readers', *NovT* 28 (1986), pp. 104-30.

Marchese, A., *L'officina del racconto* (Milan: Mondadori, 1983).

Marshall, I.H., *Luke: Historian and Theologian* (Exeter: Paternoster Press, 1970).

—*The Gospel of Luke: A Commentary on the Greek Text* (Exeter: Paternoster Press, 1978).

Martin, F. (ed.), *Narrative Parallels to the New Testament* (Atlanta: Scholars Press, 1980).

Martin, J.P., 'Towards a Post-Critical Paradigm', *NTS* 33 (1987), pp. 370-85.

Martin, W., *Recent Theories of Narrative* (Ithaca, NY: Cornell University Press, 1986).

Mather, P.B., 'The Search for the Living Text of the Lucan Infancy Narrative', in D.E. Groh and R. Jewett (eds.), *The Living Text* (Lanham, MD: University Press of America, 1985), pp. 123-40.

McHugh, J., 'A New Approach to the Infancy Narratives', *Marianum* 40 (1978), pp. 277-99.

—*The Mother of Jesus in the New Testament* (London: Darton, Longman & Todd, 1975).

McKnight, E.V., *Meaning in Texts: The Historical Shape of a Narrative Hermeneutics* (Philadelphia: Fortress Press, 1978).

—*Post-Modern Use of the Bible: The Emergence of Reader-Oriented Criticism* (Nashville: Abingdon Press, 1988).

—*The Bible and the Reader: An Introduction to Literary Criticism* (Philadelphia: Fortress Press, 1985).

Metzger, B.M., *A Textual Commentary on the Greek New Testament: A Companion Volume to the United Bible Societies' Greek New Testament* (New York and London: United Bible Societies, 1971).

Meynet, R., 'Dieu donne son nom à Jésus: Analyse rhétorique de Lc 1,26-56 et de 1 Sam 2,1-10', *Bib* 66 (1985), pp. 39-72.

—*Initiation à la rhétorique biblique: Qui est donc le plus grand?* (Paris: Cerf, 1982).

—*Quelle est donc cette parole? Lecture 'rhétorique' de l'évangile de Luc [1–9; 22–24]* (Paris: Cerf, 1979).

Middleton, D.F., 'The Story of Mary: Luke's Version', *New Blackfriars* 70 (1989), pp. 555-64.

Miller, D.A., *Narrative and its Discontents: Problems of Closure in the Traditional Novel* (Princeton: Princeton University Press, 1981).

Miller, R.J., 'Elijah, John and Jesus in the Gospel of Luke', *NTS* 34 (1988), pp. 611-22.

Minear, P., 'The Interpreter and the Birth Narratives', *Symbolae Biblicae Uppsalienses* 13 (1950), pp. 1-22.

—'Luke's Use of the Birth Stories', in L.E. Keck (ed.), *Studies in Luke–Acts* (Nashville: Abingdon Press, 1966), pp. 111-30.

—*To Heal and Reveal: The Prophetic Vocation according to Luke* (New York: Seabury, 1976).

Minguez, D., 'Poetica generativa del Magnificat', *Bib* 61 (1980), pp. 57-77.

Miyoshi, M., 'Jesu Darstellung oder Reinigung im Tempel unter Berücksichtigung von Nunc Dimittis', *AJBI* 4 (1978), pp. 85-115.

Moloney, F.J., 'Johannine Theology', in R.E. Brown, J.A. Fitzmyer and R.E. Murphy (eds.), *New Jerome Biblical Commentary* (London: Geoffrey Chapman, 1990), pp. 1417-26.

Moore, S.D, 'Narrative Homiletics: Lukan Rhetoric and the Making of the Reader' (PhD Dissertation, Trinity College, Dublin, 1986).

—'Are the Gospels Unified Narratives?', in K.H. Richards (ed.), *Society of Biblical Literature Seminar Papers 1987* (Atlanta: Scholars' Press, 1987), pp. 443-58.

—'Doing Gospel Criticism as/with a "Reader"', *BTB* 19 (1989), pp. 85-93.

—'Luke's Economy of Knowledge', in D.J. Lull (ed.), *Society of Biblical Literature Seminar Papers 1989* (Atlanta: Scholars Press, 1989), pp. 38-56.

—'Narrative Commentaries on the Bible: Context, Roots, and Prospects', *Forum* 3 (1987), pp. 29-62.

—'Negative Hermeneutics, Insubstantial Texts: Stanley Fish and the Biblical Interpreter', *JAAR* 54 (1986), pp. 401-13.

—*Mark and Luke in Poststructuralist Perspectives: Jesus Begins to Write* (New Haven and London: Yale University Press, 1992).

—*Literary Criticism and the Gospels: The Theoretical Challenge* (New Haven and London: Yale University Press, 1989).

Morgan, R., 'Literary Study of the Bible', in R. Morgan (with J. Barton), *Biblical Interpretation* (Oxford: Oxford University Press, 1988), pp. 203-68.

Morgenthaler, R., *Die lukanische Geschichtsschreibung als Zeugnis: Gestalt und Gehalt der Kunst des Lukas* (2 vols.; Zürich: Zwingli-Verlag, 1949).

Morris, L., *The Gospel according to St. Luke: An Introduction and Commentary* (London: Inter-Varsity Press, 1974).

Moule, C.F.D., *An Idiom-Book of New Testament Greek* (Cambridge: Cambridge University Press, 1953).

Moulton, J.H., *Einleitung in die Sprache des Neuen Testaments* (Heidelberg: Winter, 1911).

Murphy, R., 'On Shepherds', *BT* 1 (1964), pp. 986-91.

Muñoz Iglesias, S., 'Estructura y Teologia de Lucas I–II', *EstBib* 17 (1958), pp. 101-107.

—*Los Evangelios de la Infancia* (3 vols.; Madrid: Biblioteca de autores cristianos, 1986, 1987).

Neirynck, F., 'Le Messie sera un signe de contradiction', *AsSeign* 1 (1961), pp. 29-42.

Neyrey, J. H., 'Maid and Mother in Art and Literature', *BTB* 20 (1990), pp. 65-75.

Nida, E.A., J.P. Louw, A.H. Snyman and J. Cronje, *Style and Discourse, with Special Reference to the Text of the Greek New Testament* (Cape Town: Bible Society, 1983).

Nol, T., 'The Parable of the Wedding-Guest: A Narrative-Critical Interpretation', *Perspectives in Religious Studies* 16 (1989), pp. 17-27.

Nolland, J., *Luke 1–9:20* (Dallas: Word Books, 1989).

Nuttall, A.D., *A New Mimesis: Shakespeare and the Representation of Reality* (London and New York: Methuen, 1983).

Nuttall, G., *The Moment of Recognition: Luke as Story-Teller* (London: Athlone Press, 1978).

O'Fearghail, F., 'The Imitation of the Septuagint in Luke's Infancy Narrative', *Proceedings of the Irish Biblical Association* 12 (1989), pp. 58-78.

—'The Introduction to Luke–Acts: A Study of the Role of Lk 1,1-4,44 in the Composition of Luke's Two-Volume Work' (SSD dissertation, Pontifical Biblical Institute, 1986).

—'The Literary Forms of Lk 1,5-25 and 1,26-38', *Marianum* 43 (1981), pp. 321-44.

Oliver, H.H., 'The Lucan Birth Stories and the Purpose of Luke–Acts', *NTS* 10 (1963-64), pp. 202-26.

Ong, W.J., 'Beyond Objectivity: The Reader and Writer Transaction as an Altered State of Consciousness', *CEA Critic* 40 (1977), pp. 6-13.

—'The Writer's Audience is always a Fiction', in *Interfaces of the Word* (Ithaca, NY: Cornell University Press, 1977), pp. 53-81.

O'Toole, R.J., *The Unity of Luke's Theology: An Analysis of Luke–Acts* (Wilmington, DE: Michael Glazier, 1984).

Parsons, M.C., 'Narrative Closure and Openness in the Plot of the Third Gospel: The Sense of an Ending', in K.H. Richards (ed.), *Society of Biblical Literature Seminar Papers 1986* (Atlanta: Scholars Press, 1986), pp. 201-23.

—*The Departure of Jesus in Luke–Acts: The Ascension Narrative in Context* (JSNTSup, 21; Sheffield: JSOT Press, 1988).

Patrick, D., *The Rendering of God in the Old Testament* (Philadelphia: Fortress Press, 1981).

Patrick, D., and A. Scult, *Rhetoric and Biblical Interpretation* (JSOTSup, 82; Sheffield: JSOT Press, 1990).

Patrides, C.A., *The Grand Design of God: The Literary Form of the Christian View of History* (London: Routledge & Kegan Paul, 1972).

Peretto, E., 'Zaccaria, Elisabetta, Giovanni visti dal primo lettore di Luca', *Marianum* 40 (1978), pp. 350-70.

Perkins, P., 'Crisis in Jerusalem? Narrative Criticism in New Testament Studies', *TS* 50 (1989), pp. 296-313.

Perrin, N., 'The Evangelist as Author: Reflections on Method in the Study and Interpretation of the Synoptic Gospels and Acts', *BR* 17 (1972), pp. 5-18.

Perrot, C., 'Les récits de l'enfance dans la Haggada antérieure au IIe siècle de notre ère', *RSR* 55 (1967), pp. 481-518.

—*Les récits de l'enfance de Jésus: Mt 1–2 et Lc 1–2* (Paris: Cerf, 1972).

Perry, M., 'Literary Dynamics: How the Order of a Text Creates its Meanings', *Poetics Today* 1 (1979), pp. 35-64 and 311-61.

Pesch, R., 'Kind, warum hast du so an uns getan?', *BZ* 12 (1968), pp. 245-48.

Petersen, N.R., 'Literary Criticism in Biblical Studies', in R.A. Spencer (ed.), *Orientation by Disorientation: Studies in Literary Criticism and Biblical Literary Criticism* (Pittsburgh: Pickwick Press, 1980), pp. 25-50.

—'The Reader in the Gospel', *Neotestamentica* 18 (1984), pp. 38-51.

—'When the End is not the End: Literary Reflections on the Ending of Mark's Narrative', *Int* 34 (1980), pp. 151-66.

—*Literary Criticism for New Testament Critics* (Philadelphia: Fortress Press, 1978).

Plevnik, J., 'The Eyewitnesses of the Risen Jesus in Luke 24', *CBQ* 49 (1987), pp. 90-103.

Plümacher, E., *Lukas als hellenisticher Schriftsteller: Studien zur Apostelgeschichte* (Göttingen: Vandenhoeck & Ruprecht, 1972).

Plumb, J.H., *The Death of the Past* (London: Macmillan, 1969).

Plummer, A., *A Critical and Exegetical Commentary on the Gospel according to St. Luke* (New York: Scribners, 1922).

Poland, L.M., 'The New Criticism, Neoorthodoxy, and the New Testament', *Journal of Religion* 65 (1985), pp. 459-77.

—*Literary Criticism and Biblical Hermeneutics: A Critique of Formalist Approaches* (Chico, CA: Scholars Press, 1985).

Pope, R., 'Beginnings', *Georgia Review* 36 (1982), pp. 733-51.

Porter, S.E., 'Why Hasn't Reader-Response Criticism Caught on in New Testament Studies?', *Literature & Theology* 4 (1990), pp. 278-92.

Potterie, I. de la, 'κεχαριτωμένη en Lc 1,28: Etude philologique', *Bib* 68 (1987), pp. 357-82.

—'L'annunzio a Maria (Lc 1,26-38)', *Parola, Spirito e Vita* 6 (1982), pp. 55-73.

—'κεχαριτωμένη en Lc 1,28: Etude philologique et théologique', *Bib* 68 (1987), pp. 480-508.

Powell, M.A., 'The Religious Leaders in Luke: A Literary-Critical Study', *JBL* 109 (1990), pp. 93-110.

—*What is Narrative Criticism?* (Minneapolis: Fortress Press, 1990).

Power, M.A. 'Who Were They Who "Understood Not"?', *ITQ* 7 (1922), pp. 261-81, 444-59.

Praeder, S.M., 'Luke–Acts and the Ancient Novel', in K.H. Richards (ed.), *Society of Biblical Literature Seminar Papers 1981* (Chico, CA: Scholars Press, 1981), pp. 269-92.

Pratt, M.L., *Toward a Speech Act Theory of Literary Discourse* (Bloomington: Indiana University Press, 1977).

Prickett, S., 'The Status of Biblical Narrative', *Pacifica* 2 (1989), pp. 26-46.

—*Words and the Word: Language, Poetics and Biblical Interpretation* (Cambridge: Cambridge University Press, 1986).

Prince, G., 'Introduction à l'étude du narrataire', *Poétique* 14 (1971), pp. 178-96.

—'Narrative Analysis and Narratology, *New Literary History* 13 (1981–82), pp. 179-88.

—*A Dictionary of Narratology* (Lincoln: University of Nebraska Press, 1988).

—*Narratology: The Form and Functioning of Narrative* (Berlin, New York and Amsterdam: Mouton Publishers, 1982).

Pugliatti, P., *Lo sguardo nel racconto: Teoria e prassi del punto di vista* (Bologna: Zanichelli, 1985).

Rabinowitz, P.J., Truth in Fiction: A Re-examination of Audiences, *Critical Inquiry* 4 (1977), pp. 121-41.

Radl, W., *Das Lukas-Evangelium* (Darmstadt: Wissenschaftliche Buchgesellschaft, 1988).

Räisänen, H., *Die Mutter Jesu im Neuen Testament* (Helsinki: Suomalainen Tiedeakatemia, 1969).

Ramsey, G.W., 'Plots, Gaps, Repetitions and Ambiguity in Luke 15', *Perspectives in Religious Studies* 17 (1990), pp. 33-42.

Rasco, E., *La teologia de Lucas: Origen, desarollo, orientaciones* (Rome: Gregorian University Press, 1976).

Ray, W., *Literary Meaning: From Phenomenology to Deconstruction* (Oxford: Basil Blackwell, 1984).

Reed, W.L., 'A Poetics of the Bible: Problems and Possibilities', *Literature & Theology* 1 (1987), pp. 154-66.

Rees, C.J. van, and H. Verdaasdonk, 'Reading a Text vs. Analyzing a Text', *Poetics* 6 (1977), pp. 55-76.

Rengstorf, K.H., *Das Evangelium nach Lukas* (Göttingen: Vandenhoeck & Ruprecht, 1962).

Resseguie, J.L., 'Defamiliarization and the Gospels', *BTB* 20 (1990), pp. 147-53.

—'Point of View in the Central Section of Luke (9:51–19:44)', *JETS* 25 (1982), pp. 41-47.

—'Reader-Response Criticism and the Synoptic Gospels', *JAAR* 52 (1984), pp. 307-24.

Rhoads, D., 'Narrative Criticism and the Gospel of Mark', *JAAR* 50 (1982), pp. 411-34.

Rhoads, D., and D. Michie, *Mark as Story: An Introduction to the Narrative of a Gospel* (Philadelphia: Fortress Press, 1982).

Ricoeur, P., 'The Narrative Function', *Semeia* 13 (1978), pp. 177-202.

—*Interpretation Theory: Discourse and the Surplus of Meaning* (Fort Worth: Texas Christian University Press, 1976).

—*Temps et récit* (3 vols.; Paris: Seuil, 1983, 1985, 1988).

Rimmon-Kenan, S., *Narrative Fiction: Contemporary Poetics* (London: Methuen, 1983).

Ringgren, H., *The Faith of Qumran* (Philadelphia: Fortress Press, 1963).

Riva, F., 'L'esegesi narrativa: dimensioni ermeneutiche', *RivB* 37 (1989), pp. 129-60.

Rivken, E., 'Messiah, Jewish', *IDBSup*, pp. 588-91.

Roberts Gaventa, B., 'The Peril of Modernizing Henry Joel Cadbury', in K.H. Richards (ed.), *Society of Biblical Literature Seminar Papers 1987* (Atlanta: Scholars Press, 1987), pp. 64-79.

Robinson, J.M., 'The Gospels as Narrative', in F. McConnell (ed.), *The Bible and the Narrative Tradition* (New York and Oxford: Oxford University Press, 1986), pp. 97-112.

Ronen, R., 'La focalisation dans les mondes fictionnels', *Poétique* 83 (1990), pp. 305-22.

Ruddick, C.T., 'Birth Narratives in Genesis and Luke', *NovT* 12 (1970), pp. 343-48.

Ruthrof, H., 'Aspects of a Phenomenological View of Narrative', *Journal of Narrative Technique* 4 (1974), pp. 87-99.

—*The Reader's Construction of Narrative* (London and Boston: Routledge & Kegan Paul, 1981).

Ryken, L., 'Literary Criticism of the Bible: Some Fallacies', in K.R.R. Gros Louis, J.S. Ackerman and T.S. Warshaw (eds.), *Literary Interpretations of Biblical Narratives* (Nashville: Abingdon Press, 1974), pp. 24-40.

Ryoo, S.W., *The Lucan Birth Narratives and the Theological Unity and Purpose of Luke–Acts* (ThD dissertation, Boston University, 1969).

Sacks, S., *Fiction and the Shape of Belief* (Berkeley and Los Angeles: University of California Press, 1964).

Sahlin, H., *Der Messias und das Gottesvolk* (Uppsala: Alqvist, 1945).

Said, E., *Beginnings* (New York: Basic Books, 1975).

Sanders, J.T. 'The Prophetic Use of Scriptures in Luke–Acts', in C.A. Evans and W.F. Stinespring (eds.), *Early Jewish and Christian Exegesis* (Atlanta: Scholars Press, 1987), pp. 191-98.

Schlatter, A., *Das Evangelium des Lukas* (Stuttgart: Calwer Verlag, 1960).

Schmid, J., *Das Evangelium nach Lukas* (Regensburg: Pustet, 1955).

Schmithals, W., 'Die Weinachtsgeschichte: Lukas 2,1-20', in G. Ebeling (ed.), *Festschrift für Ernst Fuchs* (Tübingen: Mohr, 1973), pp. 281-97.

Schneidau, H.N., 'Biblical Narrative and Modern Consciousness', in F. McConnell (ed.), *The Bible and the Narrative Tradition* (New York and Oxford: Oxford University Press, 1986), pp. 132-50.

—*Sacred Discontent: The Bible and Western Tradition* (Baton Rouge: Louisiana State University Press, 1976).

Schneider, G., 'Der Zweck des lukanischen Doppelwerks', *BZ* 21 (1977), pp. 45-66.

—'Zur Bedeutung von καθεξῆς im lukanischen Doppelwerks', *ZNW* 68 (1977), pp. 128-31.

—*Das Evangelium nach Lukas* (2 vols.; Gütersloh: Gütersloher Verlagshaus, 1977).

Scholes, R., 'Cognition and the Implied Reader', *Diacritics* 5 (1975), pp. 13-15.

—*Textual Power: Literary Theory and the Teaching of English* (New Haven and London: Yale University Press, 1985).

Scholes, R., and R. Kellogg, *The Nature of Narrative* (New York: Oxford University Press, 1966).

Schramm, T., *Der Markus-stoff bei Lukas: Eine literarkritische und redaktions-geschichtliche Untersuchung* (Cambridge: Cambridge University Press, 1971).

Schubert, P., 'The Structure and Significance of Luke 24', in W. Eltester (ed.), *Neutestamentliche Studien für Rudolph Bultmann* (Berlin: Töpelmann, 1957), pp. 165-86.

Schulz, S., 'Gottes Vorsehung bei Lukas', *ZNW* 54 (1963), pp. 104-16.

Schürmann, H., 'Aufbau, Eigenart und Geschichtwert der Vorgeschichte von Lukas 1–2', *BK* 21 (1966), pp. 106-11.

—*Das Lukasevangelium: Erster Teil: Kommentar zu Kap. 1,1–9,50* (Freiburg: Herder, 1969).

Schweizer, E., *The Good News according to Luke* (trans. D.E. Green; London: SPCK, 1984).

Scott, B.B., 'How to Mismanage a Miracle: Reader-Response Criticism', in K.H. Richards (ed.), *Society of Biblical Literature Seminar Papers* 1983 (Chico, CA: Scholars Press, 1983), pp. 439-49.

Scott, N.A., *The Poetics of Belief* (Chapel Hill and London: University of North Carolina Press, 1985).

Searle, J.R., *Speech Acts: An Essay in the Philosophy of Language* (Cambridge: Cambridge University Press, 1969).

Segbroek, T. van, *The Gospel of Luke: A Cumulative Bibliography* (Leuven: University Press, 1989).

Selden, R., *A Reader's Guide to Contemporary Literary Theory* (Lexington: University Press of Kentucky, 1985).

Serra, A., *E C'Era La Madre di Gesù: Saggi di Esegesi Biblico-Mariana [1978–1988]* (Milan: Edizioni Cens Marianum, 1989).

—*Sapienza e Contemplazione di Maria secondo Luca 2,19.51b* (Roma: Scripta Pontificiae Facultatis Theologicae Marianum, 1982).

Sheeley, S.M., 'Narrative Asides and Narrative Authority in Luke–Acts', *BTB* 18 (1988), pp. 102-107.

Simon, U., *Story and Faith in the Biblical Narrative* (London: SPCK, 1975).

Slatoff, W., *With Respect to Readers: Dimensions of Literary Response* (Ithaca, NY: Cornell University Press, 1970).

Sobosan, J., 'Completion of Prophecy: Jesus in Lk 1:32-33', *BTB* 4 (1974), pp. 317-23.

Spadafora, F., 'Et ipsi non intellexerunt (Lc 2,50)', *Divinitas* 11 (1967), pp. 55-70.

Spitta, F., 'Die chronologische Notizen und die Hymnen in Lc 1 u. 2', *ZNW* 7 (1906), pp. 281-317.

Staley, J.L., *The Print's First Kiss: A Rhetorical Investigation of the Implied Reader in the Fourth Gospel* (Atlanta: Scholars Press, 1988).

Standaert, B., 'L'art de composer dans l'oeuvre de Luc', in F. Refoulé (ed.), *A Cause de l'Evangile* (Paris: Cerf, 1985), pp. 323-47.

Stanzel, F.K., *A Theory of Narrative* (trans. C. Goedsche; Cambridge: Cambridge University Press, 1986).

Steiner, G., ' "Critic"/"Reader" ', *New Literary History* 10 (1979), pp. 423-52.

Sterling, G.E., 'Luke–Acts and Apologetic Historiography', in D.J. Lull (ed.), *Society of Biblical Literature Seminar Papers 1989* (Atlanta: Scholars Press, 1989), pp. 326-42.

Sternberg, M., *Expositional Modes and Temporal Ordering in Fiction* (Baltimore and London: Johns Hopkins University Press, 1978).

—*The Poetics of Biblical Narrative: Ideological Literature and the Drama of Reading* (Bloomington: Indiana University Press, 1985).

Stock, K., 'Die Berufung Marias', *Bib* 61 (1980), pp. 457-91.

—'Maria nel Tempio (Lc 2,22-52)', *Parola, Spirito e Vita* 6 (1982), pp. 114-25.

Sykes, S.W., 'The Role of Story in the Christian Religion: An Hypothesis', *Literature & Theology* 1 (1987), pp. 19-28.

Sylva, D.D., 'The Cryptic Clause *en tois tou patros mou dei einai me* in Lk 2 49b', *ZNW* 78 (1987), pp. 132-40.

—'Ierousalêm and Hierosoluma in Luke–Acts', *ZNW* 74 (1983), pp. 207-21.

Talbert, C.H., 'Prophecies of Future Greatness: The Contribution of Greco-Roman Biographies to an Understanding of Luke 1,5-4,15', in J.L. Crenshaw and S. Sandmel (eds.), *The Divine Helmsman* (New York: Ktav, 1980), pp. 129-42.

—*Literary Patterns, Theological Themes and the Genre of Luke–Acts* (Missoula, MT: Scholars Press, 1974).

—*Luke and the Gnostics* (Nashville: Abingdon Press, 1966).

—'Promise and Fulfillment in Lukan Theology', in C.H. Talbert (ed.), *Luke–Acts* (New York: Crossroad, 1984), pp. 91-103.

—*Reading Luke: A Literary and Theological Commentary on the Third Gospel* (New York: Crossroad, 1982).

—Review of *The Gospel of Luke Vol. II (X-XXIV)* by J.A. Fitzmyer, *CBQ* 48 (1986), pp. 336-38.

Tannehill, R.C., 'Israel in Luke–Acts: A Tragic Story', *JBL* 104 (1985), pp. 69-85.

—'The Gospel of Mark as Narrative Christology', *Semeia* 16 (1979), pp. 57-95.

—'The Magnificat as Poem', *JBL* 93 (1974), pp. 263-75.

—*The Narrative Unity of Luke–Acts: A Literary Interpretation*. I. *Luke* (Philadelphia: Fortress Press, 1986).

—*The Narrative Unity of Luke–Acts: A Literary Interpretation*. II. *Acts* (Sonoma, CA: Polebridge Press, 1990).

Tatum, W.B., 'The Epoch of Israel: Luke I–II and the Theological Plan of Acts', *NTS* 13 (1966–67), pp. 184-95.

Tiede, D.L., 'Glory to Thy People Israel: Luke–Acts and the Jews', in K.H. Richards (ed.), *Society of Biblical Literature Seminar Papers 1986* (Atlanta: Scholars Press, 1986), pp. 142-51.

—*Luke* (Minneapolis: Augsburg, 1988).

—*Prophecy and History in Luke–Acts* (Philadelphia: Fortress Press, 1980).

Todorov, T., *Symbolism and Interpretation* (trans. C. Porter; Ithaca, NY: Cornell University Press, 1982).

—*The Poetics of Prose* (trans. R. Howard; Ithaca, NY: Cornell University Press, 1977).

Tompkins, J.P., 'An Introduction to Reader-Response Criticism', in J.P. Tompkins (ed.), *Reader-Response Criticism: From Formalism to Post-Structuralism* (Baltimore and London: Johns Hopkins University Press, 1980), pp. ix-xxvi.

—'The Reader in History: The Changing Shape of Literary Response', in J.P. Tompkins (ed.), *Reader-Response Criticism: From Formalism to Post-Structuralism* (Baltimore and London: Johns Hopkins University Press, 1980), pp. 201-32.

Torgovnick, M., *Closure in the Novel* (Princeton: Princeton University Press, 1981).

Trémel, B., 'Le signe du nouveau-né dans la mangeoire: A propos de Luc 2,1-20', in *Mélanges Dominique Barthélémy* (Freiburg: Editions Universitaires; Göttingen: Vandenhoeck & Ruprecht, 1981), pp. 593-612.

Tyson, J. B., *The Death of Jesus in Luke–Acts* (Columbia: University of South Carolina Press, 1986).

Unnik, W.C. van, 'Die rechte Bedeutung des Wortes "treffen", Lukas II,19', in *Sparsa Collecta: The Collected Essays of W.C. van Unnik I* (Leiden: Brill, 1973), pp. 72-91.

—'Eléments artistiques dans l'évangile de Luc', in F. Neirynck (ed.), *L'Evangile de Luc: Problèmes littéraires et théologiques* (Gembloux: Duculot, 1973), pp. 129-40.

Uspensky, B., *A Poetics of Composition: The Structure of the Artistic Text and Typology of a Compositional Form* (trans. V. Zavarin and S. Wittig; Berkeley and Los Angeles: University of California Press, 1973).

Vanhoye, A., 'Structure du "Benedictus"', *NTS* 12 (1965–66), pp. 382-89.

Vermes, G., *Jesus the Jew* (London: Collins, 1973).

Vogels, H., 'Zur Textgeschichte von Lc 1,34ff.', *ZNW* 43 (1950–51), pp. 256-60.

Vorster, W.S., 'The New Testament and Narratology', *Journal of Literary Studies* 2 (1986), pp. 42-62.

Votaw, C.W., *The Gospels and the Contemporary Biographies in the Greco-Roman World* (Philadelphia: Fortress Press, 1970).

Wagner, G. (ed.), *An Exegetical Bibliography of the New Testament* (Macon: Mercer University Press, 1985).

Watson, G., 'The Sense of a Beginning', *Sewanee Review* 86 (1978), pp. 539-48.

Watson, N., 'Reception Theory and Biblical Exegesis', *AusBR* 36 (1988), pp. 45-56.

White, H., 'Figuring the Nature of the Times Deceased: Literary Theory and Historical Writing', in R. Cohen (ed.), *The Future of Literary Theory* (New York and London: Routledge, 1989), pp. 19-43.

—'The Question of Narrative in Contemporary Historical Theory', *History and Theory* 23 (1984), pp. 1-33.

—'The Value of Narrativity in the Representation of Reality', *Inquiry* 7 (1980), pp. 5-27.

—*The Content of the Form* (Baltimore and London: Johns Hopkins University Press, 1987).

Wilder, A.N., *Early Christian Rhetoric* (London: SCM Press, 1964).

—'Story and Story-World', *Int* 37 (1983), pp. 353-64.

—'The Gospels as Narrative', *Int* 34 (1980), pp. 296-99.

—*The New Voice: Religion, Literature, Hermeneutics* (New York: Herder & Herder, 1969).

—*Theopoetic: Theology and the Religious Imagination* (Philadelphia: Fortress Press, 1976).

Wilson, R., 'The Bright Chimera: Character as a Literary Term', *Critical Inquiry* 5 (1979), pp. 725-49.

Wilson, S.G., *The Gentiles and the Gentile Mission in Luke–Acts* (Cambridge: Cambridge University Press, 1973).

Winandy, J., 'La prophétie de Siméon (Lc II,34-35)', *RB* 72 (1965), pp. 321-51.

—*Autour de la naissance de Jésus. Accomplissement et prophétie* (Paris: Cerf, 1970).

Wink, W., *John the Baptist in the Gospel Tradition* (Cambridge: Cambridge University Press, 1968).

Winter, P., 'Lukanische Miszellen', *ZNW* 49 (1958), pp. 65-77.

—'On the Margin of Luke I–II', *ST* 12 (1958), pp. 103-107.

Wright, T.R., 'Regenerating Narrative: The Gospels as Fiction', *Religious Studies* 20 (1984), pp. 389-400.

—*Theology and Literature* (Oxford: Basil Blackwell, 1988).

Wuellner, W., 'Where is Rhetorical Criticism Taking Us?', *CBQ* 49 (1987), pp. 448-63.

Zahn, T., *Das Evangelium des Lucas ausgelegt* (Leipzig: Deichert, 1930).

Zerwick, M., *Biblical Greek* (trans. J. Smith; Rome: Biblical Institute Press, 1963).

Ziolkowski, T., 'Literature and the Bible: A Comparatist's Appeal', in R. Detweiler (ed.), *Art/Literature/Religion: Life on the Borders* (Chico, CA: Scholars Press, 1983), pp. 181-90.

Zuck, J.E., 'Tales of Wonder: Biblical Narrative, Myth, and Fairy Stories', *JAAR* 44 (1976), pp. 299-308.

INDEXES

INDEX OF REFERENCES

OLD TESTAMENT

OTHER ANCIENT REFERENCES

INDEX OF AUTHORS

JOURNAL FOR THE STUDY OF THE NEW TESTAMENT

Supplement Series